shakespeare's twenty-first-century economics

shakespeare's twenty-first-century economics

The Morality of Love and Money

Frederick Turner

New York   Oxford

Oxford University Press

1999

Oxford University Press

Oxford   New York

Athens   Auckland   Bangkok   Bogotá   Buenos Aires   Calcutta
Cape Town   Chennai   Dar es Salaam   Delhi   Florence   Hong Kong   Istanbul
Karachi   Kuala Lumpur   Madrid   Melbourne   Mexico City   Mumbai
Nairobi   Paris   São Paulo   Singapore   Taipei   Tokyo   Toronto   Warsaw

and associated companies in
Berlin   Ibadan

Published by Oxford University Press, Inc.
198 Madison Avenue, New York, New York 10016

Library of Congress Cataloging-in-Publication Data
Turner, Frederick, 1943–
Shakespeare's Twenty-First-Century economics : the morality of
love and money / Frederick Turner.
p.   cm.
Includes bibliographical references and index.
ISBN 0-19-512861-3
1. Shakespeare, William, 1564–1616—Knowledge—Economics.
2. Economics and literature—England—History—16th century.
3. Economics and literature—England—History—17th century.
4. Didactic drama, English—History and criticism.   5. Shakespeare,
William, 1564–1616—Ethics.   6. Economics—Moral and ethical
aspects.   7. Economics in literature.   8. Ethics in literature.
9. Money in literature.   I. Title.
PR3021.T87   1999
822.3'3—dc21   98-31242

1 3 5 7 9 8 6 4 2

Printed in the United States of America
on acid-free paper

acknowledgments

The idea that it might be conceivable to turn my thirty years of thinking and teaching about Shakespeare's economics into a book first came to me at Michael Benedikt's extraordinary symposium "The Question of Economic Value" at the Institute for American Architecture and Design at the University of Texas at Austin. His symposium enabled me to meet a remarkable group of people, all of whom I wish to thank here, including someone I have long admired, Ilya Prigogine.

Mark Shell's fascinating essay on *The Merchant of Venice*, "The Wether and the Ewe," which we published many years ago in *The Kenyon Review* when I was one of its editors, and his ongoing work on literature and economics were seminal to this book, though a reader who has read us both will see that we have taken different tacks on the subject. *The Kenyon Review* also published an essay on gifts by Lewis Hyde, which later turned up as part of his fine book on the subject; again, my differences from him do not diminish my gratitude for his insights. My friends Alexander Argyros and Koen dePryck, in conversation and in their brilliant critical writings, expanded for me the envelope of the permissible.

I would like to thank a number of other people whose ideas have assisted me in writing this book. The Fellows of the Dallas Institute of Humanities and Culture have provided for me an intellectual context both bold enough and traditional enough so that I could grow—I would especially like to thank Gail Thomas. Many colleagues at the University of Texas at Dallas have contributed insights. Harriet Rubin helped me focus my ideas. My editors at *Harper's, Reason, The Wilson Quarterly, The Missouri Review,*

American Enterprise, The Humanist, and especially James Cooper of *The American Arts Quarterly*—and several others—have given me the room to explore. Michael Lind has been the perfect intellectual companion in this exploration. I have learned a large part of what I know about ecological and gardening matters from William R. Jordan III. My brother, the medical physicist Robert Turner, has educated me in more ways than even he knows, as has my mother, the anthropologist Edith L. B. Turner. My wife, Mei Lin Chang, herself a wise and precise editor and translator, has been a constant source of insight. I also wish to thank my sons, Daniel and Benjamin, who have so often alerted me to ideas and books that I needed to know. In the later stages of the writing of this book, my excellent graduate students pitched in to help. They include Alan Akmakjian, Rudri Bhatt, David Camacho, Ronald Cantrell, Patrick Godfrey, Ellen Hinson, Susan Lovett, Heather Stobaugh, Arthur Tabbert, Walt Turner, and Pentipa Younvanich. And as a poet I would like also to thank the magnificent community of poets and artists of which it is my honor to be part.

This book is not aimed primarily at professional Shakespeare scholars (though it could not have been written without them). It thus lacks the scholarly apparatus, the armor of citation, the reservations and suspended judgments of professional caution, and much of the specialized critical vocabulary of an academic monograph. The book is intended for intelligent people in all walks of life who feel the need for a deeper consideration of their lives as economic beings; for people morally perplexed in personal relationships involving money; for the broad public that is now showing so remarkable an interest in Shakespeare; for lovers of literature and drama; for those with a keen philosophical curiosity about the foundations of value; and for people in the new disciplines of business administration, management, and information science, whose job it is to thimk about how we will conduct our financial and personal affairs in the future. But behind any work such as this there looms the grand tradition of two centuries of Shakespeare criticism, and I must offer my deep thanks to all the scholars on whose shoulders any present-day interpreter of Shakespeare must stand.

Parts of this book have appeared in a different form in *The Missouri Review, Reason,* and *American Behavioral Scientist.* All Shakespeare quotations are taken from *The Complete Signet Classic Shakespeare,* edited by Sylvan Barnet, Harcourt Brace Jovanovitch, New York, 1972. Line numbers refer to the first line of the cited passage.

contents

shakespeare's twenty-first-century economics

1

INTRODUCTION

Understanding Money

Personal and Financial Bonds

"I love your majesty / According to my bond," says Cordelia to her father, King Lear, at the beginning of Shakespeare's great play (I.i.92). This sounds like a rather chilly thing to say to one's father, especially if he has just asked you to declare how much you love him, as Lear has done a few minutes earlier. Yet as the play turns out, Cordelia proves to be an exemplary and loving daughter. What is going on? What, particularly, does she mean by "bond"? The word itself contains a fascinating amalgam of positive and negative connotations. Perhaps we should explore again the nature of the bond and all that comes with it.

Bonds, at the most fundamental level, form the essential structure of the universe. The "fair chain of love" that Chaucer describes in "The Knight's Tale" as linking the whole universe together, that "love that moves the sun and the other stars," as Dante put it, was for Shakespeare's time the first principle of physical existence. Our own contemporary science is not so very different in its assumptions. The quantum coherence that ensures the linkage of particle pairs and begins to shape a definite universe out of a mess of pure probability is perhaps the most basic bond. Quarks bond together to make protons and neutrons. Atoms form chemical bonds, and those bonds can make up the complex structures of the DNA molecule, the cell, and the living organism. The parent-offspring bond is fundamental to most species of social animals, and involves an often intricate exchange of goods and services, including the promise of limited biological immortality through offspring and thus the pursuit by the parent of interests extending beyond its own life span. Many species also rely on a close pair-bond between the breeding male and female, with ritual behaviors that ethologists (such as Konrad Lorenz) have suggested express emotions of love, comradeship, jealousy, and loyalty not unlike our own. All bonds involve an exchange, from the gluon passed between two interacting subatomic particles to the food and grooming supplied by a male bird or mammal to its mate, and the dowry or brideprice and mutual service provided by a husband and wife.

When lower types of bonds are applied to higher organisms, the result is often morally complex. The literal bondage of a prisoner by ropes or chains, whose binding power is merely mechanical, overrules the freedom of choice proper to a human being and is justifiable only if the prisoner would otherwise subject other humans to bondage. The bondage of a slave is morally evil. The bondage of drunks, addicts, or sexual compulsives to their habit reduces them in some respects to the status of an animal. But on the other hand the freely entered physical constraints of one who is in training for athletic achievement or undergoing a chosen spiritual discipline are the very essence of human freedom. Likewise, for a human to enter a loving bondage to anything less than human can be demeaning; but artists, lovers, patriots, and priests incarnate value into the world when they make oil paint depict a human face, or treasure a wedding ring, or save a flag, or bless a wafer of bread and a cup of wine. It can be a noble decision to endow lesser objects with symbolic meaning, but it is always a fraught one.

Most problematic of all, perhaps, is the nature of financial bonds. It is the aim of this book to restore economic relations to their proper place in the hierarchy of value-creating bonds, using Shakespeare's profound understanding of them as a guide.

Bonds and Money

What is a financial bond? For one thing, the terrifying contract that Antonio, the merchant of Venice, signs with the moneylender Shylock, guaranteeing Shylock a pound of the merchant's flesh if he does not pay up. So Shakespeare is well aware of the dark side of bonds. But if he is right about Cordelia, there must be a corresponding goodness about bonds that we are failing to acknowledge and give proper credit. And there must therefore be a kind of difficulty in thinking about bonds that is blinding us to their potential benefits.

The difficulty becomes most obvious when we consider that money itself is a kind of bond. A financial bond—that is, a contract guaranteeing the repayment of a debt by a debtor to a creditor—can be and often is a negotiable financial instrument that can be used like money. A banknote is such a bond, issued by a bank and promising its acceptance as legal tender, but without a specified creditor—the bearer of the banknote is the creditor. The moment that rulers began to mint and stamp coins with an inscription guaranteeing their weight, the value of those coins began to change from the barter value of the precious metal they contained to the credit value of the promise—the bond—implied in their inscription. And at this point such coins began to become money, true currency, rather than convenient ingots of specie. The ancient practice of clipping or filing coins and melting down the scrapings and the modern practice of collecting coins in the hope that their metal value will come to exceed their face value are both ways of exploiting the difference between barter value and bond value.

But if money is a kind of bond—indeed, the most common and pervasive kind—we run straight into three thousand years of hostile prejudice against money and its owners whenever we try to find out what might be good about bonds. Money is the root of all evil, we say, citing the Bible (though what the apostle Paul said was "the *love of* money is the root of all evil"). Socrates describes the city of merchants in *The Republic* as a city of pigs. Jesus scourged the moneylenders from the temple and said that it was harder for a rich man to enter the kingdom of heaven than for a camel to pass through the eye of a needle. The one theme that unites the political Left, from liberals to revolutionary Marxists, is dislike for the rich and a feeling of benevolence toward the poor. Indian, Chinese, and Japanese religious traditions alike exalt poverty and warn of the spiritual dangers of wealth. If we fancy ourselves as aristocrats, we consider ourselves to be above the crude nouveau riche concern with money and trade. If we feel ourselves to be oppressed workers, we tell ourselves that filthy lucre rules the world and that the wealthy got their riches by exploiting the poor. If we are sturdy middle-class folk we despise the ostentation of wealth and its moral corruptions. If we are intellectuals or academics we all too often believe in class struggle and taxes to dissolve the inequities of our society and would like to do away with the pleasures of wealth altogether (except for books, classical CDs, fine wines, gourmet food, etc., which the rich don't appreciate anyway). If we actually are rich, we pretend to be one of the other groups in order to survive.

Yet at the same time there is hardly one of us who would not be richer if we had the chance. Even holy and unworldly persons, like Mother Teresa and the Dalai Lama, raise money to pursue their goals of mercy and charity. We all want this evil money, and strive to join the pigs and bloated top-hatted capitalists who possess it. We are all hypocrites! So we feel deeply ambivalent, uncomfortable, and angry when we are asked to think about what might be good about bonds, especially the embarrassing kind of bond called money. What this book proposes to do is to sort out very carefully what is indeed good about bonds, to examine the dangers and pitfalls in their use that the anti-money tradition warns about, and to find a way of thinking about the economic element of our lives that is not hypocritical.

The Root of All Evil

Suppose we make a list of the various forms of human social organization. The list might include tribes, city-states, churches and other religious organizations, feudal domains, ancient empires, nations, international ideological movements, colonial plantation empires, business companies, and so on. The recent past has shown us the hideous carnage of tribal and religious wars in Rwanda, Nigeria, Kashmir, Bosnia, the Middle East, and elsewhere; but such atrocities are as old as humankind. The cruelty of the ancient empire is chronicled in bas-reliefs and stelae from all over the world depicting the sacrifice of holocausts of prisoners. In the bloody wars among Greek, Italian, and Mesoamerican cities, which left so many of them for archaeologists to discover, we can see the destructive powers of the city-state in action. The Wars of the Roses and the warlord periods of Japan and China illustrate the savagery of the feudal system. Planter empires gave us the horrors of slavery and colonialism. But the prize for the most murderous of all human regimes must surely be divided between the nation-state and the international ideological movement. Over time nationalism has probably caused the deaths of more people, but communism and Nazism, the two main ideological contenders, have perhaps killed more persons per decade than any other system of human organization.

Significantly, the business company, which is based on bonds and money, by any calculation ranks right at the bottom of this list. Its worst crimes, mostly in the nineteenth century, consist in the exploitation of child labor, the creation of unsafe working conditions, and the occasional shooting of union members. But this is bagatelle compared to the exploits of other systems. Even Marxists agree that the horrors of the factory and tenement may not have been objectively as damaging as the rural squalor and famine from which the industrial proletariat had fled. When any other form of human organization wants to get rid of some of its members, it kills them; when a business does, it fires them. The distinction is an important one: the reader would certainly prefer being a victim of corporate downsizing to being a victim of tribal, national, religious, or ideological downsizing as they have been practiced through the centuries. The reason that we feel so especially betrayed when businesses resort to force and fraud is precisely because in doing so they violate the rules we set for them and they set for themselves; the reason that we accept such practices from the state is that we have tacitly conceded to it the right to commit them.

Certainly the business economy has historically sought to get advantage by allying itself with racist ethnic loyalties, with religious proselytizing efforts, with nationalism, with international ideology, with colonial planters, even—in Japan—with old feudal dynasties; and its deep difference from the colonial empire only became clear in the American Civil War, when the planter/colonial South took on the corporate/industrial North. But the fundamental interest of the business company, that is, whatever increases profit for the owners, largely coincides with the material interests of the human species: a peaceful wealthy world population with as few political, cultural, and tariff boundaries as possible, politically stabilized by perceived fairness and equality, which can supply an educated workforce and masses of consumers with money to spend, in a natural environment that is healthy and rich in resources. We know this condition is what business likes because it prefers to invest in societies that promote it. The bloody and coercive methods of the other forms of human organization simply don't work well for the business company in the long run, since they destroy or impoverish the market, hobble trade, hold back technological advance, restrict access to raw materials, pollute and degrade the environment, eliminate vitalizing competition, or provide inferior workers.

Business has not only done less harm than any other large-scale human institution; it is also the source of enormous benefits to our species: manufactured goods, sciences, forms of communication, medical advances, improved records, technologies, systems of organization, humanitarian values, leisure, and grand flowerings of the arts. Such benefits as literacy, law, and democracy could not have developed without the pressure of commercial enterprise. The first writings six thousand years ago in Mesopotamia were markings on seal cylinders recording business contracts. The first laws were created to prevent personal and civil strife from disrupting the flow of trade. In the writings of the seventeenth-century political philosopher John Locke, which deeply influenced the framers of our Constitution, it is quite clear that the purpose of democracy is to protect business enterprise.

Money and Gifts

And yet, and yet. What is it that makes us resist these hard facts and insist that something is terribly wrong with an exclusively business/commercial view of the world? Even if we concede, as we must, that no other form of human organization than a community of profit-seeking businesses can provide so many material benefits and protect us from so many dangers and threats, there is still something missing. Our complaints about the physical crimes of the capitalist marketplace may be unjustified. But they conceal a deeper spiritual dissatisfaction, which is rightly expressed in Jesus' sayings about camels and needles, Dives and Lazarus, and in the rejection of worldly wealth by such visionaries as Buddha, Basho, St. Francis, Li Po, Van Gogh, or our own Henry David Thoreau. The artist proves his or her integrity by starving in a garret; we do not like to think about such wealthy artists as Virgil, Raphael, Verdi, Goethe—or Shakespeare.

Three great charges are brought against the market and the bonds and contracts it employs. The first is that the market alienates us from nature. It does so, say its critics, in various senses. For radical environmentalists, nature is whatever human beings are not; and the market, with the artificial technological world it creates, is the chief sign of our separation from nature. For believers in the romantic anthropology of our times, which seeks a return to a purer, more primitive existence, the market divides us from our own true nature; if we could return to the pretechnological, preeconomic time of the hunter-gatherer, we would be in tune with nature. For Marxists, the market system traps us in an inhuman, prehuman state of necessity and thus alienates us from our true nature. Underneath all of these positions is a fundamental preference for the natural over the artificial—and the assumption that human activities, or at least those activities in which we create and exchange goods and services, are not natural.

The second charge against the market is that it alienates us from each other. Traditional moralists claim that human relationships should always be of the "I-Thou" type, where we value others not for the prospect of economic gain but for themselves. Marxists talk about "commodity fetishism," the alienation of labor, exploitation, and class struggle. Existentialists deplore the abstraction of interpersonal experience that the market imposes. Liberals are prepared to tolerate the market, but only in rigid isolation from the higher values of the community; they insist on a strict demarcation between personal rights and property rights, with a pronounced favoring of the former. Business is for them a necessary evil to be rigorously contained by regulation and permitted only because of the value of the taxes it can pay for the enlightened activities of the democratic state. All agree that economic bonds and debts are evils (even if necessary ones), and that the taking of interest on such bonds and debts compounds the evil.

The third charge is that the market alienates us from the divine. By definition, say the authorities of virtually every contemporary mainline religious denomination, the realm of the spiritual is the opposite of the realm of the economic. Grace cannot be earned but only given. Sacrifice, human and divine, mediates between God and Man—and sacrifice cannot be defined in market terms. The old idea of the Divine Economy, of the covenant between God and Man as a kind of contract, of the sacrifice of Christ as a ransom, has been swept largely under the carpet by religious progressives; and the spiritual balance sheets to be found in other world religions, such as the Hindu concept of karma or the Mayan idea of blood debt, have been studiously ignored. For mainline American theologians the market is the chief thing that disappears when we move from earth to heaven.

Thus there has been a deep rift between our culture and our economy, between our ideals of ecological purity and unconditional love on one hand, and our actual, highly successful, capitalist way of making our living on the other. That rift has damaged our personal lives by giving us unrealistic expectations of perfection and has indeed corrupted our business ethics by exempting them from the requirements of personal morality. The division of the world into two spheres, the moral and the economic, has been a self-fulfilling prophecy: perhaps the world of business is as ruthless, underhanded, and cruel as it often is precisely because we have exempted it from the realms of truth, beauty, and goodness.

Contemporary anthropology offers us a unique opportunity to make further progress in understanding the roots of human economics. Since Marx and before, it has been taken for granted that "primitive" or "aboriginal" or "natural" human economies operated purely by gift exchange and barter. According to the left-wing version of this view, when money was invented, and with it the cash economy, commodities, and the quantification of work and time, it tended to replace the old relationships of mutual obligation. It created economically expansionist societies that offered the innocent communities with which they made contact two grim alternatives: to go under or to adopt the new system. Societies that did the latter suffered the corruption and decay of their old free institutions, their arts, their religion, and their family structure. The right-wing version of this gloomy myth was somewhat more optimistic: the advent of currency and trade gave people freedom as well as alienation, equality as well as anomie, and it made possible the refinements of culture, the opportunities of civilization, and the development of republican institutions.

But it now turns out that both accounts are substantially wrong. New ethnographic research, such as is reported in *Money and the Morality of Exchange,* a pathbreaking collection of essays in economic anthropology edited by Johnny Parry and Maurice Bloch, gives a very different picture. It appears that all human societies, ranging from hunter-gatherer bands to industrial states, contain a spectrum of transactional orders, from the relatively familial, cooperative, gift-based, and uncalculated, to the relatively individualistic, competitive, impersonal, and calculated. Even nonmonetary economies possess some equivalent of the numerical monetary order, in such forms as cowrie shells, wampum, cocoa beans, or stone wheels. As technology advances, especially the technology of trading and stored value, the allocation of objects and activities between the gift-exchange area and the money-exchange area can change, often catastrophically, but the two realms themselves remain, uncomfortably tied to each other through intermediate types of exchange (such as dowry and brideprice) that carry a difficult charge of social ambiguity. No known human society has been able to escape the shame and comedy of this accommodation. According to *Money and the Morality of Exchange,* this is as true for Indians as for Madagascans, for Malays as for Andeans, for Fijians as for the people of Zimbabwe. We all tell in-law jokes.

Thus we are deprived of the easy moral conclusions that flow from the myth of an economic Eden and a subsequent Fall into our present wicked state of commodity fetishism and the alienation of the market. Instead we must accept the coexistence of personal and property values, and learn to reintegrate the world of uncalculated gifts with the world of trade and commercial exchange. This means not only accepting the role of economic interest in the realm of gift but also the moral and personal elements embedded in business dealings. We are all too aware today of the political elements in personal relationships—this is what "political correctness" is all about. But the moral horror with which we greet the intrusion of money matters into love, art, and science shows a suspicious and guilty squeamishness; perhaps we can balance the scale by understanding the generosity and goodness of the market. We must be tough-minded without losing our moral clarity and tolerant of inconsistency without abandoning the search for what is good, true, and beautiful.

In practice, trading partners, participants in auctions, and financial wheeler-dealers like the older generation of oilmen in my city of Dallas (or like most of the merchants in Shakespeare's Venice) operate on a system of mutual personal trust, reciprocity, empathy, and respect. The ad hoc terms of their handshake deals are ratified only later in the legal documents drawn up by lawyers. I have seen Budapest businessmen making deals in the Turkish Baths, where no document or laptop could survive the water and steam. Living business could not exist if it had to wait for its abstract and timeless expression in legal logic. We are deceived if we think that personal relationships cannot exist in business.

Likewise, we are fooling ourselves if we refuse to recognize the business elements in the most tender and intimate of personal relationships, such as the family. Husbands and wives, parents and children, do consciously and unconsciously estimate the economic value of their nearest and dearest, as partners, legators, and heirs. If we recognize those elements and give them their due, we can make free decisions that take them into account. But if we deny them to ourselves, we will be subliminally dominated by them, while rationalizing our actions by some noble pretence. We are crippled by the theoretical assumption that personal bonds and hardheaded business transactions must be absolutely separated. There is a wisdom in the language of bonds and obligations that insists that spiritual and emotional ties are always embodied—even incarnated, in the religious sense—in economic relations, and economic relations are the medium out of which the highest expressions of heart and spirit emerge. Money can be thought of as *negative obligation.* That is, to possess money means that all other persons are obligated to the possessor for the past benefits that the possessor has directly or indirectly conferred upon them. Money is the stored, certified, and abstracted gratitude of one's community, gratitude that can be "cashed in" for goods and services at the possessor's desire. Money is practical quantified objectified love. Despite the huge practical violations of this essential principle, it can help us unravel, though not dispel, the bad conscience and mixed feelings with which we consider even the most honest of our own financial dealings. The old meaning of "economy" is "household regimen"—a concept that unites the tender fleshly bonds of filial and marital relationships with the practical disposition of family resources, and the market dealings of a home with the public world in which it exists.

Shakespeare's Guide to the Market

Certainly the money view of things does not satisfy our spiritual needs, at least not as presently understood, interpreted, and enacted. When the cash economy of the human community loses contact with the traditional barter and gift exchange system, something profoundly valuable gets lost. Perhaps all of our violent and brutal attempts to replace economic rationality with bloody religious, ethnic, nationalistic, or ideological conquest are attempts to recover that lost sense of community and spiritual dignity. But a profound change of heart has begun. It is a change of heart partly enforced by sheer experience. Since the collapse of socialism it has become clear that we shall be living with the free market for the foreseeable future. What we need is a human economics, a capitalism with a human face; that is, a kind of market that fully expresses the moral, spiritual, and aesthetic relationships among persons and things. It is clear that we should revise our earlier mechanistic notion of economics. Must we find a new language for it?

The answer, surprisingly, is no. As Shakespeare shows, buried within our existing language of finance and business are the living meanings that we seek. Such words as "bond," "trust," "goods," "save," "equity," "value," "mean," "redeem," "redemption," "forgive," "dear," "obligation," "interest," "honor," "company," "balance," "credit," "issue," "worth," "due," "duty," "thrift," "use," "will," "partner," "deed," "fair," "owe," "ought," "treasure," "sacrifice," "risk," "royalty," "fortune," "venture," and "grace" preserve within them the values, patterns of action, qualities, abstract entities, and social emotions that characterize the gift and barter exchange systems upon which they are founded. Indeed, these words, whose meanings are inseparable from their economic content, make up a large fraction of our most fundamental ethical vocabulary.

The core questions of economics are What is value? and How is it created? These are mysterious questions, not accessible to the mathematical methods of the academic discipline of economics, which deals admirably with how "utility"—the technical term for value—is exchanged, stored, communicated, regulated, and gauged, but which remains prudently silent on the nature and origin of "utility" itself.

Perhaps poets can tell us more than economists can about what value is in itself. Poets must be always exploring the subtle chemistry of the meaning of words, and the old and new ways in which human beings come to desire and cherish that meaning. Poets spend their lives making value out of combinations of words that have no economic worth in themselves, being common property, infinitely reproducible, and devoid of rarity value. William Shakespeare, for instance, became one of the richest commoners in England—a media tycoon of his day—essentially by combining words in such a way as to persuade people to pay good money for them. Where poets blaze the trail, economists and business people can follow, usually without knowing who made the path in the first place. This book makes a large claim: that the poet Shakespeare can be a wise guide to twenty-first-century economics.

Shakespeare was a key figure, perhaps *the* key figure, in creating that Renaissance system of meanings, values, and implicit rules that eventually gave rise to the modern world market and that still underpin it. Using Shakespeare's dramatic and poetic definitions of those charged words—"bond," "trust," "good," and so on—English-speaking merchants transformed the planet and made the language of a small cold wet island the lingua franca of the world. It is no coincidence that the people who created the British Commonwealth were people who knew the plots of Shakespeare's plays, quoted

Shakespeare frequently in their own writing, had been required to read Shakespeare in school, had participated in school and amateur theater productions of his works, and had thus absorbed unconsciously his ideas about human and natural productivity, ownership, cooperation, and reciprocity. All over the world English has become the essential language for business, banking, science, telecommunications, market transactions, air traffic control, the wording of political treaties, international law, and so on. The Commonwealth was a trading empire, and its fundamental structure of joint-stock companies, the stock market, banks, business law, bonds, currency, and patents survived its political decline to become the basic organizing principles of the world's economy. Shakespeare's influence has been almost as strong in the United States: even the King and the Duke, the ignorant charlatans in *Huckleberry Finn,* are able to recall from memory enough fragments of Shakespeare to construct an entire soliloquy, and Twain's audience would have been knowledgeable enough not only to recognize the lines, but to laugh at their misquotation! As of this date five major movies based on Shakespeare's plays are playing in the United States; somewhere every day one or more of his plays are being performed in national or regional theaters and shown on cable TV. If there were no time limit on copyright, Shakespeare would surely be the highest-paid popular screen and stage writer in the country.

Shakespeare made us conceive an economy as like a theater company, a troupe of actors, whose interactions generate the plot of the play; he taught us practically how life with others is not necessarily a zero-sum game but an arena where all may profit and competition increases the payoffs for everyone. By this I mean that like a play, a political economy is made up of persons who through their very differences and conflicts make up an artistic whole that is greater than the sum of its parts. A good play has a meaning that gives value to all the characters in it—its larger significance is a kind of profit that accrues to all its members. The plot or story of the play shapes time for the characters in such a way that they take on a dignity of being— even if they are villains—that they could not have had in isolation. By watching a play we deepen our own sense of the meaning of words, because the words are illustrated by living examples. No playwright saw better than Shakespeare the inner economy of a play, the way that value is created collectively, and the deep analogy to the economics of a human community. All the world's a stage. By now many other cultures and languages have absorbed those rich and peculiar notions of trade, reciprocity, the deal, and so on that Shakespeare helped to embed in the Anglo-Saxon imagination and the practices of democratic politics that arise out of them. Shakespeare's economic language has survived the huge challenges of socialism, communism, fascism, and the other statisms that arose in reaction against its new vision of things.

But its positive contributions have not yet ceased. Until now they have been largely unconscious and unacknowledged, a habit of thought and feeling absorbed with the two or three hundred Shakespearean phrases that most English speakers know but do not know they know. For Shakespeare to make his full contribution to the next century, his wisdom must be analyzed more explicitly. This has not happened so far in the area of economics because his critics and interpreters, excellent though they often were, have usually had a blind spot as far as money was concerned. There are fine exceptions, such as Marc Shell, Kenneth Burke, Richard Weisberg, and the Law and Literature school of scholars. But in general the fact remains that until the twentieth century Shakespeare critics were gentlemen scholars, who aspired to the old values and lifestyle of the aristocracy, with its contempt for trade and its superiority to money matters; and in the twentieth century their successors were for the most part university intellectuals whose political loyalties were usually to the left of the general population, and who, as liberals, socialists, or Marxists, likewise despised the market and its values. Thus much of Shakespeare's business wisdom has been passed over in embarrassed silence, and some major misinterpretations have crept into our understanding.

Shakespeare's core insight is that human-created value is not essentially different from natural value. The market is a garden. The value that is added by manufacture and the reflection of that value in profit and interest are but a continuation of nature's own process of growth and development. As I shall show in chapter 2, the creative processes that produce a wildflower, a domesticated animal like a dog or horse, a yeasty loaf of bread, a violin, a house, a clock, and a poem are not in Shakespeare's opinion fundamentally different. They are all nature naturing, giving birth to new and more valuable forms of existence by recombining old ones. And if it is natural for value to increase, then it is also natural for the symbolic store of that value, money, to increase by compound interest. Shakespeare proposes a kind of gardening economics, a technique of *growing* value rather than extracting and exploiting existing stores of it embodied in raw materials such as topsoil, ores, and fossil fuels, or in the youthful strength of the laborer.

For Shakespeare economic exchange is the embodiment of human moral relations. He does not make a strict distinction between personal rights and property rights. For him personal love cannot be divided from the bonds of property and service that embody it. In *As You Like It* Shakespeare defines marriage as a "blessed bond of board and bed," in which three "b" words, "blessed" (the emotional and spiritual element), "board" (the material and economic element), and "bed" (the sexual and reproductive element), are likewise combined in a fourth, the "bond" of the nuptial contract (V.iv.142). The intangible elements of the contract—love, spiritual communion, friendship—can be cashed, or in Shakespeare's suggestive word, "redeemed," in material terms. For Shakespeare value must be embodied to exist, just as the inscription denoting the denomination of a coin is embodied in the intrinsic value of the metal of which it is made.

In *The Merchant of Venice* Shakespeare correctly implies that the word "market" is related to the word "mercy." Both come from the name of the Roman god of messengers and commerce, Mercury. The mercy of the market is real. Those who in the Marxist tradition persist in seeing the market as impersonal and merciless are comparing it by implication with the intimate world of uncounted cost and unquestioned trust that they believe exists in the family, in a friendship, in a traditional tribal village, or in a nonprofit organization dedicated to some higher voluntary purpose or liberal art. Perhaps the market is less forgiving than such communities, though anthropologists, sociologists, and novelists have charted the often ruthless politics and unyielding cruelty of families, friendships, villages, and universities. But communities of this kind are not the alternative to the market, nor has the market shown any sign of putting an end to them—they flourish still as they always did, and their sphere in society is proportionately no smaller in relation to the market than it ever was. The market is the place where one can begin to communicate with strangers, where one can negotiate, where there is time to haggle and latitude for error, where a loan can be prolonged because the lender wants his money back, where defeat does not mean extinction but the opportunity to pull off a better deal another day. It encourages a basic level of civility and requires of those who would profit by it a preparedness to take risks in trusting others, even if the risk taking is the margin for error in the quantification of risk itself when one is estimating the interest one should charge on a loan. The Shakespearean theater was a kind of marketplace; and that market was one of the preconditions for the emergence of democratic politics. In fact we could say that true democracy is the political expression of the Shakespearean market.

Even the human and the divine, in Shakespeare's Christianity, are engaged in a kind of purchase or ransom—and this view is more in line with the theology of the other major religions than are the antimaterialistic views of the modern mainline Christian sects. The Covenant is also a contract, a bond. Sacrifice is not the opposite of trade, but the *way* humans trade with God. As humans, we are indebted financially, ecologically, morally, and spiritually; and those various forms of debt are all deeply entwined. This sense of debt is at the core of both Shakespeare's comedy and his tragedy. Our mortal search for redemption is, in his plays, in part an attempt to repay what we owe and thus regain the pledge, or security, that we signed over in return for the leasehold of our lives. What is that pledge? and in what coin do we repay? Can we repay? These are the central questions of religion. The "lig" in obligation—ligament, ligature, bond—is etymologically the same as the "lig" in religion.

This book makes three arguments, following Shakespeare. First, that human art, production, and exchange are a continuation of natural creativity and reproduction, not a rupture of them. Second, that our human bonds with one another, even the most ethical and personal, cannot be detached from the values and bonds of the market. And third, that there is a mysterious dispensation according to which our born condition of debt can be transformed into one of grace. These three arguments may be taken as refutations of the three reproaches to the market offered by its critics: that the market necessarily alienates us from nature, from each other, and from God.

2

"great creating nature"

How Human Economics Grows Out of Natural Increase

The Economics of the Industrial Revolution

The previous chapter argued that we must change our thinking about economic bonds and money, so that our moral and personal lives need no longer be at odds with our means of economic support. In this chapter I shall show how the mechanistic science and technology of the eighteenth and nineteenth centuries divorced our economy from its traditional relationship with natural productivity, how contemporary biological science, complexity theory, and synergetic production methods are on the way to restoring our economic connection with nature, and how Shakespeare can help us manage the transition from one to the other. If bonds are essentially exploitative, as in the Industrial Revolution model, then Cordelia is wrong to love her father according to her bond. But the play insists that she is right, which means that there must be a form of bond and a kind of productive activity that is not exploitative.

Since the Industrial Revolution of the late eighteenth and early nineteenth century the dominant model of industry, and thus of profit, has been one of the exploitation of natural resources. In the traditional mode of subsistence and husbandry, farmers and peasants labored like Adam in the Old Testament to make the earth fruitful. But the new class of entrepreneurs rejected this ancient neolithic mode of thought. The lords of the mines, cotton mills, and railroads wanted a faster accumulation of capital. To be fair, the best of them were nurtured on Enlightenment ideals of freedom, equality, and human brotherhood, acculturated to a Romantic literature that emphasized the fulfilment of desire and the actualization of human potential. Progressive spirits of this kind, the eighteenth-century pottery king and philosopher Josiah Wedgwood, for example, wanted not only to make money but also to inaugurate a culture and society that would liberate the human race from drudgery and oppression. But progress depended upon the conquest of nature. Thus they accelerated economic activity by felling forests, burning fossil fuels, damming rivers, tearing up the earth for mines and construction, and finally harnessing the substance of human life by time and work studies. Instead of living inefficiently—as they saw it—off the interest generated by natural increase, they broke into nature's capital assets and dismantled them to create an urban world.

Given the science available to the first industrialists, this model made perfect sense; no alternative would have been "realistic." The Newtonian physics bequeathed by the eighteenth century to the nineteenth had portrayed the universe as a piece of clockwork. Clockwork has two characteristics: it is predictable and deterministic in its operations (the whole virtue of a clock is predictability!); and it runs down. Living things are just another part of the machine; their growth and development is merely a temporary gain made at the cost of a greater diminution in natural order elsewhere, and with the prospect of extinction when those resources give out. If we are part of the universe, then we too are deterministic, and biological, economic, and historical laws determine what we do. If the universe is running down, then we are in competition with one another and with nature for a diminishing stockpile of usable energy.

The nineteenth-century science of thermodynamics triumphantly confirmed this analysis: disorder (entropy) increases irreversibly with time, and we are here, as Matthew Arnold put it, "upon a darkling plain / Where ignorant armies clash by night"—the light is growing dimmer and chaos mounts. Thus our only defense as human beings is to burn up the available order in the natural universe at a rate that is faster than the natural decay of the world, so as to fuel human progress and enlightenment. Capitalists and socialists alike tacitly accepted this eventually despairing view of the world—Tennyson's pessimism about the fall of the Round Table in *Idylls of the King* is of a piece with Marx's vision of class struggle in *Das Kapital*. Civilizations decline and fall; and the social classes are locked in a relentless conflict over resources and labor. Malthus foresaw a final collapse as the human population overwhelmed the natural resources of the planet, Wagner portrayed the final victory of the forces of economic darkness in the *Götterdämmerung,* Hardy shook his fist at God for it, and Spengler gave it historical form in *The Decline of the West.*

We in the twentieth century have largely inherited this view of the world, despite the fact that it is now, as I shall show, so incomplete as to be scientifically obsolete. Whenever we speak of dwindling natural resources, of America's disproportionate consumption of energy, of sharing out the national wealth in a fairer manner, of equal pay for equal work, of liberation from biological destiny, we are unconsciously adopting the rhetoric of nineteenth-century industrial exploiters and the nineteenth-century revolutionaries who sought to despoil them of their gains. Let us be fair; the Industrial Revolution did in fact liberate a huge moiety of the world's population into a life relatively free of ignorance, famine, disease, and tyranny. The surge in the world's population in this time bears mute testimony to an enormous increase in real human welfare—fewer babies dying, people getting sick and starving to death less often, cleaner water to drink, children getting the education they need to make a living, and life expectancy doubled. If we think of the world's fossil fuels, topsoil, biodiversity, and usable ores as capital, perhaps the investment of some of that capital in four billion new human beings may be a sound one: time will tell.

But the rhetoric itself constrains and limits what we can think in it. A new scientific vision of the world is emerging, one that has much in common with the traditions of husbandry and natural fruitfulness that Enlightenment science replaced, though at the same time it makes possible a rate of progress undreamed of by the peasant and the farmer. The word "progress" itself needs to be redefined. At present it is a battlefield between those who are tacitly willing to accept the natural costs of human technology and those who reject those costs on the tacit grounds that there is only so much diminishing pie to go round, and that it should be shared out fairly among human beings and the other species with which we share the planet. The problem is, their shared rhetoric rules out the possibility of a kind of progress that would *not* involve loss for any constituency, and might involve gain for all; and it discourages the development of technology that enhances the life of the whole planet, biological, economic, and spiritual. In the new view of things nature generates value by the interplay and synergy of its elements, as a stage play generates meaning through the interaction of its characters. Let us therefore explore a different definition of progress: one that sees human economic activity as a continuation of the natural process of evolution and increase. William Shakespeare is uniquely qualified to guide us in this search, as a transcendent genius in his own right, as a master of the supremely synergistic art of drama, and as an inhabitant of an age in which old ideas of husbandry and new concepts of technological progress coexisted and could be compared and combined.

The Garden Economics of *The Winter's Tale*

For Shakespeare the ideal form of economic work is gardening. In his poetic vision, gardening is the union of art and nature, where the distinction between the artificial and the natural loses its negative force.

In *The Winter's Tale* there is a little episode that has the profoundest implications. The shepherdess Perdita (who is actually a foundling foreign princess, though she does not know it) is holding a rustic feast to celebrate a successful sheepshearing. She is in love with Florizel, prince of the realm, who is courting her in disguise, against the wishes of his father King Polixenes. Polixenes, not wishing his son to marry a mere commoner, has disguised himself and his chief counselor Camillo in order to attend the feast and observe the prince and his beloved together, and to break up the liaison. None of the major characters in the scene, then, is what he or she seems; and Shakespeare is thus inviting us to see beneath surface meanings to the inner truth. Perdita, who according to custom has been giving flowers to her guests as befit their age and station in life—spring flowers for the young, summer flowers for the mature, and so on—greets her distinguished-looking unknown guests courteously.

> PERDITA: You're welcome, sir.
> Give me those flow'rs there, Dorcas. Reverend sirs,
> For you there's rosemary and rue; these keep
> Seeming and savor all the winter long.
> Grace and remembrance be to you both,
> And welcome to our shearing!
> (IV.iv.72)

Like young people in any century, Perdita thinks that anyone over forty is old, and so she gives her guests flowers suitable for septuagenarians. Rather amused, Polixenes gently teases her for this.

> POLIXENES: Shepherdess—
> A fair one are you—well you fit our ages
> With flow'rs of winter.

Perdita recovers from her embarrassment, excusing herself on the grounds that she doesn't have appropriate late summer flowers to give them:

> PERDITA: Sir, the year growing ancient,
> Not yet on summer's death, nor on the birth
> Of trembling winter, the fairest flow'rs o' th' season
> Are our carnations and streaked gillyvors,
> Which some call Nature's bastards; of that kind
> Our rustic garden's barren; and I care not
> To get slips of them.

She refuses to grow the gaudier late summer and early fall flowers, hinting that there is something improper in their ancestry. A "slip" is a cutting, from which a new plant can be propagated or cloned. Polixenes pursues the matter, intrigued by Perdita's evident discernment, eloquence, and strength of mind.

> POLIXENES: Wherefore, gentle maiden,
> Do you neglect them?

PERDITA: For I have heard it said,
There is an art, which in their piedness shares
With great creating Nature.

But now she has opened up one of the perennial questions of philosophy. What she has just said is that she objects to the art of selective breeding and hybridization by which Renaissance horticulturalists transformed simple wildflowers into elaborate multicolored blooms. Like an ardent advocate of environmental purity in our own time, she is suspicious of artificial interventions into nature; Great Creating Nature is for her a goddess like the Gaia of our own New Age philosophers. There is perhaps a further unconscious thought lurking in her mind. She has just been anxiously worrying about her own presumption in entertaining the amorous advances of a prince, whose blood and breeding are so far above what she imagines to be her own humble origins. She is embarrassed about the fine clothes she is wearing for the feast and about the rustic garments that her lover, Florizel, has taken on in order to woo her without revealing his princely identity. Nature and human art should not mix, nor should commoners and nobility; if they do, appearances become deceptive and things will not be as they seem. Perdita is innocent, straightforward, and honest, and dislikes adulteration and deceit. Her decision not to cultivate the carnations and gillyvors is based on a personal code of sincerity:

PERDITA: I'll not put
The dibble in earth, to set one slip of them;
No more than were I painted, I would wish
This youth should say 'twere well, and only therefore
Desire to breed by me.

Perdita dislikes the hybrid flowers because they use their attractive looks to gain the advantage of being reproduced instead of their more modest sisters. It is as if she were to paint herself with cosmetics in order to make Florizel cultivate her with *his* "dibble" (garden trowel). But there are wider implications still. For if Perdita is right, art itself is a profoundly questionable enterprise. The very art of drama in which she is portrayed is a fiction. An actor is playing her part—in Elizabethan times, that actor would have been a gifted prepubescent boy, and so the whole enterprise is fraught with dissimulation. And what is art? For Shakespeare the word had an enormous range of related meanings, which had not disentangled themselves from each other. It could mean "art" in the contemporary sense of what we find in an art gallery, a book of poetry, a symphony hall, or a theater. But it was also a normal term for skill or technique, and by extension for technology, machinery, and mechanical devices of all kinds; and it also meant magic, alchemy, and the mystical sciences of astrology and prognostication. It could also mean deceptive practice or cunning imposture.

The ambivalence and complexity implicit in Perdita's use of the term are surely quite familiar in our own times. At present we are struggling with the ethical and health implications of the science of genetic engineering by means of recombinant DNA. Should we buy the new genetically altered tomatoes on the grocery shelves, or drink the milk produced with the aid of bovine hormones? What about the strawberries with their chimeric pesticide genes, or the experimental fruit flies with eyes growing out of their legs and antennae, the patented strains of cancerous mice? We must balance the benefits of insulin, thyroid hormones, oil-spill-eating bacteria, interferon, and gene-grown taxol against the specter of laboratory killer viruses; gene therapy for inherited diseases against sinister eugenic schemes to improve the human gene pool; in vitro fertilization and implantation against the legal and kinship dilemmas that result when the birth mother is not the same as the genetic mother. Reading Shakespeare we become aware that our problems are not new; Perdita's unease prefigures ours. Indeed, since the neolithic agricultural revolution, when we first began selecting plants and animals to breed future stock, we have been in the business of genetic engineering and recombinant DNA. Our humblest domestic and culinary techniques are just as "unnatural" as the activities of the biochemists. Brewer's yeast, sourdough, ginger ale plants, and cheese mites are all out-and-out examples of human tinkering with natural genetic processes. When we divide a clump of irises in the garden, we are literally practicing clone technology; when we enter a pedigree dog or cat or pigeon in a show, we are practicing eugenics on an entire species. Worse still, when we choose what we believe to be an exceptionally kind, intelligent, attractive, healthy, and honest person to be our mate and bear or sire our children, we are engaged in human eugenics on our own local scale. There is no escape.

Thus Perdita cannot evade the fact that as a tool-using animal—the "dibble" she uses for gardening is a cunning little technological device—she must alter nature in order to survive. She needs "art" in its technological sense. Likewise, as a social, role-performing animal she must put on appearances—her festive party dress—in order to coexist with other humans (the theatrical sense of "art"). Yet she has a point. It is only nature that is creative, that has the power to grow and reproduce; and it is only when one deals with the inner person rather than the outer social mask that one can obtain true commitment and trustworthy sincerity from someone. The implication here is that inner trust is somehow related to the living power of growth and reproduction—an idea that Shakespeare reinforces when he has Florizel, in the same scene, plight his troth to Perdita:

> FLORIZEL: It cannot fail, but by
> The violation of my faith, and then
> Let Nature crush the sides o' th' earth together,
> And mar the seeds within.
> (IV.iv.479)

How may this contradiction between nature and art be resolved? Polixenes'
reply to Perdita reveals a wisdom that we could do well to take to heart. Recall that she has just disparaged the gillyvors on the grounds that there is an
art that went into their ancestry.

> POLIXENES: Say there be;
> Yet Nature is made better by no mean
> But Nature makes that mean; so over that art
> Which you say adds to Nature, is an art
> That Nature makes. You see, sweet maid, we marry
> A gentler scion to the wildest stock,
> And make conceive a bark of baser kind
> By bud of nobler race. This is an art
> Which does mend Nature, change it rather; but
> The art itself is Nature.
> (IV.iv.88)

The image that Polixenes uses to explain the relationship between nature
and art (or rather, perhaps, between potentially artful nature and fundamentally natural art) is the horticultural technology of grafting. This is what he
means when he speaks of marrying a "gentler scion to the wildest stock." A
gardener or vineyard tender will cut off the upper stem of a vigorous wild
plant and bind to the stock that remains the stem and upper branches of a
more delicate hybrid plant. Nature is accommodating enough to allow the
graft to "take," and the two plants are fused into one. The resulting combination has the virtues of both—the resistance to disease, pests, and frost of
the wild stock, and the hybrid's desired characteristics of productiveness, excellence of fruit or flower, or perfume. "A bark of baser kind" (the wild
stock or root) is made to "conceive" (become pregnant) by a "bud of nobler
race" (the hybrid cultivar). The Elizabethan word "conceive" had for them
as for us the further meaning "to engender a new idea," so Shakespeare is
also suggesting that there is a natural continuity between the miracle of
sexual fertility and the even greater miracle of imaginative creativity.

The main point of Polixenes' remarks is that the art of genetic engineering by which we improve nature, or even change it, was itself created by nature. The plain ancestral gillyvors have the genetic potential to produce the
gaudy streaks that attract the eyes of men and women, and persuade human
gardeners to propagate them. Humans become a way for streaked gillyvors
to make more streaked gillyvors, to extend the diversity of the gillyvor
species by branching out a new breed specially adapted to the environment
of human culture. The gillyvor is by nature an art-using plant. And we humans are by nature art-using animals. We survived to reproduce because we
had the capacity to make tools like sheep hooks or dibbles and breed domestic species like sheep or gillyvors for our own purposes. Moreover, our capacity to make fictions—to tell lies and put on disguises and mount plays

and enhance our looks by clothing or cosmetics—is likewise a natural talent, like the eagle's to fly or the mole's to dig. It is of a piece with our ability to express our thoughts in words, and to build families, tribes, cities, and nations.

It is also the foundation of all economic activity. Human art, human fiction, human invention, and human technology are not unnatural forces that have suddenly supervened upon nature, but are the natural continuation of nature's own evolutionary process. Since they are natural productive forces in their own right, they participate in nature's own mysterious capacity to grow and reproduce. Furthermore, human economic production cannot be separated from human reproduction; the family is still the primary unit of economic cooperation, and marriage is the major means of distributing the wealth that accrues to production. Interestingly enough under the circumstances (against his father's wishes Florizel intends a marriage between a cultivated prince and a wild shepherdess), Polixenes uses metaphors of social class to describe the graft—"gentler," "baser," "nobler." Even now we use the technical grafting term "scion" (the cutting that is grafted to the stock) to refer to the offspring of illustrious families. But the implication is that there is no necessary harm in marriages between the social classes. In fact Polixenes has shown the fallacy in his own objection to his son's proposed union.

But his immediate purpose is to show Perdita that her hard-and-fast distinction between sterile insincere art and creative honest nature will not hold up. Nature will accept the graft of the wild and the artificial: nature can be artistic, art can be natural. Art and appearances can possess the same sincerity, faithfulness, and inner trustworthiness that Florizel compares to the seeds of the earth. This does not mean, of course, that untruths and disguises are always harmless. To the contrary. After all, Polixenes has disguised himself with the harmful intent of breaking up his son's marriage. Though he will later repent of his anger when he finds out that Perdita is exactly the kind of grafted hybrid he has described—a princess by birth, cut off from her ancestral roots and grafted onto the stock of a peasant family—in the meantime lies and deception are quite as dangerous and harmful as they are anywhere else in Shakespeare's plays. Nevertheless, it is in disguises and subterfuges also that Florizel and Perdita escape the wrath of the king. There is nothing wrong in themselves with fictions, contrivances, and masks, nor are such things unique to human society: the gillyvors mask themselves in order to be cultivated.

So the issue has changed profoundly. It is no longer a matter of having to choose between the innocent creative sincerity of nature and the sophisticated sterile deceptions of art—a choice in which we would be forced to abandon all the advantages of technology, consciousness, language, and social communication if we were to opt for moral purity. Art and nature are one: we must now use our moral and aesthetic judgment to choose between courses of action, not some simple formula that labels one artificial and the other natural. The past course of nature as we can discern it in the evolution of plants, animals, and humans—and even, today, in the cosmos of physics and chemistry—can act as a suggestive and potent guide in making such decisions. But the decision we make will itself be part of nature, and it will take its place beside other natural events, both beneficial and destructive. When we choose to alter nature by a technological intervention, or when we choose to alter society by some new fiction, we should do so with the whole tradition of natural evolution in mind. But we cannot abdicate the prerogative of choice itself that nature has endowed us with.

And such decisions do not extend only to matters of horticulture and other technologies, nor even to our social and economic arrangements, as the whole sexual subtext of this wonderfully subtle passage of Shakespeare implies. Even in matters of human reproduction there is no comfortable dividing line between art and nature. The very choice of marriage partner is itself a reproductive technology, favoring one set of human characteristics over another in the propagation of the species. If in the future we develop biotechnological means for healing or improving the genome of the human embryo, this capability will be new only in its scope and speed, not in its essentially difficult and problematic character. After all, a woman who chooses for the father of her children a good, honest, and intelligent man is discriminating against some other potential mate whom she has consciously or unconsciously judged less worthy of continuing the species. But this also means that we should not be squeamish in continuing to improve our control over our own genetic future. The damage, so to speak, has already been done; even before human beings came along, nature, like the gillivors that use their colors to attract bees that will help them reproduce, had already been taking over control of its own evolution.

Investment and Evolution in the Sonnets

Nature is the realm of growth; but as Shakespeare was well aware, it is also the realm of decay. The nineteenth-century thermodynamic view of the world as irreversibly running down is still true as far as it goes. Indeed, this idea is the central problem that Shakespeare addresses in the Sonnets.

> When I consider everything that grows
> Holds in perfection but a little moment . . .
> (15)

> When I have seen by Time's fell hand defaced
> The rich proud cost of outworn buried age,
> When sometime lofty towers I see down-razed,
> And brass eternal slave to mortal rage;
> When I have seen the hungry ocean gain
> Advantage on the kingdom of the shore,
> And the firm soil win of the wat'ry main,

viduality of a loved human being that we miss when it is gone; and that individuality is the product of sexual reproduction, which creates a unique recombination of genes for each new birth. In other words, the process of sexual reproduction that Shakespeare recommends to preserve his friend's beauty is the guarantee that his individuality, the essence of his beauty, is irreproducible! Shakespeare's second answer to the problem of time is proposed at first as an inadequate stopgap measure; parenthood is still "a mightier way" to "make war upon this bloody tyrant Time." But as he examines it, the new answer makes more and more sense.

It is to eternize his friend's beauty in poetry, in the very art by which Shakespeare mourns its passing:

> But thy eternal summer shall not fade,
> Nor lose possession of that fair thou ow'st,
> Nor shall Death brag thou wand'rest in his shade,
> When in eternal lines to time thou grow'st.
> So long as men can breathe or eyes can see,
> So long lives this, and this gives life to thee.
> (18)

We today are reading those lines, so the solution has worked for four hundred years at least. What is especially significant is that poetry is being described as a higher form of sexual reproduction. Both are what Shakespeare, in Sonnet 16, calls "the lines of life that life repair." These lines of life are the lineage of a family, which replaces the dying with the newborn. But they are also, in context, the lines that a portraitist uses to eternalize the features of a sitter; and they are, most fundamentally, the lines of poetry. It is as if the poet has guessed that the genetic code that specifies the shape of our bodies is a line or thread, like the long thread of letters that make up a poem. DNA is indeed a thread of nucleotides, which spell out the "words" and "sentences" of the genes, which in turn determine the proteins that make up the human body. The words in which this beautiful relationship is being conducted find for themselves a form of repeated rhymes and metrical rhythms that are able to reprint themselves in memory and books, as DNA does by peeling its double helix apart and printing the sequence of nucleotides anew upon the raw material within the cell. But poetry is a higher form of reproduction, for it can capture and preserve the mind and individuality of an organism, not just its bodily composition. Living reproduction can outwear the enduring metals and stone with which we build monuments to defy the effects of time. But poetry, which is even more spiritual, intangible, and apparently fragile, is more enduring still:

> Not marble, nor the gilded monuments
> Of princes, shall outlive this pow'rful rhyme,
> But you shall shine more bright in these contents
> Than unswept stone, besmeared with sluttish time.
> (55)

What Shakespeare now does is *graft* the new, cultural form of reproduction upon the old, biological form:

> And, all in war with Time for love of you,
> As he takes from you, I engraft you new.
> (15)

Thus poetry is to living reproduction what living reproduction is to the enduring hardness of the stone and metal out of which we build monuments to defy time's decay. Poetry is grafted onto natural inheritance, so that both the generic and unconscious elements of what we wish to preserve, and also the individual and self-aware elements, are protected.

Poetry can thus transcend the process of decay described by nineteenth-century thermodynamics. Suppose we were trying to arrange a line from Sonnet 18 in the most thermodynamically ordered way, that is with the least entropy. We cannot, for the sake of argument, break up the words into letters or the letters into line segments. The first thing we would do, which is the only sort of thing a strict thermodynamicist could do, is order the words alphabetically: "a compare day I Shall summer's thee to ?" As far as thermodynamics is concerned, such an arrangement would be more ordered than the arrangement, "Shall I compare thee to a summer's day?" as composed by Shakespeare. Here, in a capsule, is the difference between the deterministic linear order that decays with time and nonlinear emergent order that can resist or reverse its effects.

We could even test the thermodynamic order of the first arrangement by a further experiment. Suppose we coded the words in terms of gas molecules, arranged in a row, the hottest ones corresponding to the beginning of the alphabet, the coldest ones to the end, and so on in alphabetical order. If left to themselves in a closed vessel the molecules would, because of the increase of entropy over time, rearrange themselves into random alphabetical order (the hot and cold would get evenly mixed). Just as in a steam engine, where the energy gradient between hot steam and cold steam, or hot steam and cold air, can be used to do work, one would be able to employ the movement of molecules, as the alphabetized "sonnet" rearranged itself, to perform some (very tiny) mechanical task. The poem would be, in William Carlos Williams's phrase, "a machine made of words." And as with any machine, it would take somewhat more energy to put the molecules back into alphabetical order, because of the second law of thermodynamics.

As arranged in Sonnet 18 those words are already in more or less "random" alphabetical order. Yet most human beings would rightly assert that the sonnet order is infinitely more ordered than the thermodynamic, linear, alphabetical one. The information-theory definition of a system with high thermodynamic order (low entropy) is that it takes as few bits of information as possible to specify it, while it takes many bits to specify a high-entropy, low-order system. Indeed, it would take few bits to specify the alphabetical order, and many to specify the sonnet order: hundreds of books have been written about Shakespeare's sonnets, and they are not exhausted yet.

For a reader of poetry this is not a sign of the poem's randomness but rather of its exquisite order. In other respects the poem does seem to exhibit the characteristics of order. If highly damaged by being rearranged, it could be almost perfectly reconstituted by a person who knew Shakespeare's other sonnets and the rules of grammar, logic, and especially poetic meter. One would need only perhaps a fragment of the lost original, showing its meter and a rhyme, and this, together with a syllable-count of the whole, would be more than enough to reconstruct the sonnet. The sonnet can "do work": it has deeply influenced human culture and has helped to transform the lives of many students and lovers. It is an active force in the world precisely because it does not have the low-entropy simplicity of the alphabetical order that might enable it to do mechanical work. Thus the force of beauty is of an entirely different nature from the force of power. The answer to Shakespeare's anguished question

> Since brass, nor stone, nor earth, nor boundless sea,
> But sad mortality o'ersways their power,
> How with this rage shall beauty hold a plea,
> Whose action is no stronger than a flower?
> (65)

is that beauty is more powerful than power, because beauty renews and propagates itself unendingly, while power, however destructive locally and temporarily, must always run down and decay into randomness.

Natural Profit

What does all this mean for economics, which is the primary focus of this book, and for business, which is its primary target? Shakespeare's vision of an economics of natural fecundity can help us move from the thermodynamic pessimism of the Industrial Revolution to a new vision of life-affirming economic progress. As I have already suggested, the nineteenth-century notion of the world as containing a diminishing stockpile of natural value is rapidly becoming obsolete. Certainly, in thermodynamic fashion, stone and metal wear out in time. The "hungry ocean" gains "advantage on the kingdom of the shore," but then the "firm soil," in the form of encroaching sand dunes or salt marshes, takes over what was once the ocean's. It is a zero-sum game; one realm's gain is another's loss, and meanwhile chaos itself increases a little at the expense of both—"state itself confounded to decay." But in a living ecosystem, on the other hand, one species' gain is not necessarily another species' loss. The story of biological evolution is largely one of cooperation, synergy, symbiosis. And competition, even natural violence, can be just a fiercer form of cooperation. As the Eskimos say, the wolf protects the herd: prey species such as caribou rely upon their predators to cull out unfit individuals and preserve the genetic vigor of the survivors. What is waste for one species is food and fuel for another; what is death for one species (such as Douglas firs) is the womb and cradle of others (funguses and beetles).

There is no reason that human manufacturing should not fit itself comfortably into the creative increase of life. Living things grow in a rhythm limited only by their previous increment of growth—that is, in one cycle of growth they can add to their size by a proportion somewhere between none at all and doubling their previous size. The best sustainable rate of growth seems to be at a ratio of about 61.8% in each cycle. This ratio is known as the "golden ratio" or ϕ, and is obtained very simply by creating a series of numbers, known as the Fibonnaci series, each of which is the sum of the two previous numbers, and then working out how fast they increase. For example, if we begin with 1, the next number in the series must also be 1—that is, 1 plus zero (there was no previous term in the series). The next number is 2 (1 + 1). The next is 3 (2 + 1), the next 5 (3 + 2), the next 8, the next 13, the next 21, and so on. If we divide 21 into 13, to obtain the ratio of increase, we get about .619 . . . , and the ratio gets closer and closer to ϕ as the numbers increase. Leonardo Fibonnaci, the discoverer of this series, obtained it by trying to figure out how many rabbits he would get from a single breeding pair after a given number of generations. This growth rhythm expresses itself elegantly in the spirals of seashells and sunflower heads, and in the fronds of ferns, the branchings of trees, and throughout the realms of life. Thus, 61.8% is nature's own profit margin, and this is surely enough for the most enthusiastic business entrepreneur. The trick is to get in sync with nature's own highly efficient processes, while still fulfilling one's human goals. The art of doing this is called gardening or husbandry. We need a gardening economics.

But even before life emerged, the universe was already capable of spontaneously generating new forms of organization, new forms and structures. Before life, new kinds of crystals, polymers, and other complex molecular structures were already precipitating out of the universe as it expanded and cooled. New atomic nuclei were condensing in the hot wombs of young stars. Each fresh creation carries its own requirements for existence, even its own primitive and emergent values. And this enormous natural increase—what we might call natural profit—is achieved without violating any of the gloomy laws of thermodynamics that so depressed our ancestors in the nineteenth century. Usable energy is still running down, and thermodynamic disorder is still increasing with time. The chemist Ilya Prigogine has shown, however, that in open systems far-from-equilibrium states can arise by chance and that these far-from-equilibrium states can in turn give spontaneous birth to new forms of organization that solve the problems presented by the disequilibrium. Living organisms are the classic examples of such forms. What Prigogine calls the "dissipative systems" of chemistry and life—and human culture—use this phenomenon of self-organization to finesse the process of decay, turning the increase of disorder into the increase of information. They then need only trivial amounts of energy to order that information in more and more elegant ways. Thus there is a net increase of usable knowledge that outpaces the increase of physical disorder.

Here again a kind of "gardening economics" suggests itself. Industry need no longer burn huge amounts of natural order to force its will upon matter and thus turn out its mass-produced product. Instead, it might discover the far-from-equilibrium situations that crop up throughout nature and find ways to tweak existing natural processes so as to bring about economically desirable results. In fact industry has already begun doing this on a large scale, as the expansion of the biotechnological sector of contemporary business demonstrates. Industry is also making extensive use of catalytic chemistry, chaotic mixing processes, and the like—those processes in the inorganic world that anticipate the ingenious economy of life. Just as microscopic chips of silicon can now efficiently control the roar of a mighty dump-truck engine, so we can use the efficient leverages offered to us by nature itself to harness the grand natural forces of our living universe. Industrial chemistry loves to exploit those states of matter at the boundaries between the solid, liquid, gaseous, and plasma states or between different crystalline or chemical configurations, where, far from equilibrium, only a small change of temperature, light, chemistry, or pressure can produce large results, giving us devices such as doped silicon computer chips, catalytic converters, self-adjusting sunglasses, liquid crystal displays, efficient fuel injection, or highly sensitive measuring devices such as the home pregnancy test. It took a huge expense of coal and oil and iron ore to develop the cybernetic control systems that now require only a few ounces of silicon and a tiny flow of current to maintain, and that are in turn radically diminishing our need for fossil fuels and ores.

As we have followed it, Shakespeare's reasoning endorses the control and readaptation of natural processes for human purposes. Bioengineering, even including the altering of human genes, is in theory ethically defensible, since nature has already been blamelessly engaged in such activities for billions of years, and the ability to perform them ourselves was given to us by nature. Even to marry is to deflect the evolutionary process, by however small a degree. This argument has immediate practical implications. For instance, the opposition voiced by Jeremy Rifkin and various church groups against the patenting of biomedical processes involving human genes (*Newsweek*, May 29, 1995, etc.) is clearly invalid by Shakespeare's logic. Their argument is that God made living organisms and that thus human beings can only claim as intellectual property artifacts that are dead. There is a disguised version of this idea in Steven Spielberg's and Michael Crichton's *Jurassic Park*. In the light of what we have learned from Shakespeare, we can see that such a line of reasoning will not hold up and leads immediately to absurdities. It would, for instance, make it illegal to sell thoroughbred horses and cattle or put them out to stud, to market meats and vegetables in a grocery store (all normal grocery foods are the result of genetic alteration by selective breeding of plants or animals), or even to charge students for tuition (the "product" of a school or university is the knowledge embedded in the students' brain cells). To be absolutely literalistic, such logic would even forbid marriage, since marriage connects economic obligations with selective reproductive planning.

This is not to say that *any* proposed genetic intervention is permissible. Genetics is a fantastically complex subject, and it is extremely difficult to predict the consequences of actions in this area. The ethics governing any weighty, far-reaching decision apply more strongly to biogenetic intervention than anywhere else. The work should be fail-safe, and every possible consequence should be examined. But on the other hand, all human decisions are subject to unpredictable consequences. This is the tragic field of action. The deep footprint I leave running across the wet field nearby may trip a child and break her neck. Every time a couple get married and start a family, they are taking enormous risks. Would the parents of Adolf Hitler have decided to have children if they had known the result? Could one imagine any worse catastrophe than the birth of this man, generated by routine gene recombination in sexual reproduction? The use of gene technology, licensed and regulated by patent, looks tame by comparison. Indeed, the constraints of customer safety and business goodwill may be the best safeguards against the misuse of a technology that is going to be developed whether we like it or not.

Economic enterprise, then, can imitate and participate in the natural productiveness of living and other nonlinear dynamical systems. But there is a further implication in the passages from the Sonnets and *The Winter's Tale* cited here that suggests there is a productiveness in art and poetry that, when grafted onto life, can outdo the productivity of life itself. If industry models itself upon thermodynamics, it will extract smaller and smaller amounts of value from a dying world. If it models itself upon life, it will create a sustainable planetary economy. But if it grafts onto the life model the further model of art and poetry, it will begin to achieve miracles.

Shakespeare's philosophy of natural and human productivity thus has further contemporary relevance, concerning the nature of advertising. Both in the Sonnets and *The Winter's Tale* he shows that the ideas and appearances of art are not necessarily deceptions concealing the truth, but can be new truths in themselves or revelations of old truths. Perdita's rejection of the gillyvors is based partly on her sense that they advertise, they sell the sizzle rather than the steak. Many today likewise decry advertising as the creation of artificial desires. Marxists talk of "commodity fetishism" and condemn the consumerism that they see as the result. But again, Shakespeare shows us that the art and poetry that recommend something to us and mediate our relationship to it—its advertisements—are not essentially different from the inner structures of information that shape and order the thing itself. And they are no less legitimate in themselves. DNA is a kind of poetry, which organizes insensitive matter into appetite, passion, desire. The inorganic world would consider the motivations of living organisms to be artificial, inauthentic, fetishistic. Life is matter that advertises, that sells the sizzle,

that disguises itself in elegant genetic and bodily structures in order to survive. Again, this is not to say that all life, all art, all advertising are beneficial
and should be encouraged. Cancers are alive; and art and advertising can tell
lies. By their fruits ye shall judge them, said Jesus; we must discriminate between the good and the bad in the area of genetic, poetic, or corporate fictions as in any other area. There is a deeper truth in good and valid fictions
that overwhelms their literal inaccuracy, and it is this by which we judge
them. The deeper truth has two aspects: it honestly portrays the nature of
the evolutionary process that generated the fiction in the first place; and it
makes possible the richest interplay of free beings in the future.

Part of the challenge and promise of the Sonnets and *The Winter's Tale*
for business is to resolve the oppositions between art and technology, art
and life, production and creativity, natural increase and profit, advertising
and production, just as Shakespeare resolves them in his poetry. After all,
Shakespeare is today a thriving industry, with an annual turnover of billions
of dollars. This is not bad for a business that is four hundred years old and
puts out a product that requires almost no raw materials, uses only minute
amounts of energy, and is environmentally safe.

The "sizzle" of Shakespeare's plays, the quality of charmingly complex
yet harmonious integration that sells the product, is beauty. In the coming
struggle between political power and commercial wealth-creation, business
will do wrong to borrow the coercive weapons of government, the policy of
thermodynamic force. Its best strategy will be to adopt what Shakespeare
calls the action of a flower. The bonds of political power are coercive even in
a democracy; democracy's superiority over all other forms of political rule is
only that the monopoly over violence that we accord to government is controlled by a majority rather than a minority. But the bonds of commercial
exchange are entered into voluntarily and are suasive rather than coercive in
their nature. To the extent that they are coercive, to that extent the system is
not working, and its bonds give up the natural productiveness and creativity
to which they are the heirs. The market will prove its superiority to the vote
precisely to the extent that it will draw its participants by the attraction of
beauty, rather than drive them by the compulsion of force. The best contract
will be like a good marriage, or a good relationship between parent and
child. Such bonds, and the terrifying negations that can confront them, are
the subject of the next chapter.

3

"nothing will come of nothing"

The Love Bond and the Meaning of the Zero

Garden Economics and Its Enemies

As we have seen, the Sonnets and *The Winter's Tale* develop a concept of nature as a process of creativity and growth, where human invention and imagination are a continuation of nature's own tradition of self-transcendence. But this faith in nature is achieved in the teeth of what seems to be a much more persuasive idea: that nature is instead a mechanistic process of cause and effect, gradually running down over time, and that human beings are part of the same process. What would our ethics look like if we adopted this view? Three hundred years before European philosophers of the nineteenth and twentieth centuries such as Nietzsche, Marx, Schopenhauer, and Sartre found their own answers to this question, Shakespeare had already explored it in his great tragedy *King Lear*.

If nature is indeed as hostile to human ideals as those European existentialists feared, then human moral conduct and human art can only be achieved by defying nature—by asserting an impractical ethics and aesthetics unconditioned by material interests and the motivations of our animal bodies. Thus we must either resign ourselves to a world of savage competition for access to the dwindling resources of the world, or be prepared for the inevitable tragic sacrifice that results from unconditional love. The "garden economics" of the last chapter, which are the basis of Shakespeare's very different solution, do not require such tragic choices (though they demand a discipline of love and art that is just as exacting). But Shakespeare is willing, with his enormous and genial intellectual tolerance, to give a voice to both. In *King Lear* the two views of nature clash, with tragic results. Some of the characters, such as Cordelia, Kent, and Edgar, believe in the garden economics. Others, such as Regan, Goneril, Edmund, Oswald, and Cornwall, believe in the survival of the fittest. Unfortunately, the latter are able to enforce their view of the world: both Lear and Gloucester, who at the outset control the kingdom, reject their own instinctive belief in the garden, and adopt the deterministic and rationalistic theories of the ruthless politicians. Thus the rhetoric that comes to dominate the play leaves almost no alternative to a good person such as Cordelia but for tragic loving sacrifice, even though her worldview in itself is one of optimism and growth.

The key words in the play, in which all these issues are bound up, are "nothing" and "bond." For the evil and misguided folk in the play who believe in the reductionistic, mechanistic, thermodynamic account of the universe, nothing is the dead end that attracts all natural events and all human dealings. To be left with nothing is to be the final loser, and therefore the only sensible policy is to accumulate all the possessions and power one can, at the expense of one's neighbors and even one's own family. A good person with this view would be forced to accept destruction uncomplainingly at the hands of the wicked. But there is another view in the play, that nothing is not a dead end at all, but the origin, the source, the fertile opening of all new creation; nothing is the womb of nature, not its grave. Despite the political defeat of this view, it somehow prevails in the end, thanks largely to the efforts of Edgar, who reduces himself to nothing and becomes in consequence a potent moral artist, a positive source of new growth.

The other key word in the play is "bond." For the expedient Machiavellians in the play, bonds are either literal bonds—ropes to tie up a prisoner for torture—or mere social conventions maintained by the weak-minded and credulous to be broken by the strong and realistic when the right moment comes. Such social bonds are for them the tissue of foolish trust that binds the wealthy in their illusions, a view that resembles in some ways the attitudes of nineteenth- and twentieth-century communists and leftists to the "illusions" and contract laws of the bourgeoisie. The clear-minded dispossessed should expropriate these expropriators, as Marx declared. *King Lear* is after all the story of a revolution.

But for the more humane characters in the play, bonds, while not promising the infinite wonders of unconditional love, are the humble but trustworthy assurances of real human caring. Such bond relationships as daughter to father, husband to wife, master to faithful retainer, because they are mutual and loop back reciprocally upon themselves, contain within them the same mysteries of unpredictable growth and profit that we have already found in the natural processes Shakespeare celebrates in the Sonnets and *The Winter's Tale*. What these bonds apparently lack in disinterested, one-way devotion, they more than make up for in their two-way depth of living tenderness, as King Lear will learn at terrible cost.

A Brief History of the Zero

Lear has just signed away two thirds of his kingdom to his two eldest daughters, after they have given him the elaborate and superlative professions of unconditional love he had asked them for. "Now," says Lear to his favorite daughter, Cordelia, "what can you say to draw / A third more opulent than your sisters? Speak."

CORDELIA: Nothing, my lord.

LEAR: Nothing?

CORDELIA: Nothing.

LEAR: Nothing will come of nothing. Speak again.

CORDELIA: Unhappy that I am, I cannot heave
My heart into my mouth. I love your majesty
According to my bond, no more nor less.
(I.i.87)

When Lear says "nothing will come of nothing," what he means is that if Cordelia says nothing, she will get nothing. He is also unconsciously echoing the central idea of Aristotle's physics, which would have been familiar in its Latin form to every Elizabethan schoolboy: "Ex nihilo nihil fit"—out of nothing nothing is made. But this was not the only account of the nature of creation. An alternative view to Aristotle's also existed at the time, based on the biblical account of creation, in which the universe was created by God's word out of nothing at all. In the writings of the scientist Thomas Hariot, an obscure contemporary genius and probably an acquaintance of Shakespeare's, there is a marginal note that puts the issue nicely: "Ex nihilo nihil fit; sed omnia fint ex nihilo"—out of nothing nothing is made; but everything is made out of nothing.

This may seem like a dry point of metaphysics; but for Shakespeare in some mysterious way the nature of love between two people is related to the question of how the universe is created. If Lear is wrong, or only half-right, in subscribing to Aristotle's principle that everything must have a prior cause, an antecedent—that there is nothing new under the sun—perhaps his error has something very important to do with the huge and tragic errors he makes in misjudging his daughters. Understanding Lear's error, we may be better able to understand why Cordelia implicitly contradicts him in her answer, and what she means by loving him according to her bond. Clearly Lear is deeply in error when he punishes Cordelia for her answer by depriving her of the share of his kingdom he had intended as her dowry. If the result of his reasoning is wrong, then perhaps the premise on which it is based—nothing will come of nothing—is wrong too. And if we can get this whole issue clear in our minds, we may have come a long way in resolving our own deepest personal problems about the relationship of love and property and the true meaning of bonds.

The crucial problem is what the word "nothing" means. This problem is not as easy as it seems. In Plato's *Sophist* the best minds of classical Greece had come to grief on it. After all, the very word nothing is something already, and thus it contradicts itself. The mathematical sign for zero had to be invented and defined before any progress in mathematics could be possible; the Romans had no zero, and thus it is almost impossible to do anything except simple addition, subtraction, and multiplication in Roman numerals. The zero was invented first by the Mayan astronomer-priests of the Yucatan, six hundred years before it appears in the Old World among the Hindus. It is represented by a shell or a flower: in the vigesimal system of counting (in twenties rather than in tens) it is denoted by the suffix *-alli* for multiples of the base twenty. It did not emerge in the Old World until around the sixth century AD in Cambodia; it had been adopted by Arabic mathematicians by the tenth century. In fact our word "zero" comes from the Arabic "sifr" (from which we also get "cypher"). Despite centuries of contact between Islam and Christian Europe, the zero did not make its way into Christendom until the fourteenth century, and it was only in Shakespeare's time that its full power as a concept and as a source of mathematical ideas began to be realized. Thomas Hariot conducted a correspondence with the French mathematician Ferdinand Vieta about it, a correspondence out of which came the principles of modern algebra. The essential invention was to carry all the terms in an equation over to one side, leaving zero on the other. Thus the solution to an equation such as $3x^2 - x = 10 - 14x$ is arrived at by rearranging the terms thus: $3x^2 - x + 14x - 10 = 0$, reducing this to $3x^2 + 13x - 10 = 0$, and redescribing it as $(x + 5) * (3x - 2) = 0$. Since either $x + 5$ or $3x - 2$ must equal zero, x must either be -5 or $2/3$, and if the only possible solution is a positive number, we know that x is $2/3$. It is not necessary to follow the math of this to see that the zero plays an almost magical part in this calculation, appearing on the right as the terms are moved over to the left, and then disappearing after it has done its work.

Shakespeare, whose curiosity and knowledge sometimes seem universal, and who was among the first generation in England to be educated in the new Arab math, was keenly interested in the zero. When Lear's Fool wants to find the ultimate description of the nonexistence to which Lear has reduced himself by giving away his kingdom, he says to his master: "Now thou art an O without a figure" (I.iv.193). What he means is that if Lear had a figure or digit, say 8 or 2 or 5, followed by a zero (an "O"), then he would have eighty or twenty or fifty; but as it is, he has only the zero, he has nothing. Or rather, *is* nothing. There is something utterly chilling about this image; the Fool is insisting on a meaning for zero that is not simply as a conventional placeholding sign to signify tens or hundreds or thousands, but the mysterious void itself. The O of an egg, the silver crown coin, the king's golden crown, the wholeness of the kingdom, and the bald head of the old man are all described as broken and emptied:

FOOL: Nuncle, give me an egg, and I'll give thee two crowns.

LEAR: What two crowns shall they be?

FOOL: Why, after I have cut the egg i' th' middle and eat up the meat, the two crowns of the egg. When thou clovest thy crown i' th' middle and gav'st away both parts, thou bor'st thine ass on thy back o'er the dirt. Thou hadst little wit in thy bald crown when thou gav'st thy golden one away.
(I.iv.157)

But the zero, frightening as it is in its emptiness, was proving in Shake-speare's time to be an enormously productive concept. Shortly after the zero entered Europe, geometrical perspective was invented in Italy, and with it the whole tradition that has developed since of picturing three-dimensional scenes in the arts and planning three-dimensional shapes in engineering. The very notion of objectivity and impartial unbiased observation is hard to imagine without the related notion of perspective. Perspective drawing is based normally upon the establishment of a vanishing point on the drawing surface, toward which all the objects in the scene diminish according to their distance from the viewer. The vanishing point itself is an infinite distance away in the imaged scene. The reader might test this by taking a camera and looking down a street through the viewfinder. The vanishing point is where the edges of the pavement, sidewalk, and rooflines converge. It moves in re-lation to the observer's position and angle of view. Thus the vanishing point, where the size of all pictured objects diminishes to zero, is in some sense the mirror image in the picture of the observer. The picture, moreover, is like a window through which the observer sees the world, but which separates the viewer from the world. So to make a realistic scene, the self of the viewer must be metaphorically reduced to zero and removed from the scene it is viewing. This is exactly what happens to King Lear himself when his two el-dest daughters turn against him: he is exiled to the heath, and his establish-ment of retainers is successively reduced from one hundred to fifty to twenty-five to ten to five to one; finally Regan brings him down to nothing: "What need one?"

The vanishing point is the visual equivalent of the zero in mathematics and could not have entered European consciousness without the new under-standing of the concept of nothingness that the zero represented. Another example of the uses of nothingness was in finance. The key breakthrough here was the introduction of double-entry bookkeeping, also in the Renais-sance. The whole point of double-entry bookkeeping is that the two sides of the account book must balance out to nothing. In an asset account, the sum of assets on one side and liabilities plus proprietorship on the other must be zero. Once this concept was in place, the way was open for paper money, money not based on reserves of a precious metal, and finally the highly ab-stract forms of future or conditional money that flow at light speed in ones and zeroes through the fiber optics of contemporary stock market computers. An earlier essay of mine, "The School of Night," discusses some of these developments in the Elizabethan context. Sigurd Burckhardt has an interesting essay, entitled "The Quality of Nothing in *King Lear*," that develops some of these themes in a different direction, and Brian Rotman, in his fascinating little book on the subject, *Signifying Nothing: The Semiotics of Zero,* adds another example of the zero concept: the rest symbol in music. The rest signifies the absence of a sound, and anchors the system of musical notation and equal-tempered tuning that is now standard. Thus the conscious observing self, the mathematical zero, the sound of silence, the point of infinite distance, and the financial balance of a business enterprise are all slightly different versions of the same idea.

What are we to make of this remarkable invention of the zero, what Rotman calls the "meta-sign," the sign that both negates and refers to all other signs? The usual academic view (which Rotman adopts) derives essentially from the thought of Karl Marx. That is, the Renaissance saw the rise of a great perversion in human economic relationships, whereby the owners of the means of production were able to exploit the labor of the workers. Property owners buy the labor of their employees with the abstract currency of money, thereby alienating artisans from the fruits of their labor. Meanwhile the owners cream off some of the value of the work, accumulating it as capital. Capital can then be lent out at interest, thereby generating unearned power to command goods and services and conferring upon the monied a disproportionate share of social power. The introduction of the zero in mathematics, visual representation, and accounting was a key factor in destroying the ancient world of immediate human ties, craftsmanship, harmonious relationships with nature, and a rich and satisfying life in close contact with reality. All the evils of contemporary civilization followed: the dematerialization of money into paper and electrons, the abstract systems of penal, military, and medical authority, alienating scientific worldviews, a mechanized technological existence, racism, sexual oppression, consumerism, and ecological catastrophe.

A devastating indictment. But if it is true, then there can be no question but that we should abolish stock markets, make private corporations illegal, get rid of the practice of taking interest on loans, nationalize all productive enterprise, and either return to the gold standard or find some way to eliminate money as we know it altogether. The world has in the last few decades decisively rejected this policy and the view of things it implies. Often heroically, often in the teeth of armed oppression commanding all the national organs of propaganda, often leaderless, ordinary people in every continent threw out their socialist or communist benefactors and opted for stock markets, bank loans, private enterprise, capitalist currency, and the chance to make millions of dollars and retire on the proceeds. The people have voted with their feet—and with their vote, when they got it—and it is part of the purpose of this book to show the wisdom of the emerging worldview that has resulted from their decision.

But intellectuals and artists have tended to go the other way. The poet Ezra Pound, among others, thought it all through in the years following the Great Depression. Usury, he believed, was the source of all evil: it was the way that nothing (the mere possession of a sum of money) could unnaturally propagate something (the interest charged on a loan). This view led him step-by-step from a tolerant humanism to a rabid anti-Semitism. Pound is usually described as a fascist; but as Tim Redman has shown in his important book *Pound and Italian Fascism,* his thought derived quite as much from Lenin's as it did from Mussolini's. Indeed, at this distance it is becoming clear that the quarrel between the communists and the fascists was a family quarrel, and that its bitterness and cruelty were the result of what Freud called "the narcissism of small differences." Despite the fact that Pound would have been considered a war criminal if he had not been judged insane, most contemporary academics in the humanities and social sciences still believe in some version of his account. In various guises it has been fatally attractive to many fashionable thinkers, including Heidegger, Sartre, Foucault, Benjamin, and Derrida, and is unquestioned at such gatherings as the Modern Language Association. But though it carries some grains of truth, it is essentially false, as I shall show.

Cordelia's Bond

If we are to be faithful to the imagination of the world's peoples, we must find an economic system different from the one proposed by the discredited revolutionaries of the last two centuries, one that is based on bonds but that will still fulfill the moral and spiritual demands of our higher nature. When Cordelia tries to explain to her father what she means by loving him "according to her bond," she uses the language of balanced accounts to do so:

> Good my lord,
> You have begot me, bred me, loved me. I
> Return those duties back as are right fit,
> Obey you, love you, and most honor you.
> (I.i.95)

In other words, her love and her debt to her father should cancel out to zero. Many of Shakespeare's interpreters in the last two hundred years have been scandalized by this apparently cold assessment of filial duty. Usually they put the blame on Lear himself, and explain that in asking his daughters to sell their love and putting his kingdom up for auction he is buying in to the new capitalist system of exchange. Cordelia, they maintain, cannot or will not make the right answer, that love is unconditional and unrelated to matters of property, because she knows she will lose to her sisters in such a contest.

But this interpretation is plainly lame. It portrays King Lear, the ancient patriarch who swears by the goddess of nature,

> . . . the sacred radiance of the sun,
> The mysteries of Hecate and the night,
> By all the operation of the orbs
> From whom we do exist and cease to be . . .
> (I.i.109)

—this commander of knights, this believer in honor, astrology, blood, and family—as a cold, cost-efficient corporate manager whose attempt at divestiture does not pay off. Cordelia is made to say exactly the opposite of what she means. Regan and Goneril, who swear that their love is incommensurate with any earthly property or real estate, and who end up committing astonishing acts of cold cruelty in pursuit of wealth and power, are made into experts on the subject of love. This interpretation simply ignores the play, its words, its characterization, its plot. Indeed, the grotesque stretch of this reading is the sign of a worldview that is almost at breaking point, and that is being defended at greater and greater intellectual cost.

How, then, are we to understand this terrifyingly great play if it is Cordelia, the pattern of human love, tenderness, truth, and goodness, who introduces the idea of nothing and who loves according to her bond? And what does this understanding imply about how we should assess the meaning of the zero and the role it has played in the evolution of our political economy and culture?

Let us follow the thought of the play, as it gradually works out the tragic Western fallacy of dividing higher spiritual values from lower materialistic ones. We begin with the apparent common sense of Lear's "Nothing will come of nothing." In this view of nature, as we have seen, everything comes to be as a result of a prior cause; everything is a quid pro quo, and no new thing can come into being. The world, or even a part of it such as the geographical area of Lear's kingdom, is like a pie that can be divided up but can only grow at the cost of a diminution elsewhere. Nature, according to Lear's favorite philosopher, Aristotle, gives birth only within the limits of existing species of things, unless the process is disrupted, in which case an unnatural monster or prodigy is born. There is a natural form of love that is but the prudent attachment of an animal to the source of its livelihood; but obviously there is no place for unconditional love in the terms of such a world, since any act profiting another must be the result of a prior cause, can only be payment for a past or prospective benefit. Nevertheless, it is unconditional love that Lear demands: a love that must be somehow outside the material world and its motivations, where, as he puts it, "nature doth with merit challenge" (I.i.53).

In taking this line Lear is in fact contradicting his own stated beliefs. Lear has until now subscribed to a natural religion, which maintains that nature herself implants in the soul a capacity for self-sacrifice for blood kin. In terms of the crude "survival of the fittest" view of things (which in Shakespeare's time had already received its political expression in the works of Machiavelli), such a view would be sentimental claptrap. We now know from the fascinating researches of the sociobiologists that Lear's natural religion is actually not far off the mark: genetic fitness can include altruism toward close kin, and group selection among highly social species with reciprocal resource exchange systems can even perhaps promote some measure of self-sacrifice for the community. But Lear is getting old, and he is terrified of abandonment. He wants something more reliable than natural reciprocity; if nothing can come from nothing, perhaps Cordelia will stop loving him when his power to help her and her children is gone. In his panic he finds the Machiavellian theory of human motivation a better description of his ultimate fears than any natural morality can provide and thus demands of his daughters a supernatural devotion, an unconditional love that transcends reciprocity and bonds.

Of course, such a demand is foolish in its own terms. How could a tendency to irrational self-sacrifice survive in nature, without supernatural intervention to provide a happy ending? And if such supernatural intervention is to be expected, can the self-sacrifice be genuine? It is these contradictions that Cordelia exposes when she speaks in her annoyingly commonsense way about bonds and duties. The fallacy of Lear's view of the world becomes swiftly apparent when he divides his kingdom. Surely unconditional, disinterested love should be rewarded! What is more deserving of reward? Accordingly he gives a third of his kingdom to each of his elder daughters, because they subscribe to the doctrine of unconditional love:

> GONERIL: Sir, I love you more than word can wield the matter;
> Dearer than eyesight, space, and liberty;
> Beyond what can be valued, rich or rare;
> No less than life, with grace, health, beauty, honor . . .
> (I.i.55)

But now, of course, Goneril and Regan have ample recompense for their love; and it is Cordelia, who refuses the doctrine of unconditional love, who gets nothing, and yet continues to love.

In the following scene, Shakespeare shows us what a nature religion would look like without bonds and duties. Edmund, the bastard son of Gloucester, one of Lear's vassals, is plotting to destroy his legitimate brother, Edgar, and usurp his inheritance. Edmund, too, is a worshiper of Mother Nature: "Thou, Nature, art my goddess; to thy law / My services are bound" (I.ii.1). But this is not the nature that guarantees the ties of kinship, what Lear calls "Propinquity and property of blood" (I.i.114). After all, says Edmund, nature is the realm of dog-eat-dog, of survival of the fittest. The human bonds that regulate property, rights, duties, and inheritance are but protections for the weak. The law of love is a slave religion. Nature adores the strong, who

> in the lusty stealth of nature, take
> More composition and fierce quality

> Than doth, within a dull, stale, tired bed,
> Go to th' creating a whole tribe of fops
> Got 'tween asleep and wake.
> (II.i.11)

The evil rationalizations of Edmund are a warning that Western civilization tragically ignored. The idealistic youth of Europe applauded when Rousseau proclaimed the nobility of the savage, when Napoleon demonstrated that he required no pope or other divine authority than his own natural strength to crown himself emperor, when Nietzsche proposed the idea of the Superman. But it wept when Hitler destroyed the Jews to make room for the Master Race. Given this view of nature, we live according to our thermodynamic appetites, and unconditional love would be simply impossible (though it might be a useful disguise if the victim could be brought to believe in it).

The belief that if we follow nature's way we will end up destroying any and all who stand in the way of our interests has a satisfying cynicism, which for much of the last two centuries has had the ring of truth. But it is false. Nature, as Shakespeare well knew, and as Charles Darwin pointed out three hundred years after him, is not in fact a dog-eat-dog world. Survival depends far more upon cooperation among and within species than on a ruthless struggle of each against all. Paradoxically, natural competition, which is perfectly real, is almost always a competition over which species, kin group, or individual can cooperate best with its neighbors for mutual benefit. Even prey species depend upon their predators. But this ecological view of nature as cooperative and instinctually loving can only make sense if the world is not a zero-sum game. Only if nature produces surplus value, only if the pie can be expanded, only if emergent properties can arise out of the interactions of matter and life can it make sense for natural beings to co-operate. Thus if nothing can come from nothing, the only intelligible nature religion would be one like Edmund's, of dog-eat-dog, and Cordelia's world of reciprocal bonds is as much of a sentimental illusion as Lear's expectation of unconditional love. We should fight tooth and nail for our own piece of the fixed or diminishing pie of natural value. But if something can come from nothing, if nature does generate surplus value, if new species of things can come into existence out of any sufficiently rich brew of interacting elements, then altruism might make perfectly good sense, and loving according to one's bond might actually be identical in effect with unconditional love.

Poor Tom's Reinvention of Nothing

When the Fool rails at Lear, recalling again and again the horrible word "nothing" and applying it to the kingdomless king, he is essentially demolishing Lear's faulty natural philosophy. If nothing can come of nothing, the light of the whole world itself would have gone out by now:

FOOL: For you know, nuncle,
           The hedge-sparrow fed the cuckoo so long
           That it had it head bit off by it young.
So out went the candle, and we were left darkling.
(I.iv.215)

But gradually a new understanding of nothing begins to emerge out of the action of the play. There may be virtues in nothing that are ignored in the Aristotelian view of things. When Edgar, the good son of Gloucester, is falsely betrayed by his brother, Edmund, he disguises himself as an insane homeless beggar, taking on the identity—or rather the lack of identity—of Poor Tom. In other words, in a dog-eat-dog, nothing-will-come-of-nothing world, perhaps the only thing for a good person to do is to become nothing:

> Whiles I may 'scape,
> I will preserve myself; and am bethought
> To take the basest and most poorest shape
> That ever penury, in contempt of man,
> Brought near to beast . . .
>   Poor Turlygod, Poor Tom,
> That's something yet: Edgar I nothing am.
> (II.iii.5)

Lear, too, must undergo a transformation into nothing, as he loses his role, his followers, his possessions, his home, and finally his sanity. But the zero is also the womb of all. Out of the nothing to which the basically good characters in the play are reduced come mysterious and beautiful things (even though they are doomed by the cruelty of those who believe in the zero-sum game). "Can you make no use of nothing?" asks the Fool. His answer is that one can indeed "have more / Than two tens to a score" (I.iv.132, 128). The implication is that one can, in certain circumstances, draw interest ("use") upon an investment of nothing.

How can this be? Must we abandon rationality, abandon our belief in reasons and causes, if we are to imagine a universe with the creativity to support generosity and love? There are now scientific answers to this question, though they were not available to Shakespeare. The first answer is implicit in Charles Darwin's theory of evolution. What he showed was that through a perfectly intelligible process of genetic variation combined with selection and inheritance, all the extraordinary and beautiful forms of living nature could come into being, together with the new ecosystems, new modes of sensation and cognition, and new social behaviors that emerged with them. In proving that new species could evolve, he refuted the ancient doctrine of Aristotle, that the species were immutable. Before there were species with eyes, sight did not exist; at a later time, eyed species possessed the power of sight. Thus sight had, somehow, come out of the unseeing; something had come from nothing. And we were not required to abandon reason to follow some such process as this: certain subcutaneous body cells were more sensitive to light than others; this sensitivity was useful to the species that bore it; the sensitivity increased as the generations passed; the protective transparent membrane of the skin turned out to refract and focus the light; this became a lens; and so on.

The crucial element in Darwin's explanation was *iteration,* the repetition over and over again of the survival test for each new generation; and this, as he understood it, required enormous lengths of time. New structures and behaviors emerged through an almost infinite repetition of the process of reproduction with small random variations. Only in the last few decades have we begun to understand the mysteries of such iterative feedback processes, as our own technical capabilities for repeating and reproducing have improved. The reader can test the effect by taking a sheet of paper printed with a regular pattern, copying it on a copy machine, copying the copy, copying that, and so on. After a sufficient number of generations new shapes and forms will begin to emerge, and the old pattern will eventually become unrecognizable. Computers, of course, can do this sort of thing very much faster, and so in recent years we have seen the extraordinary paisleys and Catherine wheels of the Mandelbrot Set, the transfixed scuds of the logistical set, and the bubbles and foams of the Newtonian square root algorithm. The inner forms of complex iterative physical systems are called "strange attractors"; examples are the Lorenz and Hénon attractors. The Nobel Prize–winning chemist Ilya Prigogine, the crystallographer Cyril Stanley Smith, and other researchers have demonstrated that nonliving natural iterative systems possess the same kind of inventiveness; and it is beginning to look as if the processes of fetal development and neural memory work on the same principle. The adult form of a living species may be said to be the strange attractor of the iterative process of its cellular development; a memory may be the strange attractor of the iterative firing of billions of brain cells.

Shakespeare could not know these things; but he was a careful observer of nature and perhaps the most meticulous of all observers of human behavior, and the basic principles of human and natural creativity were, I believe, familiar to him. We have already seen how his understanding of plant and animal breeding informs his thinking in *The Winter's Tale* and the Sonnets. Later we shall see how he develops these intuitions in *A Midsummer Night's Dream* and *Antony and Cleopatra*. In King Lear his chief argument for creation out of nothing rests on human moral experience and moral behavior, and it is this human moral creativity that we will now explore.

Once Edgar, as Poor Tom, becomes "nothing," he begins to gain a paradoxically potent role in the action of the play. He becomes the secret protector of his father, Gloucester, who has been cruelly blinded—the "o"s of his eyes turned into parenthesis-like sockets ( )—at the instigation of his nature-worshiping son, Edmund. Gloucester, bent on suicide—reducing himself to nothing—bids Poor Tom, whom he does not recognize as his loving son, to lead him to the edge of the cliffs of Dover. Edgar now uses his disguise to work an extraordinary spiritual transformation on his father, a transformation that also disquietingly includes us, the audience. As we watch, he mimes the climb toward the edge of the cliff, just as an actor would if portraying a real assisted suicide. We cannot be entirely sure if the cliff is a pretend real cliff or a pretend pretend cliff. Shakespeare gives such a clear and vertiginous description of the frightful brink and the terrifying gulf below it that the willing suspension of disbelief that we carry into the theater is fooled into accepting the precipice as real. And now Gloucester throws himself "down" and lies there unmoving, just as he would in a staged real suicide. Edgar now assumes a different role, that of the amazed traveler at the bottom of the cliff who has witnessed the fall and has now run—vainly, he believes—to assist the victim. He surely cannot be alive. Yet Gloucester revives; Edgar is anxious lest the very imagination of the fall could kill his father, yet convinced that this is the way to cure Gloucester of the deadly sin of despair. Edgar does not reveal the deception to his father. Instead, in his new character as good Samaritan, he says:

> Thy life's a miracle . . .
> Think that the clearest gods, who make them honors
> Of men's impossibilities, have preserved thee.
> (IV.vi.55,73)

In actual fact, Gloucester's life *is* a miracle, as are all of ours who have witnessed and have been part victims of Edgar's deception. To be alive at all, as I am whose intentions cause these words to appear on the screen of the word processor and as you are who read them in your own mysterious selfhood, is a miracle more astonishing than any tale of divine prodigy or supernatural intervention. The material universe has given birth to our personhood, our interiority, out of nothing—and it should come as no surprise that the only adequate language for describing the meaning of this event is religious. Perhaps there is a material explanation for the mystery of our existence, just as there is a perfectly good reason that Gloucester is alive—but in a real sense we are closer to the truth when we "think that the clearest gods" have preserved us.

What Edgar has done is neatly reversed his evil brother's original use of "nothing." At the beginning of the play Edmund started his plot against his brother by forging a letter in Edgar's handwriting that purported to be an invitation to Edmund to join Edgar in murdering their father and usurping his earldom. Edmund strategically placed himself where his father would "surprise" him, and hastily—and obviously—concealed the letter. Naturally Gloucester was curious about his son's apparent embarrassment and asked, "What paper were you reading?" In a ghastly reprise of Cordelia's first words to *her* father, Edmund replied, "Nothing, my lord" (I.ii.29). Gloucester now compelled Edmund to reveal the contents of the fake letter, Edmund protesting manfully that Edgar surely didn't mean it, that it was just a test of Edmund's loyalty, that his dear brother could not intend so terrible a crime; all of which convinced Gloucester utterly that Edgar really was disloyal. The letter in fact *was* nothing, in the sense that it was not a real letter from Edgar. Gloucester was fooled into believing that the letter—which was nothing—was really something, by Edmund's cunning insistence that it was nothing.

Now, at the cliff top, Gloucester is "fooled" by the other brother, the good one, into believing that the fake fall, which is nothing, was a real fall; and thus he comes to understand the truth, that life really is a miracle. Edmund, like Regan and Goneril, claimed unconditional love for his father, which masked a ruthless attempt to destroy his father's life. Edgar puts on the mask of Poor Tom, accepts payment for his service (ratifying the economic bond between them), and enacts the elaborate charade of the cliff top, in order to save his father's life.

Thus "nothing" has changed from being the inner reality of those who make protestations of unconditional love (and the destination of those who believe them), into a mysterious womb of meaning, a source of moral being. This latter sense of nothing or zero resembles remarkably a new and exciting concept in cosmological physics: the quantum vacuum. Contemporary quantum physicists now believe that empty space, far from being an inert and passive condition, is a seething ferment of emerging particles, negative and positive, known as the quantum foam. Those particles, if crushed together into the same space, into a perfectly dimensionless point, would indeed cancel each other out, the negative and the positive, the right-handed with the left-handed, to give a perfect zero. But the very meaning of space is that it is extended; there are no perfectly dimensionless points in nature. Nature is not exact and perfect, says quantum theory; it has its own limits of acuity, below which it is approximate, messy, and unstable. This instability makes of nothingness a very womb of new being. The Big Bang itself, the origin of the universe, was a product of the quantum vacuum. The only thing that nothing can *not* generate, according to the quantum cosmologists, is nothing itself!

Thus Aristotle, we now know, was wrong in saying that nothing can come from nothing. And if Aristotle was wrong, then so is Lear when he echoes Aristotle. And if we know this, then we know that we need a new economics based on the creativity of zero rather than its inertness. Strangely enough, Shakespeare has rediscovered the sense of zero that its first Mayan inventors had conceived for it: in imaging it as a seashell or a flower, they had given it the significance of fertility, potential, productiveness. There is an uncanny parallel between the images Lear's Fool uses for the zero—the fruit, the egg, the pea pod, the oyster, the snail—and the zero symbols of ancient Mesoamerica.

Only by becoming nothing—as Cordelia does when she disinherits herself with the word "nothing," as Edgar does when he becomes Poor Tom, as Gloucester does when, blinded, he comes to see the miracle of life, and as Lear himself does in the storm on the heath when he learns to sympathize with the wretched of the earth—can we become real as moral agents and creative beings. The way that Cordelia becomes nothing in this creative sense is by claiming no more for her love than simple reciprocity, promising no more than the faithful observance of a contract. She offers no more than a balancing of the books, so that credits and debts add up to zero. Within the limits of that claim and contract, paradoxically, she turns out to be capable of amazing self-sacrificial love, even to the point of risking and losing her life in the attempt to rescue her father. How do Cordelia's actions differ from the unconditional love promised but not delivered by Lear's other daughters?

False and True Infinites

Just as we have discovered two distinct senses of "nothing" in the play, so there are two distinct senses of the infinite. The infinity of love promised by Regan and Goneril is like the classical infinity of mainstream mathematics as it has been practiced since the Renaissance—an endless accumulation of points or quantities, the set of natural numbers or of zero-dimensional points on a line. Since we are by definition finite beings, promises of this kind of infinity cannot but be false. But there is another kind of infinity, corresponding to the new sense of the spatial zero or the quantum foam, which we are just beginning to understand. The old kind of infinity is defined by endless linear addition. The new kind is constructed by means of nonlinear feedback processes, such as the algorithm by which the Mandelbrot Set is generated. It can be bounded within a narrow space and yet go on developing unique new details on smaller and smaller scales. It is an interiorizing, a growth of inner articulation that is infinite in that it never recurs and never bumps up against a terminus, but finite in that at any point in time the calculation is not complete, the full detail never completed, and it can be represented by a visual arabesque that is accurate if approximate.

It is just such a "fractal" infinity that we might choose if we tried to diagram Cordelia's love for her father. It is bounded, as she insists from the outset, by the conditions of her "bond," and thus not unconditional. But within those limits it is capable of an infinite enrichment and deepening. It is able to exist in the real world—as classical infinities cannot—because its infinity is an uncompleted process, and at any point it is a work in progress, a project to date. It can be represented—that is, it can be put into practice—as classical infinity cannot. In other words, it is the kind of infinity you get in a world in which the zero is productive not passive, in which something *can* come from nothing, in which the physical and moral worlds can realize a genuine profit on the loan of existence.

These two infinities also imply two different conceptions of the divine. As soon as the old conception of linear infinity became available, it was adopted as the perfect mathematical metaphor for God, even to the point that a mere mathematical analogy had taken on the force of dogma. Almost all Christian and Muslim theologians, and many Jewish ones, used it without a second thought. But perhaps, as this analysis suggests, there are profound pitfalls in the analogy. It implies, for instance, a certain monotony and uncreativeness, and a deterministic logic whereby God would be fixed to the unchanging rail of the infinite straight line, incapable of freedom or self-transformation. There were a few who resisted this metaphor, including some of the Jewish Cabbalists, Sufi, Catholic and Protestant mystics, and William Blake, who excoriated this God of linear theory as the intellectual death-deity Urizen; and there is an antiacademic strain in Eastern Orthodox Christianity that never absorbed the idea in the first place.

But perhaps now we have a better mathematical metaphor for God. Might it not be more expressive of people's intuitions about the depth and richness and surprise of the divine to image it as a fractal, as the Strange Attractor of the universe itself, never complete because always deepening itself, always developing new inner articulation and complexity, an original source of new being rather than a closed inventory of everything? We might have to modify some of our definitions of omnipotence, omniscience, eternity, and so on, but we might get in return a conception of the divine that accords with the best, most creative, and most beautiful things we find in nature and human beings, rather than contradicts them. We would also get a God who might conceivably be involved in a genuine traffic with human beings, who might join us in covenants and promises, and react accordingly when we break them; a God that would be circumscribed but not limited by bonds of love and assumed debt.

What, then, does Shakespeare mean when he has Cordelia say "I love you according to my bond"? Let us put it in our own contemporary terms. First of all, it means something different depending on whether we are living in a nothing-will-come-of-nothing world of thermodynamic determinism and slow decay, or in a creation-out-of-nothing world where new values arise out of nonlinear interactions—in other words, whether the zero is passive or creative.

If the world is of the first kind, loving according to one's bond need mean nothing more than that one is justified in fighting tooth and nail to survive and dominate, using force and fraud, just as one claims one's ancestors did (Edmund's ethics). The strongest survive. Even if we tried to pay our debts in such a zero-sum decaying universe, we would fail, because the slow increase of entropy would mean that we would always give back less than we received. At best such a "love" would be cupboard love, a prudential cultivating of someone from whom one expects benefits, a rational calculation of future favor. Thus we would be right in objecting to Cordelia's definition of love; in such a world the only acceptable kind of love worth the name would be the pure, uncontaminated, unconditional love promised by her sisters.

This was the conclusion of Immanuel Kant, faced with the deterministic universe suggested by the mechanistic science of Newton and Laplace: ethics could not exist in a world of materialistic self-interest, and thus it must be totally divorced from the world, totally "disinterested" as we say. But if we human beings are indeed irreducibly animals, as science shows us to be, then such an ethic is simply impossible for us. Animals are part of that deterministic world. We might think we were acting out of pure motives, but actually we would be rationalizing some selfish desire, furthering the economic interests of our class, or expressing in a disguised form some repressed psychological drive. Thus in order for us to be ethical, we must deny our own intellectual integrity that tells us to accept the overwhelming scientific evidence that we are animals. Alternatively, we could divide the human being into an animal part and a mental part—but then we encounter the logical contradictions and profound psychological harmfulness of such a division. How can these two totally disparate parts have any effect on each other, whether in the form of sensation (the physical affecting the mental) or in the form of intentional action (the mental affecting the physical)? Moreover, most environmentalists tell us that the current ecological crisis will be solved only if we accept our nature and responsibilities as an animal species in a community of species. This double bind has paralyzed modern thinking for the last two hundred years.

But if the world is of the second kind, a creation-out-of-nothing world, then the bond—our acknowledgment of our reciprocal place in nature—allies us to the unending and mysterious creativity of the universe. If the world is free, we do not give up our ethical responsibility by accepting that we are part of it. In a self-organizing, evolving world, when we pay our debts we are paying in a coin that is worth more, not less, than when we took out the loan in the first place. We can accept our nature as animals— "the paragon of animals," Hamlet calls us—without accepting a dog-eat-dog role in relation to our fellows (*Hamlet*, II.ii.315). Dogs do not in fact usually eat dogs; and man is not naturally a wolf to man, except when we are persuaded by ideology that it is our duty. We are not divided into a mind and an animal. We take on both the rights and the duties of a partner in the creation of the world. In acknowledging her bond to her father, Cordelia is actually shouldering the responsibility to continue in her relationship with him the twelve-billion-year-old tradition of creative cooperation that created the universe as it is, and to do it in the special way of the human species— through conscious love and respectful care.

Perhaps that bond is not as glamorous as some romantic notion of unconditional love; but it has the advantage of being performable. Cordelia concedes practically that when she marries, at least half of her care and duty will then be due to her husband and family, which is as it should be—she is imposing conditions. But within those limits, her love can share in the infinite productiveness of nature itself. Cordelia denies that the capital Lear has invested in her is infinite, in the old linear sense, and thus that the debt she owes him is also infinite. But the interest she is prepared to pay on her bond will never cease. Perhaps her love and her debt to her father, if paid off, would cancel to zero. But she is not proposing to pay her father off, but to retain the loan and to continue paying the interest.

This conclusion implies that the contractual nature of the contemporary market economy, the world of bonds, is not necessarily as soulless and sterile as it has been made out to be. It is only soulless and sterile if one believes in a mechanistic, uncreative, and decaying physical universe. As the new/old view of the universe as alive, productive, and evolving takes root in contemporary capitalist economies, the ancient moral meanings buried in such terms as "goods," "trust," "worth," "redemption," and of course "bond" will revive and take on a new life. If nothing can come of nothing, economic activity can only be a taking and exploiting. But if everything is made out of nothing, economic activity approaches the condition of gift giving.

This conclusion raises many exciting possibilities, and also a few very thorny problems. One of the latter is the relationship between personal rights and property rights, the person and the purse; and to this question we will now turn.

4

"my purse, my person"

How Bonds Connect People and Property, Souls and Bodies

King Lear and *The Merchant of Venice*

The shocking proposition of *King Lear* is not just that love is more reliable as a reciprocal bond, with goods and services given and received, than as an unconditional one-way gift. It is that the accounting zero, the balanced books, of the reciprocal bond can become a source of infinite spiritual profit. This is the case because nature is enriching itself through its own growth and creativity, and if we accept ourselves as part of nature, we can share in that profit; and through our peculiarly human (yet no less natural) abilities of personal relationship and artistic invention we can convert that profit into moral, spiritual, and aesthetic goods as well. In *King Lear* these propositions are explored largely through the negative instance of what happens when people attempt to live as if they were not true, as if the only choices were ruthless selfishness and selfless sacrifice; and Shakespeare shows unequivocally in the case of Cordelia that an interested, bonded love is no less capable of beautiful self-sacrifice than its imagined unconditional alternative. In *The Merchant of Venice,* which is the main subject of this chapter, Shakespeare gives us a profound analysis of the positive case, in which most of the major characters accept that we are indeed animals, but no less capable of free choice than if we were angels; and that genuine human love is always *interested,* always reciprocal, but no less generous for all that.

Two profound objections immediately arise. One is that if we are mere animals, the spiritual and the generous are automatically ruled out. The other is that if we accept ourselves as part of nature, the vital distinction between personal rights and property rights, personal bonds and financial bonds, is blurred. *The Merchant of Venice* meets both these objections, and deals with them in its action and in its poetic language; and in the process arrives at a view of human love that is both realistic and deeply inspiring. However, to read the play in this way requires that we discard much of the traditional interpretation of it by literary scholars both of the gentlemanly Right and of the modernist academic Left.

The Human Animal

"Unaccommodated man," says King Lear to Poor Tom the beggar, "is no more but such a poor, bare, forked animal as thou art" (III.iv.105). This terrifyingly honest view of the human being as a mere animal haunts *King Lear* and is an important melody in the music of all of Shakespeare's plays. "Allow not nature more than nature needs, / Man's life is cheap as beast's," pleads Lear to his ruthless elder daughters when they turn on him and deprive him of all he has (II.iv.263). At the end of *King Lear* the old king holds his dead daughter Cordelia in his arms and asks, with heartbreaking simplicity, "Why should a dog, a horse, a rat, have life, / And thou no breath at all?" (V.iii.308).

Shakespeare's view of biological life and human life in particular seems to have been that life is an intricate arrangement of matter, and that the mental consciousness of human beings is a very special development of that vital complexity. In *Antony and Cleopatra* Cleopatra refers to her own conscious existence as "this knot intrinsicate / Of life" (V.ii.304). Such, roughly, is also the view of present-day biological science. Uncannily Shakespeare has guessed that the inner essence of biological life is some kind of tangle of threads that makes up a whole greater than its parts, a tangle that is untied at the moment of death: a rather exact description of the twisted knot of DNA and RNA and protein strands that constitutes the molecular basis of life.

Shakespeare's model for how such an arrangement of matter might accommodate a soul was the then-current medieval and Renaissance idea of the Great Chain of Being, with God at the top, followed by angels, humans, animals, and plants, and inanimate matter at the bottom, the contents of each category itself arranged in order of excellence. This hierarchical model applied primarily to the cosmos and secondarily to the microcosm of a human being, in which reason took the place of God, followed by the will, the passions, and the physical powers of the body. The huge and largely unappreciated virtue of the hierarchical model is that it avoids the alienating dualism of the mind/matter dichotomy, providing instead a much more subtly graded set of distinctions, and a universe of fellowship and communication. Today, after two centuries of leveling materialism, science is gravitating toward a renewal of the hierarchical model, this time one of function, evolutionary emergence, and internal structure. In this new Great Chain of Being the human body is a miraculous hierarchy of organization, from subatomic particles through atoms, molecules, organelles, cells, organs, functional units such as the digestive, cardiovascular, pulmonary, lymphatic and nervous systems, all the way up to the controlling consciousness, which might be called the strange attractor of this whole interconnected process.

This does not mean that Shakespeare was a materialist—that he would reduce the miracle of human awareness and conscience to the blind, deterministic interactions of matter or animal behavior. For one thing, as we have seen, he does not seem to have believed that matter and living organisms were blind and deterministic in the first place. He believed that all things have some qualities of spirit—plants more than inanimate matter, animals more than plants, humans more than animals. Dead matter was indeed in his view more blind and deterministic than living plants, and they more insensible and automatic than living animals; but even matter had a rudimentary vitality of its own.

For another thing, Shakespeare did not deny the existence of the soul. But for him soul arose from the interrelation of the material elements of a souled being, as the likeness depicted in a portrait arises from the dabs of color, lines, and shadings of the painting, or as a melody arises from the raw sounds of a piece of music, or as the meaning of a poem arises from the arrangement of the words. Plato himself, one of the greatest authorities on the nature of the soul, considers this view of it—though he ends up rejecting it—on his way to defining the soul as a separate, eternal, and unchanging immaterial entity in the *Phaedo*. But perhaps Plato neglected some of the most exciting characteristics of the soul defined as an "attunement," as he put it. One could, given a soul of this kind, enhance and intensify it by sacrificial moral action or careful study or the acquisition of noble skills or crafts; likewise, one could damage or extinguish the soul in oneself by cruel or dishonest behavior, cynicism, or sheer laziness. Shakespeare believes deeply in the power of habit, training, custom: in Sonnet 111 he confesses that his own nature is "subdued / To what it works in, like the dyer's hand"; Horatio says of the happy grave digger in *Hamlet* that "custom hath made it in him a property of easiness" (V.i.67); the exiled duke in *As You Like It* asks his fellow exiles in the forest "Hath not old custom made this life more sweet / Than that of painted pomp?" (II.i.2). At first blush habit seems to be a limit on our freedom, and thus on the prerogatives of the soul; but on the contrary, by deliberately planting good new habits and slowly renouncing bad old habits one can transform one's very nature. As Hamlet says to his mother, Gertrude, who is addicted to sex with her dead husband's evil brother:

> That monster custom, who all sense doth eat,
> Of habits devil, is angel yet in this,
> That to the use of actions fair and good
> He likewise gives a frock or livery
> That aptly is put on. . . .
> For use almost can change the stamp of nature . . .
> (*Hamlet*, III.iv.162)

Anyone who has trained for a sport or martial art knows how true this is both for the body and the mind. Our freedom is actually much larger than the freedom of a complete unchanging being, the Platonic soul, that acts always according to its nature; for we can alter the very reward mechanisms that impel us to act in a given way, change the very thing that decides. In *The Tempest* Shakespeare even gives us in Caliban a sort of hypothetical being, a thought experiment: someone who has the animal nature of a human being but none of the human capacity to change one's nature through education and the implantation of good habits, one "on whose nature / Nurture can never stick" (IV.i.188). Shakespeare's point is that we are not Calibans. We all contain a bit of Caliban—"this thing of darkness I / Acknowledge mine," Prospero says of him (V.i.275). But we also contain the power to change ourselves, unless we kill it by persistent evil action.

This does not by any means imply that we are born as blank slates to be inscribed by custom and training. "Use"—the usury by which we earn the profit of virtue—can "almost" change the stamp of nature, but never erase it. Shakespeare accepts that we are made out of both nature and nurture, heredity and environment. He avoids the easy reduction of human beings to either their class, upbringing, and socioeconomic background, on one hand, or their biological inheritance, neurochemistry, and evolutionary history, on the other—easy answers often appealed to by today's political Left and Right. But the twist that Shakespeare puts on this perennial conundrum is characteristically both optimistic and deeply challenging: our nature includes the opportunity to fully transform our moral nature, if we make the effort and open ourselves to the creative grace of the world, and to at least partly transform our intellectual and aesthetic capacities. Our education and social environment can supply techniques for transforming ourselves, but cannot do it for us. In other words, Shakespeare believed with Keats that we live in the vale of soul making. Our heredity gives us but the makings of a soul, our cultural background the tools to shape ourselves; but it is we, with the help of the gifts offered by the soul of the world itself, who must do the shaping. How galling this view is to racists, aristocrats, and other believers in "blood"! And likewise, how galling it is to those who wish to blame society for the poverty and destructive behavior of some of its citizens. Our blood can resist the compulsions of society and culture; our culture can bridle the egotism of the blood. The result? We are responsible for what we are.

Indeed, this being responsible for what we are is, for Shakespeare, what it means to have a soul. The soul *is* the peculiar "bond" that exists among all the elements of the body. The description a contemporary biochemist would give of the metabolic life of an organism, as the dynamic *chemical* bond among all the body's atoms, is not so different. In many ways, as we have seen, it is a far grander moral conception than the theological notion that the soul is a separately formed creation, somehow injected into a brute body at the moment of conception, quickening, or birth; because it allows for self-transformation, in other words, for redemption. And the moral beauty of the idea is entirely dependent on the view of the soul as an arrangement, a dynamic structure, of matter—in Plato's metaphor, the tuning of the instrument that is the body.

But if the person is the way the matter of the body is arranged, and if the matter of the body is no different in itself from matter not arranged in the "knot intrinsicate of life," then many legal, moral, and economic distinctions that we take for granted become suddenly more complicated than we had thought. It is precisely this distinction, between body and self, matter and soul, and all the implications attached to it, that Shakespeare investigates in *The Merchant of Venice*. A glance at some of these implications will illustrate the enormous scope and importance of the whole issue.

The Exchange System of *The Merchant of Venice*

The plot of the play is an intricate pattern of exchanges, purchases, and pledges among a remarkable range of physical, abstract, and personal entities. The three thousand ducats Bassanio borrows from Antonio is both the price Bassanio pays to enter the marriage test and the contractual equivalent of the pound of flesh Antonio signs away to Shylock. The leaden casket that Bassanio chooses—not, significantly, the ducatlike silver or gold ones—is the one that contains the portrait of Portia, which in turn stands for the right to marry her. She interprets that right as a right of possession over her property and person, symbolized by the wedding ring she gives her new husband. As the betrothed of Bassanio she then offers many times the value of the three thousand ducats to ransom the life of Antonio. In the trial Shylock claims the flesh of Antonio as property no different from the flesh of any other animal. Thus the two major plots of the play have streamed back together, both centered on Antonio's pound of flesh. Portia, by her own account the property of Bassanio, now changes her identity to that of the learned young lawyer Bellario and her public sex from female to male: yet another translation of value. In her new role she saves Antonio, making her own wit the price of his life. Mischievously she now demands Bassanio's wedding ring as the wages for this service, and he cannot refuse. Thus Antonio's pound of flesh has now been replaced by or transmuted into Portia's ring. When Portia returns to Bassanio, she demands to see the ring and feigns jealous fury at its loss, claiming that Bassanio gave it away to another woman. On hearing that he gave it to the learned lawyer who saved his friend, she swears to find that lawyer and sleep with him in revenge—of course this would mean having sex with herself, since she was the lawyer too. Finally she relents and gives Bassanio back the ring, but in a peculiar way: she gives it to Antonio to give back to Bassanio, thus bringing Antonio back into the market. So there has been a dizzying series of trades. How exchangeable are human souls and human flesh, human flesh and animal flesh, animal flesh and nonliving metal (especially the precious metal of exchange), metal and legal credit, time and

garded as the sin of homosexuality; the one made dead things repro-
the other used the living reproductive organs to perform an essentially
act.

following how Shakespeare handles love between members of the same
sex, we can arrive at a deeper view of his understanding of interest. Shakespeare did not accept Dante's harsh view of homosexuality; his view of the
matter is characteristically wise and complex. A husband pledges and gives
his "pound of flesh" to his wife for the sake of progeny. When Antonio offers a pound of flesh for his friend, there is a tactful suggestion in the play
that the feelings Antonio has for Bassanio go beyond friendship into the
realm of a deeper emotion, one that he does not fully recognize or acknowledge, but that makes itself felt in the great sigh that he heaves in the first line
of the play: "In sooth I know not why I am so sad." He knows that Bassanio
is in love with Portia, but is too noble in mind—nobler, in fact, than Shakespeare himself in the Sonnets—to admit that it grieves him to have a rival in
his friend's affections. By placing Bassanio in his debt for the expense of
wooing her, Antonio subconsciously hopes to have a share in their union.
Later Antonio says of himself, "I am a tainted wether of the flock," which
shows that he has gained some rueful insight into his own nature (IV.i.114).
But his sacrifice, the offering of his pound of flesh, is, though he cannot acknowledge it, a desperate gambit to win Bassanio back from Portia's ring.

His plan does not materialize: he ends up, moreover, being in debt to Portia for all his possessions and his very life. By changing her apparent identity
and sex Portia proves to her husband that she has all the virtues and capacities of a man as well as those of a woman; she has defeated Antonio. However, she does not triumph over him. Instead, she asks Antonio to give back
to Bassanio the wedding ring that Bassanio had given away to her own disguised self, making Antonio, her husband's best friend, the pledge of the
marriage. The meaning of this complex interchange is clear: a heterosexual
marriage of mere breeders without the deeper romantic friendship of equals
is morally inferior to true love between two persons of the same sex; but a
heterosexual marriage that *does* incorporate the kind of soul friendship a
man can bear for a man (and a woman for a woman—for instance, the love
of Portia and her companion Nerissa) is superior to both, since it takes the
supreme risk of reproduction.

What conclusions about interest are we to draw from the analogy between sexual and commercial morality? Socrates compared the taking of interest to the (same-sex) relationship of a philosopher with his young student:
the philosopher acts as a midwife for the ideas of his friend, ideas that spring
from the ideal form that the student has conceived in the womb of his mind.
Shakespeare accepted this extension of reproductive fertility into the realm
of the mind and into the realm of commerce. Friendship for Shakespeare,
then, is like an interest-yielding loan. Yet for him a gift was a still greater
thing than an earned profit, *as long as the gift itself incorporated a spiritual
profit at a higher level.* Thus an economy in which gifts were exchanged
without any increase in value was inferior to one in which profit could be

made on loans and investments, just as a "marriage of true minds" between
two people of the same sex was better than the mating of two mere breeders.
But better still was an economy of gift giving in which value exploded out of
the gifts at a rate as great as or greater than the percentage one might draw
in interest—the economic parallel of the heterosexual marriage that has incorporated the intellectual and spiritual profits of an equal, single-sex friendship. One of Shakespeare's favorite puns is between "conceiving" an idea
and "conceiving" a baby; his word for the precious coin of poetry was a
"conceit."

In a world that is essentially creative, where everything is made from
nothing—in which even the inanimate universe is not inert and dead, but
shares something of the inherent fertility of the living world and of personal
relationships—the taking of interest is perfectly natural. The creative gift
giving of lovers is not the opposite of interest taking, but a higher form of
the same universal drive to increase. Medieval and classical philosophers
who condemned interest were right only if the physical world was indeed
dead and unproductive, as they believed it to be. But if, as Shakespeare believed, the world is creative, their prohibition is mistaken. Thus in Shakespeare's profound meditation on interest and gift we can perhaps see the
soul of Europe making up its mind, as it finally did in the late Renaissance,
that the taking of interest was a legitimate and valuable instrument of
human exchange. In this light the revulsion against capitalism that occurred
in the nineteenth and twentieth centuries was a throwback to a tradition of
linear thinking that found the zero horrifying not only because of its emptiness but because of its potential productivity. The Marxist horror of "commodity fetishism" is the horror of the monotheistic iconoclast at the womb-
like fecundity of the world and the richness of its imagery.

Marriage and Property

But if marriage is like a profitable business contract, a bond, doesn't that
mean that one can buy a wife? In a sense, Bassanio does buy Portia, using
the money he has borrowed from Antonio to present himself as a suitable
match for her (indeed, he hires the servant Launcelot Gobbo away from Shylock as part of his new retinue). It would be tempting to suggest that friendship is like a loan, and marriage like full possession. But the idea is clearly
problematic. How much does a wife belong to her husband, and a husband
to a wife? When Portia gives herself away to Bassanio she says:

> This house, these servants, and this same myself
> Are yours, my lord's. I give them with this ring . . .
> (III.ii.170)

In the sexual and procreative aspects of a marriage, the conjunction of body
and soul is inescapable. Portia's ring symbolizes that ring of flesh by which

we make our entry into this world, the portal through which her husband will enter, the place where he will, in Elizabethan English, spend himself upon her. Part of his very being becomes hers to form a new being composed of both parents; like a merchant adventurer he risks himself in that dark and oceanic passage, that the profit of a child may emerge from the trade. Shakespeare emphasizes that risk by the terms to which Portia's suitors must agree if they play the lottery of the three caskets for her hand: a promise on their honor, if they fail, to live a life of permanent celibacy thereafter. This provision dramatizes the pathos of male wooing. Though in purely biological terms the work of a woman's womb is enormously more expensive than the brief contribution of the male, no male animal can be sure that his offspring are his own; and thus he must always live with the possibility that his line is doomed to die with him, and go into that biological darkness that is the deepest terror of any living thing. Among social species in which males compete for reproductive privileges almost all females reproduce, but only a fraction of the males. And whatever investment a male makes in the success of his mate's offspring must always be an act of trust, a casting of bread upon the waters. Of course the social risk taken by the wife is just as great; in Elizabethan law, she gives over to this powerful male animal the governance of her body and her possessions. This tremendous mutual risk is what Portia has in mind when she blesses Bassanio's attempt at the caskets:

> Now he goes,
> With no less presence, but with much more love,
> Than young Alcides, when he did redeem
> The virgin tribute paid by howling Troy
> To the sea monster. I stand for sacrifice.
> (III.ii.53)

Portia is the sacrificial victim offered to the great sea snake to redeem the city; Bassanio is the hero Hercules (Alcides), who risks his life to save her. The fact that Bassanio, a young nobleman whose generous habits have eaten up his inheritance, is in our terms a fortune hunter when he courts Portia, and goes into debt to his best friend to do so—and that this is no secret to Portia, to whom Bassanio has been perfectly honest—adds a further social dimension to the hazards both lovers accept in the enterprise. We have forgotten, in our age of birth control, expert natal care, sexual equality in matters of legal ownership, and easy divorce, the terrifying stakes that were placed on sexual union. It was a game of chance. Shakespeare is not squeamish about this aspect of romance; the casket episode ends with a merry wager as to which couple will conceive first. Of course it is a *wager;* in such matters we are at the mercy of chance, fortune, hazard, just as nature "intended" in setting up the great lottery of sexual reproduction. Only thus may unique individuals be created.

The irreducibly physical nature of the marriage bond is symbolized by the wedding ring. The play ends with Gratiano's pledge to his wife:

> Well, while I live I'll fear no other thing
> So sore, as keeping safe Nerissa's ring.

Gratiano is a literalist in this as in everything else (anti-Semitism is another kind of literalism, and Gratiano is also an anti-Semite). But for beings like ourselves whose very nature is a symbol, a symbolic action is a real one. When husband and wife exchange rings, flesh is manacled with metal—however lightly and decoratively—as the free soul is manacled with flesh. It is a true giving up of liberty; husband and wife truly belong to each other. Our modern experiment in marriage as a merely optional relationship has given us legal freedoms and protections at the cost of moral trivialization; perhaps it is time to combine the better elements of both. In *The Merchant of Venice* Shakespeare was feeling his way toward such a solution: when Bassanio gives his ring away to the young "lawyer"—Portia in disguise—and Portia returns the ring to him, it is clear that the marriage contract is being symbolically renegotiated in such a way as to provide the wife with an equality in the marriage not stipulated by Elizabethan law. But this renegotiation cannot be understood without a broader understanding of the relationship between property, on one hand, and kinship, tribe, and employment, on the other.

Inheritance, the Tribe, and the City

Portia's father has made the bequest of his wealth to her conditional on her obedience to him in the choice of a husband; but how just are the laws of inheritance if "the will of a dead father" can curb "the will of a living daughter" (I.ii.23)? Perhaps the most inescapable aspect of our physical materiality is our literal fleshly continuity with our parents. One's very face in the mirror is, or should be, a reminder of the act of kind between one's mother and father, by which we were engendered. And economic obligations and prerogatives come along with the biological inheritance. To the extent that we accept the money and goods that our parents pass on to us, to that extent we become their agents and representatives after their deaths, and lose a little of our own autonomy to the collective will of the lineage. But even if we accept no goods from them, we must still make do with the gifts and liabilities that come with their genes; we cannot escape them, and our moral lives are in part a continuation of theirs. We are forced, if Shakespeare is right, to accept a slightly queasy and anxious combination of purity and compromise. If we could live like perfect and ideal moral subjects, everything we did could be the product of a completely disinterested assessment of the right course of action; we would, in Immanuel Kant's terms, act in such a way that the principle of our action could be made into an ethical maxim to be obeyed by everybody. But we are always already implicated in a living body and an ongoing real history that carry with them a web of responsibilities, opportunities, limitations of perspective, and unfair advantages.

These are what is *given* to us, in both senses: given like scientific "data" (from the Latin "dare, datum," to give, given)—and given like a free gift, like that mysterious mercy that cannot be constrained or expected. The perfect moral world of Kant would be a nightmare, for nobody could give anyone a gift, gifts being unearned and therefore unfair. Or rather, the only gift one could give would be the opportunity to give a gift, that is, to make oneself lacking in some moral fashion that would require the altruistic assistance of the other. The logic of the Kantian ethical world is strange indeed. The only answer is that we must, like Portia, accept the gifts we are given, and try to be as generous and as fair-minded as we can in how we dispose of them to others. In other words, if we are born wealthy, we are born morally unfree; but we free ourselves by making gifts to others. This indeed Portia does, spectacularly and repeatedly throughout the play.

All of us, then, get our material bodies from our inheritance, our tribe. Do we therefore owe our fundamental sense of loyalty to that tribe? Does that identity define what we are? Shylock says "yes" to both questions and is horrified when his daughter marries a Christian. But both Christian salvation and the conduct of profitable business in a merchant city depend on an ability to transcend racial and tribal differences, so that, for instance, Portia can be legitimately wooed by suitors of foreign races, including a Moor from Africa, and Launcelot manages to get his negro girlfriend pregnant.

Shakespeare in his imaginary Venice is really playing with a remote and futuristic idea: of a world in which different tribes, nations, ethnic groups, and religions can live as neighbors. We in the United States are trying to construct such a society, with some success but many failures. The key seems to be that business and financial interests, the pursuit of wealth, should be vital enough to override our natural tendency to scapegoat and murder those odd-looking and smelly strangers, the members of other tribes, with their blasphemous religions and disgusting food habits. We should be more motivated to make a profit out of them than kill them, and they should feel the same way about us. The injunction to love thy neighbor has failed; as Shakespeare was well aware, Christians and Muslims, who both profess to obey this law, are no less prone to violence in motive than devotees of other religions and are usually better at it in practice. Perhaps, paradoxically, good old profit may be a more reliable route to the ideal results of harmony and cooperation. But for this one needs a city or a nation with a system of impartial justice and the will to stick to it; Shylock and Gratiano, the intolerant Jew and the intolerant Christian, must be protected from each other. At the same time, as we shall see, justice cannot operate without its partner and paradoxical opposite, mercy.

Personal Rights and Property Rights

This survey of the complex questions Shakespeare deals with in *The Merchant of Venice* should be enough to hint at the play's extraordinary relevance to present-day economic and psychosocial problems. When at the opening of the play Bassanio asks Antonio for his help in wooing Portia, Antonio replies, "My purse, my person, my extremest means / Lie all unlocked to your occasions" (I.i.138). The strange joining of purse and person appears to be a distinction between a pair of binary opposites until it is closely examined, at which point each of the pair appears to meld into the other without entirely losing its identity; and this melding is echoed in the very sound of the words.

One way of expressing the distinction is in terms of the opposition between personal rights and property rights. "A pound of man's flesh taken from a man," says Shylock,

> Is not so estimable, profitable neither,
> As flesh of muttons, beefs, or goats.
> (I.iii.162)

This macabre comparison is meant by Shylock to be taken as a joke. But it captures a central idea of the play, that personal rights cannot be easily separated from property rights. This idea is worked out through the story of Antonio's agreement with Shylock to offer a pound of his own flesh as security for the loan of three thousand ducats, which Antonio wishes in turn to lend to his friend Bassanio (this time unsecured and "disinterested"—without interest). Clearly the whole matter is problematic. Contracts ought to be kept and enforced, else a trading city like Venice (or a free-enterprise nation like the present-day United States of America) cannot exist. Antonio's flesh is his to use in commercial exchanges—or is it? Shylock argues persuasively that the distinction between life and livelihood is a cruel and hypocritical one: "You take my life / When you do take the means whereby I live" (IV.i.375). If we concede that Shylock can legally propose such a bond, and Antonio can legally agree to it, we are admitting that there is no distinction between personal rights and property rights, that there is no difference between what we own and what we are. But if we deny that Shylock and Antonio can enter such a contract, the whole concept of ownership and possession comes into question.

Karl Marx was quite willing to go this far. What we buy, he said, when we legally take possession of an object, is the human labor that has gone into its acquisition or construction. An employer owns the labor of an employee if there has been a contractual exchange of wages for work. In what way, then, Marx asked, is a wage slave different from a slave? For Marx the confusion of personal and property rights was the sign of the moral illegitimacy of private property. He wished to abolish it altogether, and we might well see the history of the last hundred years as a gigantic and tragic experiment to find out what happens when we do. The result has been ringingly clear and unambiguous. If you abolish private property—whether directly, as in the communist model, or indirectly through state ownership, central planning, the command economy, and high taxation, as in the socialist and Nazi models—you effectively give total ownership of the lives, bodies, and minds of the people over to the state. Then, because the people do not have the means of persuasion provided by property to resist tyranny, the state often turns into the fiat of a single person, like Stalin, Hitler, Mao, or Pol Pot. The state can now exact not just one pound of flesh, but the whole body, and without a contract either—hair for upholstery, skin for lamp-shades, and all. The world community has in the last few years decisively rejected this path and has declared the result of the experiment to be that private property is provably necessary. But this means that we must renew our struggle with the moral problems of property, and accept the inevitable overlap of personal and property rights.

We can, perhaps, bring home to ourselves the disturbing aspects of this issue by remembering the case of the Ford Pinto fuel tank some years ago. Ford had built a car whose fuel tank would burst into flame in a rear end impact. The effect was rare but demonstrable. Implicit in Ford's defense was a cost-benefit analysis that measured human lives in dollars: that is, to repair the defect or recall the car would cost over two million dollars per casualty. To do so was to simply remove two million dollars' worth of value from American society. The net result, once the loss had played itself out in terms of lack of goods and services for improved technology, cheaper food, cleaner air and water, medical research, education, other more cost-effective safety measures, and the general investment in the economy that would make these things possible, would be the loss of more than one human life. Of course the damage would be statistical; but such epidemiological statistics are regularly used in calculating effects like the increased cancer risk of a release of radioactivity, the environmental impact of sulphur emissions, the dangers of smoking, the death toll of a storm or heat wave, and the traffic fatalities resulting from raising the speed limit. Thus it would cost more in terms of human life to fix the gas tank than to leave it as it was. Now we can argue with the details of this case, but it is clear that there must be *some* amount of money whose loss in terms of real goods and services to the economy would mean death to a number of its citizens. In other words, there is a price to a human life—in current money, perhaps around ten million dollars. Does this mean that if one had to destroy twenty million dollars' worth of capital equipment to save a human life, we should refuse to do so, on the grounds that in so doing we would kill two people elsewhere? The conscience recoils at this; but soldiers, firefighters, and police officers are regularly expected to risk their lives to save the property of others.

And here again Shakespeare, who thought all this through and accepts the need for property, is an illuminating guide. His Venice can support its population only because it accepts some equivalence between material goods and human life, between property and personal rights.

Employment and Slavery

Though the issue of the ownership of the labor of a servant seems to be a minor one, it is actually of profound importance in the play. In what sense does a servant belong to a master? The Launcelot Gobbo subplot, in which Launcelot changes masters, explores this question. It was a live one in Shakespeare's time, when it was widely believed that the traditional feudal loyalty of servant to master, like that of family members to each other, was beginning to give way to a modern system in which money was impersonally exchanged for work. Shakespeare symbolizes this anxiety by having Old Gobbo, Launcelot's rustic father, fail to recognize his son when he visits him in the city, on account of his poor sight: as he says, it is a wise father that knows his own son! Significantly, Old Gobbo has prepared a game pie to give to Launcelot's new master, in the fashion of the old gift-exchange practice of traditional societies.

It would be easy to give a Marxist view of this episode: that the new impersonal cash and commodity exchange economy alienates family members from each other and creates a society of isolated selfish individuals. But this interpretation is too facile for the wise Shakespeare. If anything, the tendency of the play is in the opposite direction. Launcelot leaves the employ of a master, Shylock, whose only bond with him is the economic one of payment (Shylock, like a nineteenth-century industrialist of the Dickensian "Bounderby" variety, is always complaining about how much Launcelot eats and sleeps) to take up service with Bassanio, whom Launcelot genuinely admires and wishes to serve. And it only takes a few minutes for Old Gobbo to recognize his son, so the alienation of city workers from their country ancestors is not really so terrible. Thus Shakespeare is implying that the mercantile city affords greater opportunities for new personal relationships, without necessarily damaging the old ones—a conclusion quite contrary to those of most critics of capitalism.

Shylock, like Marx, sees no difference between commanding the labor of an indentured servant and owning a piece of a person's flesh—though it presents no ethical problems for Shylock.

> You have among you many a purchased slave,
> Which like your asses and your dogs and mules
> You use in abject and in slavish parts,
> Because you bought them. Shall I say to you,
> "Let them be free . . ."?
>   You will answer,
> "The slaves are ours." So do I answer you:
> The pound of flesh which I demand of him
> Is dearly bought, is mine, and I will have it.
> If you deny me, fie upon your law!
> There is no force in the decrees of Venice.
> (IV.i.90)

If the world community has rightly rejected socialism, it has also rightly rejected slavery; but it has not yet given a satisfactory reason for doing so. As we have seen, it is not enough to say that personal and property rights are completely distinct. If they are distinct, an employer cannot demand work of an employee, a con man cannot be sentenced to penal servitude for kiting a check, a surgeon cannot expect payment for grafting an artificial hip joint, a singer cannot insure her voice, an author cannot claim intellectual property in a book or assign copyright to a publisher. Clearly, enforced slavery can be condemned as a form of theft; but what about voluntarily contracted slavery, and all the gradations of indentured labor, military service, sports and show business contracts, and so on? What about Antonio's forfeiture of a pound of his own flesh? Where are the limits to one person's ownership of another, if the assignment of property rights is voluntarily entered into?

Shakespeare's answer is very subtle. At the trial in which Shylock claims his pound of flesh, Portia—who represents, as clearly as any character can, the judgment of Shakespeare himself—concedes the literal justice of Shylock's claim. The key issue is the voluntary nature of the contract: Antonio entered into it freely. The pound of flesh stands for all the ways in which we can trade over to another some part of our physical person. Shakespeare accepts that we are, paradoxically, free to give up some of our freedom to dispose of ourselves.

Thus far, however, we do not have a complete rejection of slavery, only of enforced and involuntary servitude. The violent enslavement of Africans by European, African, or Arab slave traders would indeed be condemned under this ruling; but not the selling of oneself into slavery, or even of children by parents if the children are of an age to consent to it. Such practices still exist in some countries; we come close to them ourselves in our treatment of undocumented immigrant domestic workers. Even the great African enslavement might gain some color of legitimacy from this ruling. Under the informal laws of African tribal warfare in the premodern period a captured member of a hostile tribe was the property of the chief, and this rule was tacitly accepted by victor and vanquished alike. This "legitimate" property right could in theory be transferred for a consideration to a slave trader and then to an American plantation owner. The voluntary basis of the contract cannot support the outright rejection of slavery that we need.

But Shakespeare does not stop here. Shylock is free to cut out Antonio's heart, says Portia, but only if he sheds none of Antonio's blood, and only if he takes exactly one pound, no more, no less.

> Shed thou no blood, nor cut thou less nor more
> But just a pound of flesh. If thou tak'st more
> Or less than a just pound, be it but so much
> As makes it light or heavy in the substance
> Or the division of the twentieth part
> Of one poor scruple—nay, if the scale do turn
> But in the estimation of a hair—
> Thou diest, and all thy goods are confiscate.
> (IV.i.324)

In other words, it is physically impossible for Shylock to claim his contractual property. The reason that Shylock can't get "justice" is that one cannot measure a "just" pound of flesh or "just" a pound of flesh. This is not the legal trick that it appears to be. A skeptic might point out that if Shylock had hired a particularly persnickety lawyer to draw up the bond, it might have allowed for a reasonable spillage of blood and specified a half-ounce margin of error in the weight cut off. But this is not the point. *Any* formulation in English (or any other natural language) would be subject to inexactness and ambiguity of one kind or another. Portia has just picked on one, but others can always be found; the more legal language is accumulated to guard against error, the more opportunities for double meanings, mistakes, and misinterpretations. Indeed, the recent fashion of deconstruction in academic literature departments really amounts to no more than the same—belated—realization, that all language is ambiguous if we wish it to be so. As the supreme master of language, Shakespeare knew this very well, and in several plays he makes gentle fun of legal language and its pedantic attempt to dot all the i's and cross all the t's.

The reason that even voluntarily entered and contractual slavery is wrong, then, is essentially because it is impossible! A person's soul is simply not the kind of thing that can be owned, any more than water can be caught in a sieve; not because the soul is a metaphysical and immaterial entity (which would be blind and paralysed in a world of matter), but because it is a process, a flow, an interaction; or more precisely the inner form or strange attractor of such a process. If the condition of a slave is such that the slave does not resist his enslavement, then he is not truly enslaved; some element of cooperation, voluntary agreement, mutual exchange must exist in the relationship, which the "slave" is buying into; he is not the chattel of another. He is like a conscripted soldier, who is fully at the disposal of his commanders, but he is not a slave. And if the slave is resisting his enslavement, even if in the unwilling silence of his own mind, then he is not in any legal sense the property of his "master," but rather a victim of kidnapping and coercion, whose labor is being stolen. Any contract by which he entered his servitude is void, not because it is unjust, but because it makes the category mistake of confusing a thing with a process. In other words, the "rights of Man" (to use the old sex-specific language in which they were proposed) name not an ideal of justice but a condition of reality. They belong to a mercy that is in its own sphere impossible to constrain, not to an enforceable justice. But this idea will require another chapter.

The Economics of Incarnation

Meanwhile let us consider once more the problems we have looked at in *The Merchant of Venice*—ownership; eating; interest; marriage and its symbol, the wedding ring; inheritance; tribal loyalty; hired labor; and the overriding issue of personal and property rights. What do they have in common? They all involve paradoxes and complications arising out of the issue with which this chapter began—the incarnateness of the human soul in its animal body, and the consequent inextricability of personal and property rights. What are Shakespeare's conclusions?

The reader who has encountered Shakespeare in school or university may find some of these surprising, even shocking. The major commentators on Shakespeare in the last two hundred years have come from cultural traditions that, though profoundly different from each other, shared an inveterate distaste for market capitalism. The gentlemen and literary professionals who made up the body of nineteenth-century Shakespeare criticism saw trade as a necessary evil and finance as a corruption as mysterious as it was disgusting: Anthony Trollope's epic novel on insider trading, *The Way We Live Now,* conveys the flavor well. In the twentieth century the critics are largely academics of an increasingly Marxist persuasion, for whom profit, interest, and the trading of financial instruments are the mechanisms of oppression and injustice. Literary right wingers, like Ezra Pound, were even more rabidly hostile to normal capitalist business practice.

Thus almost all the critics would like to read *The Merchant of Venice* as a subversive argument against private ownership, as a rejection of the animal roots of human economics symbolized by eating, as a condemnation of usury, as a rather ill-managed warning against marrying for money, as a protest against the restrictions of inheritance and tribal identity, as an attack on the commercialization of work, and as a straightforward endorsement of the distinction between personal and property rights, with a strong preference for personal rights. Though they are partly correct in some of their contentions, a close examination of the play shows that Shakespeare's view is much deeper, wiser, and more subtle, and can serve—as their model of its meaning cannot—as a guide for a future economics in which the strengths of market capitalism have been fully incorporated.

For Shakespeare private ownership was essential to human existence. It is more than just a matter of human dignity ("Allow not nature more than nature needs, / Man's life is cheap as beast's" [*King Lear,* II.iv.263]); it is a matter of human existence. We are human in that we can exchange and communicate with other humans and with the world of nature. We cannot perform these exchanges and communications by telepathy, and thus we must have material means for doing so—or perhaps it would be truer to say that we *do* use telepathy, and the medium of our telepathy is the physical human body and its inseparable extensions, the things we own. We are in the human and natural world to the extent that we own things. Like stage actors, who require material means for the exercise of their craft, and must exchange with each other and with the audience as the very body of their art, human beings must be incarnated into an economic world. Put this way, the proposition perhaps sounds like rather unremarkable common sense; but it contradicts two centuries of attempts to maintain an absolute distinction between the kingdom of means and the kingdom of ends, between "I-It" and "I-

Thou" relationships, between cold commodity exchange and warm personal commitments.

Shakespeare accepts the humbling fact that we must put the body tissues of other living things into our mouths, grind them up, swallow them, and eject the disgusting waste products in order to stay alive. More than that, he celebrates the pleasure and essential comedy of this act. "Dost thou think," says Sir Toby Belch in *Twelfth Night* to the Puritan Malvolio, "because thou art virtuous, there shall be no more cakes and ale?" (II.iii.116). Shakespeare's Falstaff, in *Henry IV,* is a grand compendium of fleshly existence—the quintessential communicator, actor, dweller of the world, eater and, finally eatee:

> If sack and sugar be a fault, God help the wicked! If to be old and merry be a sin, then many an old host that I know is damned. If to be fat be to be hated, then Pharaoh's lean kine are to be loved. No, my good lord: banish Peto, banish Bardolph, banish Poins; but for sweet Jack Falstaff, kind Jack Falstaff, true Jack Falstaff, valiant Jack Falstaff, and therefore more valiant being, as he is, old Jack Falstaff, banish not him thy Harry's company, banish not him thy Harry's company, banish plump Jack, and banish all the world!
> (*1 Henry IV*, II.iv.475)

Thus it is ominous when Shylock, seeking a purity and separation that deny the communion of the flesh, refuses to accept Bassanio's invitation to dinner.

> I will buy with you, sell with you, talk with you, walk with you, and so following; but I will not eat with you, drink with you, nor pray with you. (I.iii.33)

As far as he is concerned, Falstaff's merry old innkeepers are indeed damned—not because of their religion so much as because of their defiling adulteration of body and soul. "How like a fawning publican he looks," says Shylock of Antonio, who in lending money gratis mixes personal and property concerns (I.iii.38). But Shylock ends up as the exact opposite of the stereotypical grasping Jew so dear to anti-Semites; it is his final refusal to "feed upon the prodigal Christian," to take financial advantage of the defaulted bond, that is his downfall. He is not materialistic enough, not enough of a compromiser, a greedy businessman. He is acting out of principle, a genuine tragic hero, when he refuses the offer of thrice his bond.

Contrary to the conventional wisdom, Shakespeare actually *endorses* the taking of interest in the play. In the terms of the settlement of the trial, Antonio becomes the trustee of half of Shylock's wealth, which he proposes to "have in use"—that is, lend out at interest—for the benefit of Shylock's son-in-law, a proposal that the court accepts. In fact, Antonio has learned from his experience that the taking of interest is infinitely preferable to the pledging of securities such as a pound of flesh! The point is that there is nothing wrong with the taking of interest if it reasonably represents the rate of natural increase by which the universe itself generates value in cooperation with human creativity and enterprise. Only if the universe is a closed system with a diminishing stockpile of order—a view of the world shown to be both wrong and evil in consequences, as we have seen in the previous chapter—is the taking of interest the kind of parasitism that Antonio first believes it to be. Shylock the merchant is not wrong for lending money at interest, any more than Antonio the merchant is wrong for buying low and selling high; he is wrong for *not* taking interest, for refusing Bassanio's offer of thrice the value of the bond and insisting on the exact fulfillment of the pledge. Interest is simply an abstract representation of the sexual productiveness of nature; it is like the fruits of friendship as compared to the fruits of the womb. Shakespeare's implicit validation of a friendship modern psychologists would call homoerotic in feeling is deeply related to his equally prophetic validation of profitable finance.

Shakespeare's astonishing moral boldness, which his admirers have still not brought themselves to face, extends even to the matter of marrying money. "In Belmont is a lady richly left," is Bassanio's first description to Antonio of his proposed bride, Portia (I.i.161). To the dismay of centuries of critics, Shakespeare seems to have no qualms at all about Bassanio's plans, and depicts the result as an exemplary and beautiful marriage. Of course Shakespeare is well aware of the moral dangers, and he subtly disposes of them. For instance, without insisting on it in a conspicuous way, he makes it quite clear that Bassanio has not concealed his financial straits from Portia. Bassanio is deeply in love with Portia, and there is already a tacit understanding between the two. Further, as we have seen, Bassanio is taking risks just as great as Portia is in this marriage. Shakespeare gives us an obvious contrast to the sincerity and courage of Bassanio in his portraits of the other suitors, whose initial rejection of the perilous terms of the enterprise, or whose choice of the gold and silver caskets, proves them unworthy. But the fact remains that the motives of Bassanio and Portia are mixed ones, in which financial considerations play a part, and that Shakespeare applauds their union by giving them some of his most gorgeous poetry when they are together.

Shakespeare is asserting the paradox that we are only free if we knowingly incorporate our "baser" motives into our more refined ideals. In Jane Austen's *Pride and Prejudice,* a novel that both continues and extends the psychoeconomic insights of Shakespeare, Elizabeth Bennet meets Darcy, and it is plain that these two intelligent, strong, and sensitive people are destined for each other. However, they are separated by pride and prejudice, and their quarrel results in a series of misunderstandings, which leads to Elizabeth's angry rejection of Darcy's first proposal of marriage. On a visit to Darcy's country house in his absence she finds herself admiring the grandeur of the grounds and building, the loyalty Darcy inspires in his servants, the consequence and power of his position in the world. She cannot help meditating that "to be mistress of Pemberley might be something!" Even after this, she turns Darcy down one more time; but her final decision to accept his hand in marriage, though it is not compelled by the promise of a grand economic bond, does not ignore it either. Indeed, at the end of the novel, when Elizabeth's rather earnest sister Jane asks her when she first began to have warm feelings toward Darcy, she teases her sister by answering that it was when she saw his beautiful house in Derbyshire. The fact that she can joke about it both admits it as a motivation and assigns it to its proper place; the reminder of property relationships can be a good cold shower for sexual vanity.

Shakespeare solves the problem of inheritance, the baggage that comes from biological descent and bequeathed property, by means of a finesse. Essentially he rejects the moral claims of obligations that come with racial, tribal, or ethnic inherited affiliations, but accepts the rights and duties of family and dynasty, if those rights and duties are interpreted as applying to the future, not the past. That is, one does indeed owe a debt to one's parents, though not to one's tribe; but the debt to one's parents can only be paid off to one's own children. Children owe their parents loving care and respect as long as the parents do not demand the sacrifice of their children's own family and future. Shakespeare is especially prescient about the dangers of tribalism. Tribalism has become modern racism under the false color of science, and modern "multiculturalism" under the false color of sociology. Then as now it divides the city, cramps the imagination, and closes off the future too much to be a valid way of preserving continuity with the past. One cannot ignore the fact that one's body, brain, and heart have a biological history; but for Shakespeare, that history goes no further than one's family lineage.

There are problems enough there. In *The Merchant of Venice* Jessica is imprisoned by her father within her house, and she does the only thing she can: escape. Portia is also trapped, by her father's will; but she finds a way to both obey it and to subtly get around it—by having her musicians play Bassanio a song whose rhyme sound is "-ed" while he is choosing among the caskets, thus hinting that the lead casket is the right one. But she is not exactly cheating; only a man with Bassanio's discernment would notice the hint. It is this quality of discernment that Portia's father is testing for, after all; the ability to see beneath the surface, to be more than just a fortune hunter—which is also to be a successful, rather than a failed, fortune hunter. Thus the message seems to be that one may deflect the absolute letter of one's parent's bequest as long as one hews to its spirit, if that spirit is fundamentally generous to the future. The terms of Shylock's sentence insist on one thing: that he pass on his wealth at his death to his daughter's family, regardless of his tribal loyalties.

What is Shakespeare's conclusion regarding the commercialization of work? In *The Merchant of Venice* the Launcelot Gobbo subplot suggests an answer. Launcelot starts off in Shylock's employ, but accepts a better offer from Bassanio, whom he personally prefers anyway. The message is that in such normal circumstances, though we give up some personal rights in ac-

a wage, the voluntary nature of work contracts sufficiently preserves
dom of the individual that we value as defining the person. For this
to be possible, let it be noted, there must be a plurality of employ-
---, in competition with each other for the services of the employed, and this
in turn implies that there cannot be a state monopoly of employment, nor
can private monopolies be permitted. If there is only one possible employer,
we are not free. Already some sort of balance is implied between a strictly
limited state with antitrust powers and limited but independent private corporations. Shakespeare has pretty well foreseen in the context of his fictional
merchant city the commonsense shape of the modern capitalist democracy
as it has worked itself out since.

But Shakespeare has not just foreseen the world of modern commerce, he
has also given it a moral interpretation that is now of profound relevance as
we try to construct a twenty-first century that is both prosperous and humane. Ever since organized corporate business began, it has been assessed by
moralists in one of two ways: as an essentially wicked activity, by which the
rich oppress the poor and accumulate goods that are morally bad for them;
or as a morally neutral activity, that is necessary to society, that is essentially
outside the ethical code that governs personal relationships, and that can be
harnessed for good or evil ends by morally responsible agents. There exists a
third possibility, which I believe Shakespeare is exploring in this play: that
business, as the human continuation of the creative impulse of nature, is essentially a good activity, and that its mechanisms of profit, security, capital
formation, interest, debt, and so on are formalizations of fundamental moral
relationships among human beings and between humans and the rest of nature. Thus business is not a neutral moral world that must be converted to
good by moral missionaries from the church, the arts, or the university, but
an independent, though limited, source of good in itself. It is certainly cor-
ruptible, though not exceptionally so by comparison with the church, the
arts, or the university; and indeed its corruption is the worse, when it happens, because of the essential goodness of the enterprise: lilies that fester
smell far worse than weeds, says Shakespeare in Sonnet 94. Shakespeare
himself was a highly successful businessman, a partner in the Globe Theater
company, an owner of choice real estate in Stratford-on-Avon, and one of
the richest self-made men in England at the time. It is not too much of a
stretch, perhaps, to imagine Antonio's rich argosies—with their bright sails
and holds full of precious silks and spices—as the plays that Shakespeare's
company was launching several times a year, which could sink or prosper according to public whim.

Perhaps the most important conclusion Shakespeare draws is, as we have
seen, that personal and property rights are inextricable. The great symbol of
this union is the leaden casket that Bassanio must choose in order to obtain
the hand of Portia—her property, her body, and the commitment of her soul.
What is the meaning of the casket? This enclosed vessel, whose interior is
mysterious and contradicts its external appearance, is both tomb and womb.
Its gray leaden surface symbolizes death; but within there is a fair face, re-

produced in a painting, and a beautiful future. To choose it is to venture into that unknown interior, the creative matrix of woman, for the male an adventure finally greater than any purely masculine merchant journey to the ends of the earth. It is to enter the great lottery of human reproduction, and thus join what Shakespeare could not have known was a four-billion-year-old tradition of life and death on this planet. When living organisms first began to reproduce by sexual recombination, they also first began to die by programmed cell death.. That casket is the same thing as the fertile zero we explored in the previous chapter; it is what Chaucer called "Goddes foison," God's fecundity. It is also the same thing as the transforming power of life that we examined in the Sonnets and *The Winter's Tale.*

Here in *The Merchant of Venice* this death-risking vitality is interpreted as the inescapably liquid and processual nature of any bond or contract, even a legal and written one. A contract, though it contains a necessary orientation toward an eternal and unchanging perfection of clarity and justice, and implicitly stipulates the most unambiguous construction of its words at the moment of their composition and signing, is always an ongoing relationship of persons. It can work only so long as it contains enough free play, enough lubricant of inexactness, so that it does not seize up. Shakespeare identifies this property of inexactness, liquidity, preparedness for compromise between material and moral interest, with the quality of "mercy," and finds it in the world of commerce. The linguistic root of "commerce," "market," "mercantile," and "merchant" is the Latin "merces," probably meaning "the things of the god Mercury." From this root we also get the word "mercy." It is this word, so central to Portia's great speech at the trial, to which we now turn.

5

"the quality of mercy is not strained"

Why Justice Must Be Lubricated with Mercy

Solid and Liquid, Earned and Given

Our investigation of the nature of bonds has raised a fundamental paradox, the need for the coexistence of mercy and justice. The task of this chapter is not to choose one at the expense of the other, nor to demonstrate that there is no real contradiction between them. It would be entirely against the spirit of Shakespeare to do either. What Shakespeare does in *The Merchant of Venice* is to accept the necessity and the mutual contradiction of mercy and justice, and to generate a dramatic world out of their continued struggle. As he develops a poetic vocabulary of metaphors and puns and plot twists and historical and mythological allusions to embody the struggle, the legal paradox of mercy and justice opens into wider and wider fields of relevance: morality, economics, physics, human physiology and evolution, religious history, theology, linguistics, aesthetics, cosmology. The point is not so much to resolve the paradox of mercy and justice, as it is to trace Shakespeare's own demonstration of how the paradox constructs the world. The solution to its puzzles is not a neat one that would dispose of the problem once and for all, but rather the continuation of the struggle itself in the marketplace, under the sign of Mercury.

In *The Merchant of Venice* Shakespeare chooses the distinction between solid and liquid (flesh and blood), and the irreducible approximateness of any measurement of weight, as ways to make a much broader argument about justice and mercy. If Shylock had been listening to Portia's plea for mercy rather than sharpening his knife, he would have heard her explain the liquid-solid quibble before his lawsuit is destroyed by it. "The quality of mercy is not strained," she says. "It droppeth as the gentle rain from heaven / Upon the place beneath" (IV.i.183). Unlike solid matter, which stays in one place and can be constrained ("strained") by force, the world of mercy is liquid and dynamic, and thus escapes definition and control. Justice applies to the world of solids; mercy to the world of liquids.

As we have seen in chapter 3, the universe emerges from an initial state of nothingness—that is, the state, impossible to maintain, in which the minimum of change is taking place, and in which there is the minimum of commitment to any particular identity. The newborn universe fell first into the form of energy, which is change with the minimum of commitment to an identity, and then into the state of matter, which is commitment to an identity with the minimum of change. It is as if energy's nostalgia for its birthplace were reflected in its uncommitment to any fixed state—it flies away from itself radially at the speed of light—and matter's nostalgia were reflected in its attempt to minimize change and inconsistency within itself. Mercy is like energy, justice like matter. But the miracle of life is that it combines both change and commitment to a particular identity—it is both mercylike and justicelike. And it is life that is Shakespeare's primary touchstone for what is of the highest moral value.

Mercy, like grace, is always a free gift, gratis. Yet justice grinds to a halt without it. This paradox is echoed in the coexistence, within any conceivable economy, of wages and gifts, the earned and the inherited, merit and luck. "Earned" value is obvious. If the value of money comes from its "standing for" work—for time and trouble—how can that value be preserved if money can be acquired without them? We pay people for their time and trouble, and the value to us of what we earn is partly that it constitutes a banked store of other people's time and trouble that we acquired by saving and not reaping the rewards of our own. Indeed, there is a strong sense in which the "earnedness" of money is the value of money itself. If all money were given away, the rate of inflation would be infinite.

Yet what is the value of money if one cannot give it away unearned? One would be forced to spend it, since to save it is either to spend it later or to give it away unearned (if only at one's death). Without gifts, one's life would be one of buying and selling only, devoid of any kind of unaccounted-for exchanges, devoid of surprises, devoid indeed of any kind of personal or family—that is, voluntary or volunteer—activity. My daughter and my ducats would amount to the same thing, as they do for Shylock. We can almost define family life as the region where one does not charge interest on loans nor seek their repayment, and as the place where one is free to be oneself; and these two definitions are connected. In a world where all value is earned, one would not even be able to spend money upon oneself, for the self that enjoys the money is not the self that, months ago, labored for it; it is a free gift from the working self to the holiday self. I am not taking the trouble when I reward myself for it. The very passage of time requires gift giving. A large part of the value of money is the freedom to decide whether to spend it, keep it, or give it away; and perhaps the most delightful use of money is to give it away, to help or pleasure those we love. In considering such expenses, a family will often use the old phrase "that's what money's *for.*" All other uses of money are somewhat constrained; gifts approach the pure exercise of freedom. It is this freedom, this sovereignty, that Portia is thinking of when she describes mercy—which is gift giving in the context of debts and injuries—as "mightiest in the mightiest." Mercy (like gift giving) is to be found in its strongest form among those people who are least constrained by weakness or indebtedness:

> It becomes
> The thronèd monarch better than his crown.
> His scepter shows the force of temporal power,
> The attribute to awe and majesty,
> Wherein doth sit the dread and fear of kings;
> But mercy is above this scept'red sway;
> It is enthronèd in the hearts of kings,
> It is an attribute to God Himself,
> And earthly power doth then show likest God's
> When mercy seasons justice.
> (IV.i.187)

Temporal power is temporal partly in that it is temporary, that is, subject to decay over time. Mercy and gift giving, however, though they too indeed take place in time, liberate us from the decay and the constraints of linear cause and effect.

Payment is a zero-sum game; payment is only payment if the payer is impoverished by the same amount by which the payee is enriched. Not so the gift of mercy: "It is twice blest; / It blesseth him that gives and him that takes." For it is not only the giver that is enfranchised by the gift; it is also the receiver. To receive a gift, windfall, or lottery prize "out of the blue" is surely one of the greatest pleasures in the world. Many other writers and poets would agree; consider Wordsworth's *Prelude,* whose opening passages express the unburdened exhilaration of having just received a bequest that made him financially independent and free to write.

But in all this praise of gifts and mercies we must not forget the bitter truth that the gifts we give are valuable because somebody (or something) earned them. Even when the earner is not human, and the living planet—the universe in its protean generosity, the biological lineage of our forebears—supplies the gift, it took nature the long tortuous process of evolution, of trial and error, extinction and survival, to produce it. During the 1974 oil crisis somebody figured out that if we regarded a gallon of crude oil out of the ground as having been created by an industrial process requiring investment capital, energy, and raw materials, it would have cost nature roughly $100,000 to produce. In one sense this process of natural manufacture was nothing more than free play; in another sense it was compelled by cause and effect. Everything is free, and nothing is free. Nothing comes from nothing, yet everything comes from nothing. The generosity of the monarch comes from his power; but his power comes from his generosity. His mercy exists only because real punishments exist, and the convicted one to whom he offers clemency stands liable to a punishment that is justly imposed in other cases. But the monarch would not perhaps remain a monarch if his subjects did not believe him capable of mercy. Likewise, a company that gave its products away for free or even at cost would not long exist; but it would not be able to sell its product if its consumers did not feel that what they got when they bought the product was of more value to them than what they paid, and that they were thus getting at least a fraction of what they bought, for nothing.

The boundary between justice and mercy, the earned and the given, is an emotionally uncomfortable place. The discomfort, to give it its painful name, is shame. Consider, for instance, the following problems: which daughter inherits the mother's engagement ring; how to invite your spouse to make love when the onus is on him or her to make the first move; how to ask your son-in-law for repayment of the interest-free loan you made him to buy his family a house; how to punish a junior officer who is also a friend; what price Christmas gift you give to someone who has always given you a cheaper (or more expensive) gift than you have given her; whether to attend a party to which one has been kindly invited, but at which everyone will be wearing clothes obviously far more costly than one can oneself afford; how much housework a spouse should do when the other spouse earns more money; how to discourage an overenthusiastic fan; and so on. In such situations only one participant needs to feel the irresistible hot flush of shame for all the other participants to feel it too; like yawning, shame is contagious.

This emotional territory, despite its unpleasantness, is also, however, the major arena of our moral maturation, our life-altering decisions, our redeeming repentances, and, thank heaven, the most hilarious moments of our lives. The internal negotiation between justice and mercy at such times constitutes a large part of our moral identity: as long as we do not deny the experience, we are more vividly alive then than when we are in a comfortably unambiguous state. We might add to our list of shames and embarrassments almost every experience that Bassanio must deal with: how to ask his dear friend for money to woo a rival; how to get a loan from a man against whom all one's associates are ethnically prejudiced; how to court a rich lady when one is oneself penniless; how to handle a loudmouthed and racist follower (Gratiano) who is devoted to one; how to cope with the imminent death of a friend who is sacrificing himself for one's own interests; how to explain to one's wife the disappearance of one's wedding ring; and so on. Shakespeare, in loading poor Bassanio with these predicaments, is also blessing him with the opportunity for growth and insight, gifts more painful than welcome, though valuable beyond price. Shakespeare also burdens Shylock with repeated shames—the contempt of the anti-Semites in the play, his daughter's elopement, his legal outwitting by Portia, the choice between loss of his goods and loss of his religion. Unlike Bassanio, who accepts his embarrassments and turns them to graces, Shylock responds with shamed rage, which catches both our sympathy and our distaste. Of such difficult cases is great drama made.

The Stated and the Implied

We must, then, be content with the logical imperfection of any value system, legal or economic, and prepared to accept the emotional and moral consequences of that imperfection. This ambiguity carries over into the language on which we must rely when we speak of such matters. Our vocabulary for dealing with this area of experience and decision consists of a shaky set of double meanings, near puns, stretched implications, and metaphors. Shakespeare explores them in depth in *The Merchant of Venice*. All the value words are torn apart and put together again—"good," "bond," "means," "mercy," "grace," "hazard," "use," "freedom," "trust," "credit," "worth," "rich," "suit," "sum," "fortune," "venture," "rate," "thrive," "thrift," "save," "expire," "return," "forfeit," "competency," "lottery," "will," "interest," "seal," "gild," "geld," "guilt," "stones," "cost," "judgment," "pay," "profit," "loss," "pawn," "wage," "purchase," "buy," "owe," "own," "deed," "charity," "jot," "title," "dear," "deserve," "liberal," "lend"—and so on. All of these words have multiple meanings, ranging from the economic to the moral, and Shakespeare does not allow us to ignore those meanings. In yet another sense of "strained," mercy is what is left when matters of justice have been strained out of the liquid of an utterance. Justice is the hard, logical, denotative sense that can be made of a sentence in English; but mercy is the implication, the metaphorical content, the connotation, that is the heart of its meaning.

Thus the multiple meanings Shakespeare gives words in the play—those puns and quibbles that Dr. Johnson believed to be a "fatal Cleopatra" that lured Shakespeare away from the path of supreme greatness—are actually central to his message. When Shylock is pondering whether he should make the loan to Bassanio on Antonio's security, he muses out loud that Antonio is a "good man" (I.iii.12). Bassanio bristles at this, taking Shylock's remark to imply that he is in a state of doubt about whether Antonio is good in the sense of honest and honorable. Shylock reassures him, with a laugh, that he meant "good" in the sense of "good for a certain sum." But of course Shakespeare has opened up the whole issue of the meaning of "good" in such phrases as a good poem, a good deed, a good logical proof, and a good check or banknote. Are they entirely different meanings, or is there an underlying meaning in all of them? I believe Shakespeare is implying something not quite the same as either of these alternatives: that there is a hierarchy of goods, from the lowest commercial ones to the highest ethical and aesthetic ones. Though the highest goods in this hierarchy cannot be reduced to the lowest, they depend on them for their validity; meanwhile the lowest attain their goodness as goods through cooperation in a system that maintains the highest.

The word "mean" or "means" has a similar fluidity in the play. Shakespeare uses it in several senses:

> My purse, my person, my extremest means
> Lie all unlocked to your occasions
> (I.i.138)

(Antonio to Bassanio, taking "means" as financial resources);

> It is no mean happiness, therefore, to be seated in the mean
> (I.ii.7)

(Nerissa to Portia, complaining about the constraints of great wealth; here she is punning between mean as "base, low" and mean as "the golden mean, the perfect state of balance between extremes");

> But stop my house's ears—I mean my casements
> (II.v.34)

(Shylock to his daughter Jessica, ordering her to shut the windows; when Shylock catches himself using a risky figure of speech such as a metaphor, he immediately explains his meaning, which is what the word means here);

> subject to the same diseases, healed by the same means
> (III.i.59)

(Shylock again; here he uses means to mean simply the methods and instruments by which an action is carried out);

> when your honors mean to solemnize
> The bargain of your faith
> (III.ii.192)

(Gratiano to Portia and Bassanio, taking "mean" as intend).

Thus the very word for meaning itself is subject to a bewildering multiplicity of meanings. This multiplicity might seem logically to be a disadvantage, but any one of those meanings would be weakened if it were not substantiated by the subtle metaphorical presence of the others. In other words, we know better what kind of a thing the mysterious meaning of a word might be, because we know that it is something like having a tool to do something, having enough money to buy something, being in a blessed state midway between dangerous extremes, being based upon something that is low, and intending some project or completed action.

Of especial interest to my purposes in this book is the implied analogy between the meaning of a word and the value of money. Money holds value as words hold meaning. The analogy is a fertile one: words, like money, can become devalued if there are too many words chasing too little meaning; money can lose its value through overuse, like a cliché; a new financial instrument, like a new verbal trope or figure of speech, can embody a rich concentration of value, but can also be a false amplification of an inadequate fundamental. Nouns are useful in two opposed ways: as indicators naming particular objects or persons, and as generalizations linking whole classes of referents; likewise, money value can take the useful form of a limited financial instrument such as a share of stock in a company, or the equally useful form of liquid cash, valid for any exchange within a given national economic community. Syntactical words are like derivatives and other financial instruments. The analogy also explains why the disappointed critics of the capitalist market system turned to the deconstruction of verbal meaning after the failure of Marxist economics. Like Puritans smashing idolatrous stained glass and holy images in the pursuit of an unmediated contact with the divine, the Marxists and their postmodern successors sought to smash the currency and language that they believed alienated us from economic and textual reality.

If meanings did not need words for their embodiment, but could exist in a world of pure telepathic explicitness, then each meaning could remain limpid and uncontaminated by any other. However, in such a world metaphors could not exist, and double meanings could never arise that might trouble the perfection of silent communion and require actual speech to sort out the misunderstanding. Since language grows through metaphor and through the sound changes and confusions implicit in its embodiment in speech, a world of pure meaning would need no language and could not produce one.

> Such harmony is in immortal souls,
> But whilst this muddy vesture of decay
> Doth grossly close it in, we cannot hear it
> (V.i.63)

says Lorenzo to Jessica near the end of *The Merchant of Venice*. But immediately he calls for earthly music to welcome Portia home, and a few lines later she herself demonstrates the fallacy of the purely immaterial unheard music of the heavens:

> Nothing is good, I see, without respect;
> Methinks it sounds much sweeter than by day.
>
> NERISSA: Silence bestows that virtue on it, madam.
>
> PORTIA: The crow doth sing as sweetly as the lark
> When neither is attended; and I think
> The nightingale, if she should sing by day

When every goose is cackling, would be thought
No better a musician than the wren.
How many things by season seasoned are
To their right praise and true perfection!
(V.i.99)

In other words, a material world is needed, like the lovely imagined garden
of Portia's country house, when the birds are just beginning their dawn chorus, a world within which meanings and values can encounter each other
and give each other substance and reality. The need for context ("respect")
to make meaning does not contradict the fact that things *do* have a "right
praise and true perfection." Meaning itself cannot exist without referents
and without the risk of contamination that a world of referents brings with
it: contamination by the physicality of things, as a note of music is contami-
nated (but also given being) by the imperfections of the instrument that
plays it; and contamination of meanings by each other, as when two notes
mingle to produce a discord or a harmony—a pun or an enriching metaphor.
So just as the quantum vacuum, as we have seen, cannot choose but issue
forth into a physical universe, so a world of pure meaning, if it is to be
meaningful, must issue forth into a world of physical expression. Portia uses
two words for the physical context that makes the melody of meaning real:
one is "respect," which includes both the need for observers and the moral
relationship between persons; and the other is "season," repeated immediately as the verb "seasons." "Seasons," we will recall, is the word she has
used to describe the relationship between justice and mercy:

And earthly power doth then show likest God's
When mercy seasons justice.
(IV.i.195)

So the very word itself is given meaning by its prior context, by its existence
in time with other objects and other words, in the world of seasons and sea-
sonings. The spiritual must be incarnated in the physical; the divine Father
issues forth as the Word. The name of the great lawyer who sends "Bellario"
(Portia in disguise) to defend Antonio is, interestingly enough, Balthazar.
Traditionally Balthazar was one of the three Magi, Zoroastrian priest-kings,
who attended the birth of Christ; his gift to the incarnate god, the infant
child, was a casket of gold. Thus her mission is associated with the incarnation of the infinite into fleshly human form, and with the human response of
a rich gift. Though Portia, as Bassanio's portal to paradise, is disguised as a
leaden casket, Bassanio sees her, as the eye of heaven would rightly see her,
as a golden one.

Though the seasoning of mercy is needed to generate words in the first
place, for ordinary practical purposes—as when we are dealing with the just
resolution of contracts, or weighing and dividing matter in an accurate
way—justice is sufficient. The ambiguities of language are trivial and unim-

portant when there is a basic and broad agreement on the meaning of the rules, and when the application of the rules does not destructively interfere with the making and interpreting of those rules. If Antonio and Shylock were conducting a normal contract dispute, the fiction that legal language is exact is perfectly sufficient. If we had to live with deconstructed language all the time, it would be like living in the sea with no dry land—worse, it would be like *being* a liquid also, without even the solid structure of a jellyfish. We can move only because the hard struts of our bones are there for the soft gels of our muscles to pull against. Linear logic is essential for the minimal necessary control of our environment. But when it comes to contracts that are nonlinear—that involve the very flesh and blood of one of the parties, for instance—an element of mercy enters into the picture. And it does so not because it *ought* to, which would be justice, but because it cannot be prevented from doing so—mercy is not strained.

Exactness and Approximateness: The Quantum Paradox

This kind of reasoning makes mercy very much more important, and more effective, than we might have thought. The point becomes clear when we look at the second legal quibble that Portia uses to get Antonio off (the first was the liquid-solid quibble). It is impossible to weigh out an exact pound of anything. As far as present-day physics is concerned, Shakespeare is absolutely right. Many things in the universe can indeed be measured, to almost any desired degree of accuracy. Science and technological civilization depend upon it. But there will always be a point where the measurement becomes approximate. Quantum mechanics describes that approximateness. When the smallest possible divisions on the measuring stick are as large as or larger than what is to be measured, as when we reach the minimum sizes of physical matter, the error can be relatively huge. When the measuring process interferes with the object to be measured, as when we try to photograph an elementary particle using a flash whose photons are as big as the particle itself, and which disrupt or displace the particle, we get quantum uncertainty. The wave nature of matter is more basic than its particle nature—as Einstein showed, matter is reducible to energy, which comes in waves—and thus when we try to measure a wave to tolerances finer than the distance the wave vibrates, or at a clock interval shorter than the time period of its oscillation, we are measuring nothing at all. Justice, in Shakespeare's sense of the word, applies to what can be accurately measured; mercy, to what cannot be measured—"strained" in yet another sense, caught within a rectilinear grid. The universe is more basically probabilistic and approximate than it is determinate and exact, even though it has achieved remarkable exactness and solidity in the course of its evolution. Mercy is more fundamental, then, than justice. Justice floats upon an ocean of mercy; mercy is the fine structure and basic stuff out of which justice is fabricated.

Another way of putting this point is in terms of tolerance. Tolerance is a technical term in engineering, referring to the amount of "give" or free play in a machine. If we accept Shakespeare's description of mercy as the essential inexactness of the world and of the language we use to talk about it, then mercy is the tolerance, the give, of the universe. The more perfect a machine is, the finer its tolerances. Car manufacturers advertise their products by rolling ball bearings along their joints to demonstrate the minuteness of their tolerances. But if the tolerance, inexactness, or mercy of the machine shrinks to zero—if its justness becomes complete—then something remarkable happens. The machine freezes up and cannot move. It ceases to perform its function; ceases, in fact, to be a machine! Likewise, the only way for solids to mix with each other—and thus for new compounds to form—is through the liquid state. If they are to combine, either they must be dissolved in a liquid, or they must be melted down. There must be a space for the lubricating oil of mercy, as it were, in order for justice to work as justice at all; there must be a solvent of mercy to allow solids to interact.

Thus Shakespeare's solution to the problem of slavery, as it is raised in Shylock's defense of his bond with Antonio, is twofold. Justice clearly forbids involuntary slavery, but cannot forbid legal voluntary slavery; it is mercy that forbids legal voluntary slavery, by making it impossible. Mercy is a liquid that cannot be strained; but if that liquid is drained off, the legal machine of justice cannot move. Mercy at this level is the prerequisite of justice itself; and the power of mercy as a critique of any exact legal language is so great that legality is defenseless against mercy when mercy's fundamental logic is engaged. On the other hand, mercy cannot help but generate justice; a world without justice is the sure sign of a world without mercy.

However, it is all very well in theory to talk about the need for a combination of justice and mercy, an indissoluble union of property rights and personal rights. In practice such a combination is fiendishly paradoxical. It is out of such paradoxes that *The Merchant of Venice*—perhaps Shakespeare's most intellectually brilliant play—is constructed. Mercy is by its nature a free gift, and a free gift is by definition undeserved—if it were deserved, it would not be a gift but wages, reciprocation, and just reward. If I give a gift to one person, I am not giving it to another, and am thus discriminating against the other. I am in a quiet way being unjust to all those from whom I withheld my gift. Likewise, if I am a convicted criminal, and the judge extends clemency to me and commutes my sentence, I have either deserved that clemency by mitigating circumstances, or not. If I have deserved it, then the commutation of the normal penalty is just, not merciful, and any other prisoner convicted of the same crime with the same mitigating circumstances should in justice receive the same reduction of sentence, and the legislature should amend the law accordingly. Only if I have *not* deserved the clemency can the judge's reduction of sentence be deemed merciful, for it would be a free unearned gift. If the reduction were earned, the judge would be compelled in justice to award it. Thus mercy is in a literal sense unjust. At the end of the trial scene in *The Merchant of Venice,* Shylock stands under penalty of death for seeking the life of Antonio. His sentence is mercifully commuted thrice: first, into the forfeiture of all his possessions, second, by payment of a fine and punitive damages amounting to half his possessions; and third, by the return of those possessions on condition that half of them be held in trust for his daughter and son-in-law.

Jews, Christians, and the Justice-Mercy Problem

Clearly Shakespeare is morally ahead of his time. One aspect of the play, however, has rightly given recent critics of the play enormous problems. It is the final proviso of Shylock's sentence. Shylock is a Jew, and Antonio's mercy to him is conditional upon Shylock's agreeing to convert to Christianity. An understanding of historical context is of vital importance in grasping what Shakespeare means here. Shakespeare has not been given full credit for the fact that he is one of the greatest pioneers in humankind's long struggle to throw off the evils of racism and anti-Semitism. *Othello* is the first and still the greatest portrayal of a black tragic hero, and its complete acceptance of marriage between a black man and a white woman is three hundred years in advance of its time; the villain, Iago, is a penetrating study of the hideous moral roots and effects of racism. Likewise, Shakespeare's portrayal of Shylock, Tubal, and Jessica, the Jews in *The Merchant of Venice,* is on the whole deeply sympathetic. Shylock is indeed a grasping and miserly financier, but his rage at the injustice he is subjected to is clearly understandable in the play, and it is not the miserly financier that seeks bloody revenge but the grieved and wounded human being. We see him, as a widower, remember with anguish his dead wife, Leah, when he hears how his runaway daughter has traded for a monkey the turquoise Leah gave him when he was a bachelor. His great speeches on the humanity of Jews were the central inspiration to the passionate humanitarians of nineteenth-century England who began the process by which discrimination against Jews was gradually abolished in civilized countries:

> Hath not a Jew eyes? Hath not a Jew hands, organs, dimensions, senses, affections, passions?—fed with the same food, hurt with the same weapons, subject to the same diseases, healed by the same means, warmed and cooled by the same winter and summer as a Christian is?
> (III.i.56)

Like almost all great writers who have engaged the mystery of human character, Shakespeare began with stereotypes and then humanized them from the inside until we recognize their deep human kinship with ourselves, a kinship that compels compassion. This method is not politically correct, but it follows the organic path by which any sentient organism deepens its experience into knowledge and accurate assessment. We begin every visual or auditory investigation with a neural hypothesis, a set of expectations, a prejudice; and then, if we have the time and wisdom for it, we correct that first sketch until it cor-responds as closely as possible with the idiosyncrasy of the reality. There is no such thing as a pure, unbiased first view of anything. Such a view would be akin to perfect justice, which as we have seen cannot exist, and if it did exist would seize up and be incapable of motion. The only way we can approach a just view of things is by a process of successive approximations beginning with a simple prejudice; and the only way that process of approximations can work is through the messiness and tolerances of mercy.

The effects of *The Merchant of Venice* in gradually breaking down anti-Semitism in England, so that eventually a Jew, Benjamin Disraeli, could be elected prime minister, can be traced in theater history. Nineteenth-century British actors and directors vied with each other in presenting Shylock as a tragic, romantic, and misunderstood figure—so much so that critics pro-tested the portrayal, as a distortion of the more subtle import of the play. Likewise, Shakespeare's portrait of the ugliness of anti-Semitism in the char-acter of Gratiano has acted as a mirror to show generations of playgoers the moral blot of that comfortable prejudice. Gratiano is nominally a Christian, but is so in reality only in the sense that he belongs to one side or faction or tribe rather than another. Like his companions Salerio and Solanio, whose names begin with the Romance language roots for dirt and soil, he is merci-less toward the Jew and sadly sums up centuries of European anti-Semitism. Despite Shakespeare's evident detestation of this characteristic, the great dramatist finds himself unable to make Gratiano simply repulsive. Like many anti-Semites, Gratiano is witty, generous, a good companion, a rather lovable loudmouth, and touchingly naive. Life is so much simpler and easier for writers not touched with genius. But the point is that Gratiano's literal-ism is the intellectual equivalent of his moral mercilessness. In other words, mercy is deeply connected with the power to make and understand metaphors, to be able to trade in different kinds of entities—love for flesh for metal, and so on. The sacrifice of Christ on the cross was an act of ran-soming, of purchase, of exchange, that the Gratianos of the world—those who take tribal sides—cannot understand.

The Christian-Jewish marriage of Lorenzo and Jessica is a refutation of the tribal prejudice against intermarriage, a prejudice that would later blos-som hideously into racism. Shakespeare, like Mark Twain, was a hero of the war against prejudice; one might as well condemn *Huckleberry Finn* for its stereotype of the black man Jim as *The Merchant of Venice* for its stereotype of Shylock the Jew.

Thus the argument between Christianity and Judaism in the play is not racist or anti-Semitic. This being said, it does rest upon some factual errors, which Shakespeare could not really have corrected. Shakespeare's purpose is to have Judaism stand for justice, and Christianity for mercy. More subtly, it is also to have Judaism stand for a tribal and exclusive definition of human solidarity, while making Christianity stand for the hope of a more universal bond among humans, honored indeed more in the breach than in the obser-vance, and subject to the complications of the emerging market economy that would give it reality, but an ideal nevertheless. More subtly still, Shakespeare wishes to use the Christian-Jewish contrast as a way of exploring the inner meaning of usury, the practice of taking interest on a loan. These three issues—mercy versus justice, universal humanity versus tribal solidarity, interest-free versus interest-conditional loans—seemed to fit neatly into the conventional theological differences between Christianity and Judaism, as viewed from Renaissance England. It was not Shakespeare's fault that this view was deeply skewed.

The best Christian commentators of the time maintained that Christ came to liberate the human race from the due penalties of a divine justice that was too heavy for frail human beings to support. The Old Testament, they said, told of the regime of justice; the New Testament, with its astonishing gospel of a God who remits the just punishment of human beings by taking it upon his own shoulders, chronicles the regime of mercy. Likewise, the Old Testament told of God's chosen people, while the New extends the favor of God to all of humankind. For Shakespeare's audience, perhaps a little surprised and thoughtful at how human the Jews are in the play, and how severely Shakespeare treats the prejudice against them, conversion to Christianity would have meant liberation from a narrow, tribal, and humanly unbearable regime of justice, into a more compassionate world of mercy and justice combined. Shylock's acceptance of the mercy of the court would be in itself a conversion to Christianity, even without the explicit proviso.

According to Christian commentators, the then-prevalent Jewish practice of lending money at interest was the direct result of the "eye-for-an-eye" justice ethics and the exclusivism of the Jews as they saw it. As we have seen, medieval Christian ethics forbade the taking of interest, and though in Shakespeare's time that prohibition was relaxing, it was still an emotional and fraught moral issue. Shakespeare, not having been brought up among Jews, could not have known of the ancient and pervasive Jewish traditions of mercy, and the generous interpretation by Jewish moral authorities of those hints in the second chapter of Isaiah that the special fatherhood of Jehovah might extend to all nations, not just the chosen people. The wise rabbi in the old Jewish story explains why the stork, though a beloved and loving bird, is nevertheless considered unclean: because it cares only for its own young, its own tribe. Though Shakespeare was keenly cognizant of the prejudice against Jews, he was apparently unaware of the laws in most European countries that forbade Jews to own land and conduct certain professions, prohibitions that virtually dictated such occupations as banking and jewel trading. Shakespeare does seem to have known that Jews would not have taken interest from other Jews—Tubal lends Shylock money free of charge. But he would not have realized that the old Christian prohibition against usury had applied only to taking interest from other Christians, that Christians had always been free to charge interest against Muslims and Jews (though in practice they rarely had the occasion to do so), and that therefore Jewish and Christian attitudes toward interest and the in-group were in fact perfectly identical.

Given Shakespeare's limited knowledge of Jews, Shylock could be made to represent the arguments of an economic philosopher who attempted to base his ethics on absolute contractual justice, who gave tribal kinship special moral privileges, and who defended the taking of interest. And as we have seen, Shakespeare's conclusion is by no means a straightforward denial of Shylock's arguments. Shakespeare admits the force of contract, but insists on merciful tolerance in its application; he denies tribal privilege but endorses family commitments; and he supports the practice of interest. In other words, Shakespeare makes a much more powerful argument against those who have reproached the Jews for profiteering than the usual defense of liberals, which is to attempt to deny the charge. Instead Shakespeare ringingly defends profit as a natural and creative force, the continuity of natural fecundity into human economics. If this is what Jews did, then Europe owes to them much of its wealth and progress, and so does the world as a whole.

The Mercy of Mercury

But here we must finally come to grips with the difficult issue raised at the end of the previous chapter: how can the market be merciful? Isn't it counterintuitive that mercy—and *merci,* the French word for thanks—should come from the same linguistic root as "mercenary," "merchant," "mercantile," "commerce," and "market" itself? What does the legendary ruthlessness of the marketplace have to do with the free gifts of compassion? If, using the excellent *American Heritage Dictionary,* we follow the etymology of this root back to its Etruscan origins, we find the same ambiguity all the way down. The Old French *merci* meant forbearance to someone in one's power; the Late Latin *merces* meant reward, but also God's gratuitous compassion. The Latin *merx* meant merchandise, in the sense that merchandise was something under the purview of the god Mercury, patron of commerce.

Mercury is an extremely interesting god in this context: as well as being associated with markets, he was the divine messenger, the god of travel and of thieves, and the psychopomp, that is, the god who conducted the souls of the dead to their final destination, whether Hades or the Elysian Fields. Perhaps we can make sense of him thus: being the spirit of communication and exchange, he is that which allows whole systems of connected feedback to come into being. He is thus the patron of change, since systems can change only to the extent to which they can communicate within themselves and with other systems. Merchants, the "middlemen" of human exchange and often the carriers of news, information, new science, and socially disruptive ideas and diseases, take Mercury to be their leader. The marketplace is the place where both goods and ideas are exchanged, and thus it bears the god's name. Naturally all the illegitimate and cheating forms of communication and exchange—lying and stealing—are also under his aegis. Mercy is kin to thievery; both are unjust. Naturally, too, Mercury conducts human consciousness—itself the product of the internal communication of self-awareness and the external communication of exchange with other human beings in the marketplace of life—across the greatest threshold of change, from life to death.

When we look at some of Mercury's other attributes and associations, he becomes more interesting still. He gives his name to the metal that is liquid, quicksilver, that cannot be held in one place but runs away. Mercy—the things of Mercury—is essentially liquid, as we have already seen. In alchemy, mercury was one of the two primary opposites, sulphur—a solid—being the other, whose true union through the evolutionary process of alchemical metamorphosis produced perfect gold. Mercury's planet was the harbinger of the two great diurnal changes, day into night and night into day, and thus the link between the day world and the night world: again, Mercury is the reconciler of opposites.

Most interesting of all, he is the possessor of the caduceus, the snake-entwined rod, that ancient and modern symbol of life and its transformative powers. This talisman represents the reconciliation of order and stasis (the rod) with chaos and change (the snakes). The rod is solid and is often the symbol of justice; the snake is associated with liquid and is the great symbol of transgression. The snake itself symbolizes the polar opposites of death and healing (its venom can kill or cure), and change and immortality (it changes its skin and thus rejuvenates itself). Like the serpent of Eden, it is the breaker of the status quo, the opener of new perspectives, the originator of new levels of being and consciousness. The caduceus as a whole represents the pairing or twinning by which reproduction takes place, and the transfer of information by which that information is communicated, replicated, and immortalized. It so happens that the double helix of the two snakes is an exact model of the shape of the DNA molecule; and this is not just a coincidence, for the double helix is perhaps the best intuitive diagram of any feedback process, and DNA is the feedback process of feedback processes. Uncannily, in the symbol of the caduceus the ancient icon makers anticipated the modern discovery of the structure of DNA.

In Greek mythology the lyre of Orpheus (which he inherited from his father Apollo) was originally the invention of Hermes, the Greek version of Mercury. The lyre was the instrument by which Greek poets marked the meter of their poetry. Hermes traded the lyre for the caduceus, which had at first belonged to Apollo. If the lyre, then, is in some sense equivalent to the caduceus, we may infer that the meter of poetry is analogous to the meter of biological reproduction and evolution. This is the central insight of Rilke's *Sonnets to Orpheus*. Poetry becomes an accelerated version of evolution itself, of that miraculous feedback among variation, selection, and heredity which produced the orchid, the sperm whale, the tobacco mosaic virus, the giant panda, and the coral reef. In Rilke's Sonnet 21 (first series), the poet imagines the springtime earth as a child who has learned by heart all the poems that nature has taught her:

> Oh what her teacher taught her, all those things,
> and what's imprinted on the roots and long
> complicated stems: she sings it, she sings!
> (A. Poulin, Jr., trans.)

These are the "lines of life, that life renew." Nature is poetry, poetry is nature. Perhaps indeed this is the meaning of the myth of Orpheus, the first poet in the Greek mythology, who, like Solomon, or like Vyasa, the mythical poet of the *Mahabharata,* could speak the languages of animals and plants and stones. Orpheus' journey to the underworld and back (as Virgil says, any fool can go down there, but to return—this is the labor, this is the task) is more than just a search for his lost wife, Eurydice. It is also a rediscovery of our roots in nature. Or rather, the search for his lost wife *means* the recovery of the organic connection with the rest of the universe. The point is that Orpheus can make his journey only because he possesses and can use his lyre, the instrument by which Greek poets kept the measure of their meter. It is the lyre that opens the gates of the underworld; and it is when Orpheus fails to trust its magic and looks back to see if Eurydice is following, that he tragically loses her forever. Other versions of this talisman are the magic flute of Mozart and da Ponte, the golden bough of Virgil, the staff of Moses (also a combination of rod and snake), the drum of the Asiatic shamans, the Celtic harp, the rattle of the Bantu spirit-doctor, the bagpipe of the ancient Magyar bards.

Perhaps we can find out what the wisdom of the ancients can tell us about the market by viewing it as the domain of Mercury. Shakespeare himself plainly did the same. In *The Winter's Tale* he creates the unforgettable character Autolycus, who is a wandering small trader, a haunter of fairs and markets, seller of trinkets, and occasional thief and con man. Autolycus describes himself as "littered under Mercury" (IV.iii.25). Autolycus is in a sense a distant relative of Edgar, the Poor Tom of *King Lear,* another homeless outcast who paradoxically helps to restore the moral balance of a world gone mad. It is through the agency of Autolycus that the lovers are united, the estranged kings of Bohemia and Sicily are restored to friendship, and the lost daughter Perdita is given back to her grieving father, Leontes. Reading between the lines, Shakespeare implies that despite the deceptions of the market, it is only through the market's communicative agency—whose spirit the Romans called Mercury—that the miscarriages and frozen deadlocks of justice can be dissolved into merciful resolution.

So the mercy of the market is real. Liberal neo-Marxists might concede much of this but remain suspicious of those financial instruments, such as futures, junk bonds, and derivatives, that have cut loose to some extent from the fundamentals of actual economic efficiency. What about the injustices that happen when financial bubbles burst through the abuse of short selling, when clever speculators artificially manipulate the market, when leveraged buyouts based on junk bonds result in thousands losing their jobs? But the problem here is not the nature of the market but the human capacity for reflexibility in general. We sell short or place puts in exactly the same way that we examine our own motives and our motives for examining our motives, and try to predict how our spouse or friend will react to our estimate of what his or her reaction will be. We are a subtle and self-referential species, and much of what we are consists in emergent properties arising from our second thoughts about ourselves and each other. As Alexander Argyros has pointed out in his fine book *A Blessed Rage for Order*, the apparent abstraction of the financial market is not different from the second and third order psychological effects that we can find in a novel or on the psychoanalyst's couch. Perhaps we should even celebrate that complexity rather than deplore it. The solution to the abuse of human reflexivity, in the market as elsewhere, is not to abolish it but to control it by an even deeper and more subtle reflexivity, as Portia does when she finds the loopholes in Shylock's contract.

One of the oldest reproaches that is brought against the market is that it is unfair, that it gives unearned advantages to some and undeserved handicaps to others. *The Merchant of Venice* makes us understand that this unfairness is systemic to any living economic system. The market is the place where the given and the earned negotiate, mate, and find their way toward their mutual solution, which is the increase of value and the emergence of new kinds of value. It is only if there is something given, something granted, something unmerited, something mercifully uncounted, that the market has material upon which to go to work. And what is given and unmerited is by definition unfair. The most perfect meritocracy is based on the entirely unfair allocation of human talents at birth—it is quite as unjust to base success in life on genetically given intelligence as on genetically given skin pigmentation. Does this mean that we should just accept the unfairness of life and countenance racism just as we countenance the preference given by the Nobel Prize committee and the National Basketball Association to natural talent? Of course not.

The miracle of the market is that its system of negotiation and feedback actually produces mechanisms that mitigate the unfairness of life. The more buyers and sellers can participate in the market, the richer everybody gets. Using "givens" like skin color to exclude people is economically inefficient, and a market that does so will get swallowed up by one that does not. The real reason that the duke in *The Merchant of Venice* is afraid to rule arbitrarily in favor of the Christians and against Shylock is that to do so would be to kill the goose that lays the golden eggs. Germans, Spaniards, Englishmen, Africans, and Jews come to trade in Venice precisely because they can get a fair shake there; and their trade enriches Venice. Trade creates justice as the medium within which trade can operate. But justice in this context can never be absolute, because trade needs "givens," things "taken for granted," as its raw material. Trade, together with the manufacture trade inspires, continues the creative process of nature; but in taking up where nature leaves off it must accept the arbitrary provisions of what it inherits, just as Portia must accept the arbitrary provisions of her father's will.

Thus we must learn to free ourselves of the idea that freedom and fate are opposites. For two hundred years the thought of the West has pursued the idea that freedom comes from justice, from the elimination of unfairness, the squeezing-out of the last remnants of the given, the granted, the arbitrary—in other words, fate—from our collective lives. We have sought these ideals in the name of equality and berated the market for its unfairness; and time and time again we have tried to create a more just system, based on the vote rather than the market. Shakespeare suggests that this may have beeen a mistake, or at least an overcorrection. If we seek fairness, we will often produce unfairness; but if we seek a good climate for business, a practical measure of fairness will come along as a by-product. Market economies tend to be more free and egalitarian, not less, than traditional priest-and-pyramid empires or feudal aristocracies or bureaucratic centrally planned economies; not because the market is less based on the arbitrary givens of fate, but because it is a more efficient system of communication and thus wealth creation.

The market, then, is the true inheritor in human affairs of the cosmic tradition of evolutionary ecology that is the hallmark of life itself. Mercury, the god of the market, appropriately bears the caduceus, the symbol of the transformative, creative, and therapeutic powers of life.

6

"never call a true piece of gold a counterfeit"

How Does One Stamp a Value on a Coin and Make It Stick?

Face Value and Intrinsic Value

In the introductory chapter of this book we encountered the distinction between the metal value of a coin and its stamped or inscribed value. It was this distinction that enabled us to establish the idea of money as a kind of bond, a promissory note, albeit one that binds not two particular individuals with each other, but one unspecified individual—the "bearer"—with the whole community sharing a given currency. The distinction between the value of a coin as a financial instrument and its value as specie bears a close relationship to the distinctions we have investigated in the last two chapters, between the earned and the given, the willed and the accidental, the predictable and the risky, merit and luck, justice and mercy.

A mint can control exactly the nominal value stamped on its coin, and the number of coins it releases. But it cannot control the planet's concentration of metal ores by erosion, deposition, or volcanic activity; nor the luck of the prospector and the frequency of ore discoveries; nor the emergence of new technologies that either cheapen a metal by substitution or raise its price by demand. What the mint controls lies within the realm of the earned, the willed, the predictable, the merited, the just. What it does not control is under the sign of the given, the accidental, the risky, the lucky, the merciful. If the uncontrolled aspect of value raises the price of the metal above the nominal value inscribed on the coin, then the hoarding or clipping or melting down of coins will commence; if it renders the metal useless, or if an intrinsically worthless paper currency is established instead, then the economy becomes vulnerable to counterfeiting.

Of course the true picture is more complex than this. It would include such complications as the relationships among different currencies and the competition of national economies, the disproportions between available goods and available money that can cause inflation or recessionary liquidity squeezes, the role that timing and delay can play in the establishment of value. But however far we pursue the matter of economic value, we will always encounter the two poles of what we are handed by the past, or by circumstances, or by the unpredictable effects of our own actions—and what we attempt, by legal or actual means, to do about it. Even paper or electronic currency is backed by something subject to contingencies—a gold reserve, a pool of oil under the ground, a gross national product. If, in the most extreme case, the backing is a military threat that holds a population under obligation for its survival, the military's loyalty is subject to unpredictable givens. Gold, oil, gross national product, and military force are all forms of specie, in an extended sense. The main point is that there is no escape from the dilemma, no place where we can take total refuge in one kind of value, undisturbed by the other. Our lives are always a mixture of the hereditary, the given, on one hand, and the contrived, the socially constructed, on the other. No perfectly—unconditionally—loving family exists into which the thought of equity and financial obligation never penetrates; no perfectly impartial and ruthless state or corporation exists in which family loyalty and gifts (and thus nepotism and corruption) play no part. This is to put it negatively; it would be more accurate to say that just as the earned and the given, justice and mercy, maintain each other, so also do the nominal and the intrinsic worth of currency.

Perhaps this is the true significance of the original mint itself, the temple of Juno in ancient Rome where the coins of the Roman empire were struck. Juno was the wife of Jupiter, and the goddess of marriage, childbirth, home, and family. Thus she represents par excellence the realm of mercy, uncalculated gifts, the hazardous lottery of sexual reproduction, the givens of heredity and family destiny. In giving Juno's vestals control over the stamping of money, the Romans were making a point akin to that of Aeschylus in the *Oresteia*, who transforms the Furies of family revenge into the Eumenides of civic order: the impartial regime of justice, contracts, and money must be founded, paradoxically, upon the arbitrary and partial order of mercy, gift, and family inheritance. Juno was the counselor—"moneta"—from which epithet we get both mint and money. "Counselor," not "commander," an epithet more befitting her husband; her regime is one of nonlinear influence, of the long-term fructifying of wise policy through multiple agency, rather than Jove's linear power, the heroic, short-term, and sacrificial imposition of individual will together with the just acceptance of responsibility for its results. But the counselor and the commander—Juno and Jupiter—are married, and though the marriage is frequently stormy, it is eternal. Thus the mythological implications of Roman economic institutions are quite consonant with the recent anthropological picture of coexistence and cooperation between the impersonal world of market legality and the personal world of family gift exchange. Both are in contradiction to classical and Marxist economics, which picture the market as destructive to the old personal forms of community.

Whether the ancient Romans and the new economic anthropologists are right, or the classical and Marxist economists are, is still being worked out in how we create and run our institutions. The issue was not lost on Shakespeare; he was especially interested in the implications of coining, stamping, and inscription, in the relationship between the intrinsic and the nominal value of coins and contract seals, and in the deep analogies that could be found between these matters and the biological, political, and economic aspects of our lives. In *A Midsummer Night's Dream* he examines a pathological case where nominal value—justice, the willed, the contractual—has overwhelmed intrinsic value—mercy, the given, the arbitrary—in an imagined version of Athens. The play suggests ways in which the city can be healed and the balance restored.

The Seal and the Wax in *A Midsummer Night's Dream*

At the outset of the play Theseus, the mythological king of Athens famed for his wisdom as a lawgiver, is confronted with a family dispute over marriage. Egeus complains to the king that his daughter, Hermia, refuses to marry the man he has chosen to be her husband—Demetrius—and instead insists on marrying Lysander, the man who has won her heart. Enraged by his daughter's stubbornness and disobedience, Egeus invokes the ancient law of Athens, which requires that she obey her father in this matter, upon pain of death. Theseus presents this draconic choice to Hermia, adding these words:

> To you your father should be as a god,
> One that composed your beauties; yea, and one
> To whom you are but as a form in wax
> By him imprinted and within his power
> To leave the figure or disfigure it.
> (I.i.47)

In other words, the law claims that the social person of the daughter is like a seal impression stamped into hot wax, the authentic signature of her father. It was with such waxen "bulls" that official contracts were validated. Papal decrees—bulls—got their name from the seals that authenticated them. The use of seals in this way goes back thousands of years to Minoan seal rings, and further still to Mesopotamian cylindrical bulls, carved so as to leave an inscription in cuneiform when rolled across a soft clay surface, and signifying a legal mercantile contract. Coinage itself, with metal substituted for clay or wax, is another development of the bull. When Hamlet forges a document condemning his betrayers to death, he uses his dead father's seal ring to stamp it as genuine; it is at this moment that he finally takes on without reservation his filial duty to avenge the murdered king.

The image of the wax seal is superficially a symbol of absolute authority, of the reduction of human individuality to the purely conventional, the socially assigned. According to this interpretation, if Hermia accepts Theseus' suggestion that she is like passive wax to her father's stamp, she has no identity of her own. Contemporary academic thinkers in cultural studies would agree and would see the laws of Shakespeare's Athens as a straightforward example of oppressive patriarchy. Like the fictional Athenian lawgivers, such "poststructuralist" thinkers themselves maintain that our attitudes, our criteria for what constitutes reality, our very idea of what is a self, are "socially constructed," are essentially taught to us by our early education and enforced by the subtle coercion of our institutions. (How such academics themselves are able to free themselves from the great shared illusion is not adequately explained. Some say that being marginal and powerless—female or ethnically disempowered—enables one to see through the illusion, but logically such persons would be even more helpless against the brainwashing of the ideological authorities than those in positions of central power.) Thus poststructuralist thinkers do not fundamentally disagree with the notion that our identity is inscribed by society; they would just contest with the likes of Theseus his control over the inscription process and claim that if they themselves were doing the inscribing, daughters like Hermia would get more autonomy. A cynic might wonder whether such new authorities would exercise their power in any wiser and more humane fashion than the old; the track record of such liberators in this closing century, such as Lenin, Mao, and Pol Pot, is not promising.

But in fact the image of the wax impression is not, if we look at it more closely, one of pure social construction and absolute authority. The play describes the rebellion of the young people whose lives have been so dragooned by their society. They escape into the night, into the forest, into the realm of natural fertility, the land of fairy enchantment, the preconscious world of dream. It is as if the wax resisted the impression of the seal and insisted on taking its own shape; or as if the value of the metal resisted the denomination stamped on the coin. Hermia puts it quite clearly: I would rather live my life out as a celibate, she says, withdrawing my generative capacity from the service of the city, than "yield my virgin patent up / Unto his lordship, whose unwished yoke / My soul consents not to give sovereignty" (I.i.80). A patent in this sense is something spread open and made available, a permission to produce using the patented property; but the holder of the patent must take care that his "sovereigny" not abuse its privilege. Society can shape its members to some extent; but it cannot violate their essential nature without unleashing forces of destruction and creation symbolized by the fairies in the play. An artist may be able to work wonders, but she cannot make an equestrian statue out of oil paint or compose a sonnet out of musical notes; just so a legislator cannot ignore the nature of his medium, which is human beings, the givens of human life. All utopias seek to abolish those givens—Plato banished poets from his ideal republic, and Stalin starved his own peasants to death—but to do so is to deprive the state of the creative and generative forces that give it life. Theseus sees at once that the law Egeus has invoked is tyrannical, and he gives Hermia another alternative besides marriage to Demetrius or death: perpetual celibacy. But even this is clearly unacceptable, and in the end Theseus endorses the rebellion of the young lovers and gives them what they want. After all, he and his bride-to-be, the Amazon Hippolyta, did not submit to an arranged marriage but won each other in the great battle of the sexes. Their relationship is clearly one of equal mutual sovereignty and holds the promise of fertility; each is the hot wax of the other, each stamps the other with the seal of freehold, each holds the patent to the other: their wedding will be

> The sealing day between my love and me,
> For everlasting bond of fellowship.
> (I.i.84)

So those delightful, comic, and terrifying scenes in the forest that every lover of Shakespeare remembers with a peculiar shiver are in fact a kind of analysis of the givens that underlie the conscious, rational, daylight world of social legality and earned justice. It is as if Shakespeare took a microscope to the smooth, intelligible surface of our social life and revealed the fantastic caverns and labyrinthine fractal geometry of its microstructure, the indeterminate quantum glimmer of its uncertain light, the apparently arbitrary transformations of its metabolism. The play is full of the grotesque Heironymus Bosch surrealism of the nanoworld:

> Over hill, over dale,
> Thorough bush, thorough brier,
> Over park, over pale,
> Thorough flood, thorough fire,
> I do wander everywhere,
> Swifter than the moon's sphere;
> And I serve the Fairy Queen,
> To dew her orbs upon the green.
> The cowslips tall her pensioners be:
> In their gold coats spots you see;
> Those be rubies, fairy favors,
> In those freckles live their savors. . . .
> (II.i.2)

> There sleeps Titania sometime of the night,
> Lulled in these flowers with dances and delight;

And there the snake throws her enamelled skin,
Weed wide enough to wrap a fairy in . . .
(II.i.253)

The honey bags steal from the humblebees,
And for night tapers crop their waxen thighs,
And light them at the fiery glowworm's eyes . . .
(III.i.168)

Sometime a horse I'll be, sometime a hound,
A hog, a headless bear, sometime a fire;
And neigh, and bark, and grunt, and roar, and burn,
Like horse, hound, hog, bear, fire, at every turn. . . .
(III.i.107)

We have descended into the dim realms of DNA, into the great "Heraclitean fire" of nature, as Gerard Manley Hopkins put it, into the psychic universe of mammals, reptiles, and insects. We see the wax of formal seals and contracts and patents in its natural state, as the secretion of honeybees. In this world the ordinary clarity and certainty of perception are put aside; the eyes can be deceived, vision can alter unpredictably: things seem "small and undistinguishable, / Like far-off mountains turnèd into clouds" (IV.i.188). It is as if we had lost the bold optical synthesis of ordinary daylight vision and had descended to the lower levels of neural processing. Those levels are normally automatic and unconscious, but they are here revealed, as the impressionist painters revealed them, in order to remind us not to take our consensual commonsense reality too much for granted. Likewise, the young Athenians and we, the audience, are plunged in these scenes into a dreamlike state, where the hippocampus, the brain's messy kitchen of associations, somehow produces the coherence of everyday memory. Beneath the apparently uniform and featureless surface of the wax seal is a mysterious world of biology, chemistry, and atomic structure, which can support those odd changes of state, from solid to liquid and back. These changes—exemplified in the various states of candle wax—so enchanted Descartes fifty years after Shakespeare's time that he built an entire skeptical philosophy upon them. When the abstract justice of the city becomes tyrannical, when the inscription of nominal value becomes a lie, we must subject our socially constructionist assumptions to a Pyrrhonic testing to destruction, fly back to the givens of nature and human nature, and find our freedom there.

The issue of how pliant human beings are to the constructions of society is still a live one. At present our government bureaucracy and educational system are still operating under the assumption that human beings at birth are more or less indistinguishable, blank slates to be inscribed by society. Inequality, poverty, social conflict, crime, and unhappiness must therefore be the fault of society, and its citizenry should gladly offer their taxes to pay governmental and educational experts to reprogram our errant culture. Like the laws of Theseus' Athens, they ignore the genetic givens that make us individuals, that interact with the cultural environment to generate an emergent soul that can contest both its biological and its social programming. Meanwhile a strong challenge is being mounted to the received ideas of social construction we have labored under since the sixties. Genetic, anthropological, and neurobiological science is giving us a picture of a human animal that is stubbornly its own individual from birth.

But we should not make the mistake of going back to the dog-eat-dog individualism of classic liberalism, of the apostles of pure economic competition. For humans became human, as we now know, through a five-million-year process of evolution in which our emerging social and cultural systems were already the major selective pressure shaping our bodies and brains. In other words, we are not fundamentally wild animals with hypertrophied intelligence forced by economic necessity to contract into an unnatural condition of society (as Hobbes, Rousseau, and Freud believed), but domesticated animals, formed like dogs and horses to serve humankind, with an inbuilt need for gregariousness and cultural norms. The fact that we domesticated ourselves, by selectively awarding reproductive privileges to the culturally adept and withdrawing them from the sociopaths, in no way alters the fact that we are animals with social instincts. Shakespeare seems, like Aristotle, to have intuited this fact, and thus he trusts human individuals, on the whole, to arrange their own affairs in a reasonably social way if there is a legal ball field that is more or less level. Their trust is to be contrasted with the basic mistrust of human nature evinced both by dog-eat-dog individualists such as Thomas Hobbes (who require coercive government force to keep people from each other's throats) and by bureaucratic social constructionists (who demand politically correct education to reprogram the citizen).

This is why Shakespeare does not leave his lovers out in the forest, as for instance a Romantic poet, faced with the same story material, might have been tempted to do. Our nature, Shakespeare feels, paradoxically requires a human society and culture to complete it and satisfy it. Out in the forest the lovers are credulous literalists, as are all other animals compared to human beings. Shakespeare arranges that a group of amateur actors, headed by the harrassed director Peter Quince and the egomaniac actor Bully Bottom, are also in the forest at the same time as the lovers, rehearsing their play. Shakespeare's irrepressible comedy has full sweep. The players' chief anxiety is that their prospective audience will be alarmed by the tragic and terrible events they mean to portray; they have a touching and totally unjustified faith in their own verisimilitude and are trying to reduce the realism of their performance so as to protect the sensibilities of their patrons. Bottom wants to play the part of the lion that has apparently eaten the hero; on being cautioned that his roaring will "fright the ladies," he promises to roar "as gently as any sucking dove" and to allow his face to be seen in the neck of the lion costume (I.ii.79). We are rightly incredulous that any real audience, especially of sophisticated aristocrats, such as this one would be, could be as naive as Bottom fears. But in actual comic fact, the aristocratic lovers be-

come in the forest just such a hayseed audience before the fantastic performance of their own romantic dreams.

Shakespeare symbolizes the fickle obsessions of young infatuation—a
nice word here, literally "making fatuous"—by the device of having the
fairies smear magic love-juice on the lovers' eyes, whereupon their victims
instantly fall into doting worship of the first living being they see. "Lord,
what fools these mortals be," chuckles Puck, the director of the little performance that has so deceived them (III.ii.115). This is the trouble with living
in the forest, with giving oneself over to the night world of the unconscious,
of retreating to the natural microstructure of human life. One becomes stu-
pid, incapable of reason, of objectivity, of detachment from one's own interests. Pathetically, like advanced Alzheimer's cases, they cannot even recognize their disability. After one such transformation, Lysander intones:

> The will of man is by his reason swayed
> And reason says you are the worthier maid.
> (II.ii.115)

The great pity of this beastlike earnestness is that one is then unable to see
the joke, and the whole rich and lovely comedy and tragedy of the world becomes invisible. As Keats lamented to the nightingale, if he were to shuck off
the burden of consciousness he would no longer be able to appreciate its
midnight song and would "to thy high requiem become a sod." We need to
go back to the city to recover our human birthright of reason, reflection, and
appreciation, bred into us by millennia of ritual, art, and human intercourse.
The objectivity, clarity, and moral independence we learn in the city are
worth the candle, so long as we do not sacrifice to them the fertile and creative powers of emotion and imagination.

Another way of putting all this is to say that if the inscription of a coin or
seal alone is not sufficient for our purposes, the intrinsic value of coin metal
or the intrinsic natural adhesive properties of sealing wax is not either. We
need the metal and wax to express our economic and legal meanings besides.
And in any case we do not use wax or metal in their natural state as ore or
honeycomb. The metal and wax of human nature are already selected and
transformed by human agency. The inscription, the "third nature" that a
material takes when it is struck or stamped, is demanded by its "second nature" as a smelted precious alloy or a pigmented processed glue; likewise,
human flesh and blood, bred to human culture over millennia, demand
cities, laws, and canons of proof. The wax or metal will reject an improper
stamp; not because they reject all stamps, but because they crave the right
kind of stamp.

At the end of *A Midsummer Night's Dream* the love tangle with which
the play began is sorted out. The four lovers—Hermia (who loves Lysander),
Lysander (who loves Hermia), Demetrius (who also loves Hermia), and Helena (who loves Demetrius) learn from their immersion in the night forest
what their true feelings are. The net result is that Demetrius gives up his vain

pursuit of Hermia and turns his affections to Helena, who loves him, and who, as we learn by the way, had been the object of his affections before he met Hermia. Theseus accepts nature's disposition of the case over the protests of Egeus, Hermia's father. It would seem as if nature had won the contest with social construction; but it is, after all, Theseus the lawgiver alone who can make the judgment and legitimate the marriages, and his verdict is based not on natural inclination but on reason. What we have here is a model of wise rule, that recognizes the role of nature in human decisions and, when appropriate, validates the hot wax of nature's process with the inscription of legal and property rights.

One might object that if the institutions of society only rubber-stamp decisions already made by people's natural inclinations, justice is a travesty, a face-saving way of bowing to the inevitable. This objection would only be valid if human beings did not already have a social nature and a genetically imprinted conscience whose dictates are reflected, without much variation, in the moral codes of all religions. What saves Theseus' way of dealing with the problem from mere moral relativism is its foundation upon natural law. Theseus does not accept all personal inclinations and desires as legitimate; in fact, he is rejecting Egeus' quite irrational and fundamentally animalistic desire to control his own daughter against her happiness and his own posterity. Theseus' way is to work with nature to improve it, as his fine disquisition on dog breeding implies:

> My hounds are bred out of the Spartan kind,
> So flewed, so sanded; and their heads are hung
> With ears that sweep away the morning dew;
> Crook-kneed, and dew-lapped like Thessalian bulls;
> Slow in pursuit, but matched in mouth like bells,
> Each under each.
> (IV.i.120)

Notice that the hounds are not bred just for efficiency, but for beauty and harmony of voice as well. Or perhaps we could say that Theseus has arranged it so that beauty and harmony have become the most efficient way for the organism to reproduce; he is the most potent force of Darwinian selection in the dogs' environment, after all!

In permitting the marriages of the four lovers—and in celebrating his own—Theseus is in a sense practicing eugenics, the improvement of human stock by selective breeding. But we need not be horrified by this way of putting it. For after all, he is endorsing the free-enterprise eugenics of people's own love choices and giving that system of selective breeding preference over any state-run system. The way he breeds for beauty and harmony in the population of his city is by creating a social and legal evironment in which fine young people can meet and fall in love and marry, and can justly demand a share of the accumulated wealth of older generations to support their work of reproduction. In this way the bonds of society and property

are reconciled with the bonds of affection and desire; and out of the min-
gling of those two imperious compulsions arises the mysterious flower of
freedom. This mystery is suggested when one sheet of sheer silk is placed
over another, and a new, volatile, unpredictable rainbow pattern of moiré
waves arises out of the diffraction and interference of two strict, deterministic, rectilinear grids. Or—to return to our original metaphor—out of the
combinations of specie and stamp, of wax and seal, come the essential connections and obligations that give humans a place in the world, and the autonomy as civil beings that comes with that place.

In the final scene, the amateur actors put on a lamentably funny performance of their tragic play. It is pure entertainment; the sophisticated audience makes fun of the ridiculous theatrics, and yet the ridicule is in a generous spirit. As Theseus says of all such performances, "The best in this kind
are but shadows; and the worst are no worse, if imagination amend them."
The "silly stuff" they are watching is not unlike the silly stuff we ourselves
perform when under the influence of strong emotions (V.i.210). The institutions and celebrations of the city make it possible for us to reflect upon our
natural folly and to transform its shame into comedy. The superimposition
of conventional inscription upon natural matter gives birth to *play*, in three
senses: game playing, the "free play" of physical systems, and drama. The
audience of Quince's play are passing the time; they have just celebrated
their weddings and have not yet consummated them. A decent respect for
civilized custom creates this brief interim before the satisfaction of natural
sexual drives; and this delay is the domain of art, however clumsy and ab-
surd that art may be.

At last the newly married couples drift off to bed, leaving the great hall
of Theseus' palace to the flickering light of its fading fireplaces and the mysterious moonlight pouring in through the windows. And now the fairies
reappear—for the fairies live not only in the forest, but also in the city, in the
home, at the bottom of the garden, behind the door, under the bed. As humans, we are never far from the forces of nature that underlie our rational
daylight lives and populate our dreams. The fairies bless the issue of those
marriages, which are being consummated even as Puck addresses the real
audience across the footlights in his epilogue, breaking the conventional bar-
rier between fiction and reality. For Shakespeare true marriage, the "blessed
bond of board and bed," is the most potent symbol and example of the
union of fiction and reality, culture and nature, stamped inscription and raw
material, justice and gift.

The Counterfeit King

But the properties that emerge out of this union—consciousness, calculation,
reflection—also make possible new kinds of abuses, especially deceit. That
deceitfulness can turn and attack the very legitimacy of the bond itself, and
when it does, we call it counterfeiting. In *A Midsummer Night's Dream*,

which is a comedy, there is no question as to the legitimacy of Theseus' rule; the mythological background of the play is explicit about Theseus' royal blood and his earned leadership as the savior of his people and the slayer of the Minotaur. Theseus is genuine: he has proved in battle that he is more powerful than the bull-headed man-monster of the Minoan labyrinth who symbolizes the brutish aspects of human nature. In *A Midsummer Night's Dream* the ferocious Minotaur reappears farcically and innocuously as Bottom the Weaver transformed by the fairies into an ass; human beings are therapeutically reminded of their animality in their dreams, their love affairs, and their art. This is the realm of comedy, where there is always a legitimate city to return to; our given animal bodies are the raw material of a society that is generally successful in controlling them. In terms of the metaphor of the wax seal and the metal coin, the play concerns a dispute about how far the raw material of human beings can be bent out of shape by civilized legal constraints, and what redressive resources—dream, art, imagination, humor—exist to put things right when the rules of the city overreach themselves.

But what if there is a serious question about the legitimacy of the stamp or inscription with which the raw material is impressed? Who has the right to mint a coin? What if the king, whose image is on the coin, is not a legitimate king? What makes a king legitimate anyway? A sufficiently large number of counterfeit coins will debase a currency; a counterfeit king can debase a whole commonwealth. What if there were no legitimate city to return to after one's adventures in the forest? These problems cannot be handled in the mode of comedy; instead, they form the core of Shakespeare's great series of history plays, *Richard II, Henry IV* (parts one and two), and *Henry V.*

In the Battle of Shrewsbury, which forms the climax of *Henry IV, Part One,* Henry IV uses a tactic that secures victory over the rebel armies arrayed against him, but that smacks of dishonor and symbolizes all too graphically the political problems of his regime. He has a number of his followers put on his own heraldry and coat armor, effectively disguising themselves as the king himself. Several of these fakes are killed by Douglas, his Scottish opponent. The king survives to see his enemies slain or captured; but the rebellions continue, because the doubt as to Henry's legitimacy remains. Nobody can tell for sure which is the real king, and there are many claimants to the throne. The problem lies in the history of Henry's rise to power. Henry usurped the throne from Richard II, and though Richard had himself been a weak, venal, and treacherous king with royal blood on his own hands, and though Richard had formally abdicated his throne, ceding it to Henry, nevertheless the sacred chain of descent has been broken. Henry is a counterfeit king.

This is not to say he is not a good king in many ways. He has the mettle, discipline, and intelligence of a true king—his blood, in Shakespeare's metaphor, is vigorous and potent. He has the right metal to be king, but the inscription has been improperly acquired, and thus his coinage, so to speak, is suspect. Shakespeare plays with this idea throughout all four plays, punning on the colloquial terms for the coins of the realm—"crown" (five shillings), "royal" (ten shillings), "cross" (the inscription on the "tails" side of various coins), and "sovereign" (one pound). How can the English monarchy, Shakespeare asks, recover its legitimacy? And how can its economy regain its vigor and stabilize its currency, and so renew the basic fertility of its soil, its productiveness, and its health in the international markets (symbolized by participation in Europe's great project of the Crusades)? The plays are full of references to the financial instabilities of civil war economies. One can "buy land now as cheap as stinking mack'rel;" worse, one can "buy maidenheads as they buy hobnails, by the hundreds" (II.iv.362, 365). Hotspur, before the battle, puns on "crown" (the top of the head) and "crown" (the coin):

> We must have bloody noses and cracked crowns,
> And pass them current too.
> (II.iii.92)

The implication is that to engage in rebellion is to use as legal tender (pass current) a coin that is cracked and thus defaced and devalued.

All of these anxieties are summed up in Henry's first speech to his lords in *Henry IV, Part One.*

> So shaken as we are, so wan with care,
> Find we a time for frighted peace to pant
> And breathe short-winded accents of new broils
> To be commenced in stronds afar remote.
> No more the thirsty entrance of this soil
> Shall daub her lips with her own children's blood,
> No more shall trenching war channel her fields,
> Nor bruise her flow'rets with the armèd hoofs
> Of hostile paces. . . .
>   Therefore, friends,
> As far as to the sepulcher of Christ—
> Whose soldier now, under whose blessèd cross
> We are impressèd and engaged to fight—
> Forthwith a power of English shall we levy,
> Whose arms were molded in their mother's womb
> To chase these pagans in those holy fields
> Over whose acres walked those blessèd feet
> Which fourteen hundred years ago were nailed
> For our advantage on the bitter cross.
> (I.i.1)

The metaphor Henry uses for the soldiers' service to God in the Crusades is a mixed one. The soldiers are "engaged," a word like "mortgaged," implying the pledge of personal property or person itself as security for a sum of money. The passage also refers to the "impressing," or we would say "press-ganging" of soldiers by forced conscription into an army, and the acceptance by the recruit of payment—the "cross" or the "king's shilling"— for his military service. And of course all this is based on the by now familiar process of pressing or stamping a coin, the British warrior shaped in the mold of the British womb and the cross of the British military uniform. In the ideal state of the kingdom, the "blood" to which Henry alludes so graphically at the beginning of his speech, the true wax or metal of England, must be properly molded and stamped with the cross of royal legitimacy if it is to carry value. But the poetic imagery of sacrifice—Christ's, the crusader's—implies that the only way the sacrifice of English blood in civil war can be stopped is paradoxically by more sacrifice. What sacrifice can redeem the pawned crown of England? This is the question, the poetic work that the plays set for themselves.

For Americans at the end of the twentieth century these issues may well seem remote and politically antiquated. Did not we, after all, reject the coinage of the British king, and ban in our Bill of Rights the practice of forced conscription? Did we not throw the tea into Boston Harbor, in protest against the sovereign stamp of duty? Our nation was founded—was it not?—on the principle of allowing the raw material of a nation, the people, to govern and inscribe and stamp themselves. In *Walden,* within earshot of Concord Bridge, Thoreau insists,

> You may melt your metals and cast them into the most beautiful moulds you can; they will never excite me like the forms which this molten earth flows out into.
> (Merrill Standard Edition, 1969, p. 330)

But America has always struggled with the anguish of legitimacy. As Thoreau wrote, we were preparing for the bloodiest civil war in human history. And in our own times we have seen the murder of a "king," John F. Kennedy, the uneasy accession of a successor, Lyndon B. Johnson, who was hounded from office to be replaced by a Richard of our own, who was in turn deposed and who, betrayer and betrayed as he was, rests uneasily on the national conscience. We have, indeed, a legal, exact, and apparently impersonal system of voting and succession of power; but beneath that system is the gigantic hidden flow of national feeling, uncertainly plumbed by polls, that can render helpless a president with great official power, can protect him from legal prosecution for his misdeeds, or give huge potency to an ex-president, a general, a Speaker of the House, or a private citizen with moral authority. Our ancient tribal roots are not mocked, and we all yearn for the wise and generous leader who will retell our national myth in the way that we need, who will rejuvenate our rituals, who will demand efficacious sacrifices, and get them. The very health of our economy demands the morale such a leader provides. Of course this need in us is dangerous—it can produce Hitlers as well as Lincolns—but it is there, and it will not go away, and we had better know its ways. And this is what we can learn from Shakespeare—the mythical and ritual depths of politics. Those depths are also the foundations of the national wealth, the health of our currency, the context of our personal and family relationships.

Prince Hal, who must succeed his father as Henry V, faces a crisis of legitimacy not unlike that which confronted the American colonists after their victory over the British. Indeed, this issue has dogged the United States to this very day, in the form of the distinction between the president as the chief executive representing the policies of the majority party and the president as head of state—a role haunted by the ghost of the British monarchy. Can the sovereign be merely the most recent winner in the political struggle? Surely not. Prince Hal must legitimately succeed to a crown that was not itself legitimately attained by succession. Though Hal is of kingly metal, the inscription or stamp of his sovereignty has been defaced. How does one make a counterfeit coin (made of genuine metal) into a true "crown" or "royal" or "sovereign" of the realm?

The Sacrifice

The answer, when we express it in terms of coinage, is obvious: remelt the coin, and restamp it with a legitimate head of state. The answer is less obvious when when we try to put it in terms of public policy and the necessary rituals of succession. Hal knows that the solution is not to join his father in the unscrupulous Realpolitik and treachery by which he maintains an uneasy seat on the throne. Hal seeks out an alternative father, one who is apparently free of all the hypocrisies of social power and who embodies the ease and creativity of nature itself. He finds this alternative father in the fat highwayman Falstaff. Falstaff's solution to Hal's problem is that if nature has given a man kingly metal, the stamp doesn't matter: "Never call a true piece of gold a counterfeit," says Falstaff to Hal; "Thou art essentially made without seeming so" (II.iv.496). If Hal is a true piece of gold, he cannot be a counterfeit king. He is truly made out of sovereign essence and has no need to appear so. Ignore the stamp of rules and regulations, says Falstaff, live by gifts not earnings, thumb your nose at justice with its killjoy accountings; "we that take purses go by the moon and the seven stars, and not by Phoebus, he, that wand'ring knight so fair" (I.ii.14). Phoebus is Apollo, the god of daylight and reason—the Logos, the word, the inscription by which we impress nature and make it serve us. Who needs him, demands Falstaff, when we can have the moon's perpetually borrowed light?

Falstaff is a misuser of the king's press, that is, someone who recruits soldiers in an illegal fashion for private profit, using the writ and seal authority of the monarchy. The word "press" itself alerts us to the deep relationship between the acts of minting and of conscription: both are ways to imprint, or impress, or stamp, the free material of nature for state use. The connection is underlined when Falstaff pretends to be dead on the battlefield in order to save his life. His defense against the charge of being a counterfeiter is that he is after all alive, and that life itself has a genuineness that trumps any kind of civilized, inscribed value, any such "trim reckoning" as honesty or honor (V.i.135). He argues that in denying the Apolline prerogative to stamp the raw material of life, he is himself genuine metal. The paradox is summed up in Falstaff's very name: he is a "false staff." Does this mean that he is the wrong kind of support for a king, or that he is no mere staff, but a caduceus or Moses-staff, that is also a living snake? Or both? To counterfeit a counterfeit is to be genuine. If, Falstaff points out, death is the counterfeit of life—a dead body is a mere simulacrum of a living one—to counterfeit death "is to be no counterfeit, but the true and perfect image of life indeed" (V.iv.116). Or is he a false caduceus, that is, a staff that would turn into a snake but could not turn back into a staff, like those of the Egyptian priests who competed in magic with Moses?

We have encountered this idea already, in *A Midsummer Night's Dream,* when we considered the romantic possibility that the lovers might elect to stay in the forest and never return to stuffy old Athens with its laws and traditions. Once the rigid and authoritarian staff has been changed into the vital and transgressive snake, why turn back? But the romantic solution will not work, as we have already seen. At its best, it leaves us in a forest where we are isolated from each other by the utter incommensurability of our senses with those of others, and incapable of the objectivity that makes possible both judgment and laughter. At its worst, the romantic solution—allow the stronger natures to do what they desire without check—gives us Edmund, the bastard in *King Lear,* who declares, "Thou, Nature, art my goddess," and claims for the "lusty stealth" of his nature "more composition and fierce quality" than a whole tribe of legitimate fops "got 'tween asleep and wake" (I.ii.1). Edmund is indeed charismatic, attractive, strong, and intelligent—he has kingly virtues. But he is also a moral monster who will do anything to get power, including kill his own father and brother. In our American democracy, there is nothing in constitutional principle to prevent such a man from coming to office; after all, Hitler was elected fair and square by the citizens of a nation more civilized in many ways than ours and a voting system no more liable to manipulation. All that protects us from such tyrants is the continuity of certain ritual institutions much deeper and much less well known (which, in the case of Hitler, had been destroyed by the German revolution of 1918). Shakespeare gives us fine portraits of the tyrant in the hunchback Richard III and in Macbeth; and it is only a certain basic decency and restraint that prevents Henry IV from being of the same type. Truly the means of his rise to power provide no check to his being so.

Indeed, it is Henry IV's basic decency that makes of his regime a cold, bloodless, mean-spirited affair. He is always desperately trying to legitimate his reign by dishonest means, preserving the illusion of true authority without its substance. He outsmarts and cheats his rebel subjects instead of winning their loyalty by generosity in victory as would a true king, or crushing them cheerfully as would an entirely unscrupulous tyrant. At the Battle of Shrewsbury Henry Bullingbrook himself wears the coat of arms of the king of England, but though his metal is of the right bullion to do so, he is still a counterfeiter, his bull is false; we know this because he finds it necessary to outfit his base-metal followers in the same disguise. Imagine the heroic Henry V resorting to such subterfuges! Henry IV's plottings, machinations, image manipulation, and legalistic hypocrisy are precisely what repel his son, Hal, and drive him into the arms of Falstaff.

We saw earlier that the theoretical solution to Hal's problem is to remelt the counterfeit coin of his inheritance and restamp it with a legitimate head of state. But this is in practice a long process—Hal must, for example, wait for his father to die. He cannot continue the defiling series of murders for the sake of power. Though he has already explicitly rejected his father's way, Hal's psychological coinage must take some shape in the meantime. In the deepest symbolism of the play, the placeholder head that is inscribed on Hal's coin is the Boar's Head, the sign of the tavern where he and Falstaff hang out. The boar's head should immediately remind us of those two other animal heads that we have glanced at in this chapter—the bull head of the Minotaur and the ass head of Bottom. Falstaff is the ritual king of the May, the Lord of Misrule, the embodiment of our animal nature. He is the boar, the sacrificial beast that must first be prepared for his role—the sins of the community heaped on his back—and then immolated for the health of the land.

Just in case his audience might have missed the point, Shakespeare even gives us a comic postscript, *The Merry Wives of Windsor,* in which all these themes are made explicit. In *Merry Wives,* Falstaff puts on the head of a deer, disguising himself as the ancient nature god Herne the Hunter, in order to seduce a pair of respectable married women. He enters Windsor Forest, the old domain of the English kings, where he has plotted to meet his paramours. His companions then play a trick on him, putting on a counterdisguise as fairies, hunting the hunter down like Actaeon, and tormenting him until he is forced to take off his deer head. "I do begin to perceive," says Falstaff, "that I am made an ass." "Ay," says Ford, one of the husbands Falstaff sought to have cuckolded, "and an ox too" (V.v.121). The nearly blasphemous joke—an ox and an ass attended the birth of another sacrificial god in human form—cements the relatedness of the Minotaur, Bottom, and Falstaff. It is not often that a poet will spell out his message so obligingly, providing in the form of another play a profound exegesis of the thematic relationship between *A Midsummer Night's Dream* and *Henry IV.* Somehow Shakespeare understood to their core the prehistoric animal sacrifice rituals and shamanic disguise practices that he evokes in this farcical and delightful comedy.

The first step, then, in Hal's solution to the paradox of his inherited illegitimacy is to replace the king's head with the boar's head as his personal sign, replace the fake king with the authentic beast. Falstaff is authentic in that he embodies the fundamental substance of the English national character—that substance that we find in Sir Bercilak (the jolly castellan in *Sir Gawain and the Green Knight*), in the Host and the Miller in the *Canterbury Tales,* in Dr. Johnson and Samuel Pickwick, and even in Benny Hill. John Bull is the cartoon version of this mythic figure. Falstaff is invested by Shakespeare with all the imagery of traditional animal sacrifice festivals— the roasted Manningtree ox with the pudding in his belly, the Bartholomew boar-pig, the fat kine of Pharaoh's dream, the sow that has overwhelmed all her litter but one. These are images of great meat-feasts, of satisfied hunger, of carnival (literally, flesh rites), of the fertility of the land that gives us such good things and provides us with a surplus to tide us over the winter. Falstaff is a huge relief from the starved dry politicking of the historical chronicle.

But of course so far Hal does not yet have a solution. We cannot have a man-beast for a king. The coin of the realm must have another stamp than the slavering and greedy snout of the boar. As soon as Falstaff is given the friendship of the prince, he immediately abuses it, using it to commit highway robbery with impunity and to sell draft exemptions to the soldiers he has impressed into the king's service (another example, in the light of our discussion of Henry IV's proposed draft for the Crusades, of Shakespeare's astonishing poetic economy). The problem with people who live like animals is that the big ones eat up the little ones; as Falstaff himself puts it, referring to one of the victims of his con games, "If the young dace be a bait for the old pike, I see no reason in the law of nature but I may snap at him" (2 *Henry IV,* III.ii.335).

But at least part of Hal's problem is solved. By consorting with Falstaff he has, as it were, reduced himself to a sort of Everyman; he has erased the stamp of his father and is now in the condition of Adam, with the potential to become anything he chooses:

> I am now of all humors that have showed themselves humors since the old days of goodman Adam to the pupil age of this present twelve o'clock at midnight. (II. iv. 94.)

The Boar's Head tavern is a place where Hal is liberated from his ordinary identity and can play any role he likes. It is, among other things, the space of theater art itself. In the course of the ensuing scene Hal engages in a series of amateur theatricals, taking the parts of a bartender, a rich young drunk, the rebel Harry Hotspur, his own father the king, and himself as a dissolute young prince being scolded by his father. He is actually preparing himself to be the representative of all his people, since he has become, in play, each of them in turn.

Most important of all, he has thoroughly detached himself from his identity as an interested political party in the power struggle. He is thus in a position to "renormalize," as mathematicians say, the paradoxical situation in which he has been placed as the potential inheritor of stolen property. (To renormalize is to cancel out one mathematical absurdity with another, leaving an equation of finite real quantities that can be solved.) The manner in which this task is to be performed is explained symbolically in the episode of the Gad's Hill robbery. The prince has agreed to help Falstaff and his companions rob some rich travelers on the Canterbury road. But by prearrangement Hal does not rendezvous with Falstaff; instead he waits until Falstaff has completed his holdup, and in disguise with his friend Poins he in turn robs the robbers and turns the whole affair into a joke. Later he repays the money ("with advantage"—interest) to its proper possessors. It is just in this fashion that he will restore the legitimacy of the English throne: he must in some sense steal it from the thief (his father), commit a second crime to erase the first.

This act of counterusurpation is in turn symbolized by the scene in which Hal encounters his father for the last time on Henry's deathbed. In error, Hal believes that his father is already dead, and pitying his father for the terrible burden of the crown that has destroyed him, Hal takes that same crown up from the pillow where it lies and tries it on himself, as if to wrestle with the antagonist that has defeated his father. But Henry is not yet dead; he awakens to find his son wearing the crown and bitterly upbraids him for his unseemly haste. Hal apologizes and they are reconciled at the end, but the act of counterusurpation has been symbolically performed. And the symbolism is not empty, for throughout both *Henry IV* plays Hal has been psychologically and politically distanced from his father—so much so that at one point Henry wishes aloud that his son had been exchanged in the cradle with the chief rebel, Harry Hotspur. Significantly, when Hal comes to the throne, he discards the nickname "Hal" and adopts the name of the rebel, "Harry," as his familiar appellation. Hal has robbed the robber; or, to put it in terms of coinage, he has reminted the coin of sovereignty.

But Hal does not keep the money stolen from the travelers on Gad's Hill. The very name—"God's Hill"—connotes that the events that happen there, between London and Canterbury, the civil and the spiritual capitals of Britain, are of a ritual importance matching that of the martyrdom of the Archbishop Thomas à Becket. Another Henry, the Second, had been the cause of Thomas's death in much the same fashion as Henry IV had been the death of Richard II. Hal has expiated the crime, but he must still, so to speak, make restitution, return the money. To whom does he owe the crown? The answer is, to the people of England. Hal now proceeds to pay it back, and the paying is the work of his reign. His royalty consists, so to speak, in the continuous paying of "royalties" to the people of the land, who are the authors of the authority over which he has copyright. The play in which Hal receives his true title, Henry V, is Shakespeare's vision of what a genuine king should be, that is, the leader whose constant work is the emancipation of his subjects. When Hal, now Henry V, wanders his camp on the eve of the battle of Agincourt, speaking incognito with the common soldiers and presenting himself as Harry le Roy and the servant of England, there is a distinct premonition of the ideal role of the American president, the first citizen, the ruler as recycler of sovereignty back to the people. It is a reversal of Henry IV's stratagem of disguising his followers as himself. Instead of betrayal and execution, which are the fate of rebels against the counterfeit King Henry IV, the loyal soldier who challenges the disguised Harry gets a glove full of gold coins.

The restoring of the stolen property is a process, one that is never ending, and one that constitutes the true function of sovereign rule. There is, I believe, a direct line of political theory running from Shakespeare through Hobbes and Locke to the framers of the American constitution. This line of theory is essentially economic. That is, as we have seen, the establishment of just government is fundamentally a matter of property rights and only secondarily one of political or even human rights. This idea may seem to contradict our most idealistic beliefs, that human and political rights precede property rights. Indeed they may precede them in *importance,* but, if my analysis of Shakespeare's reasoning is correct, not in order of *achievement.* Political and human rights cannot be achieved until property rights are secured.

Recent world events seem to confirm this view. The rush toward free market democracy all over the planet has provided a reality experiment in whether the goal is best achieved by establishing political and human rights first, or by creating a healthy market economy first. Nations that tried the former, preserving command economies while opening up the voting process and giving legal protection to individuals, have tended to sink into economic chaos where the actual suffering of people is greater than it would have been under a benign tyranny. The prime example is Russia, but India and some of the former Iron Curtain countries and ex-Soviet republics also spring to mind. On the other hand, nations that preserved what to us is rightly an unacceptable level of political control and suppression of individual freedom, while opening up the forces of the market and economic development, have usually crossed a threshold at which democratic institutions and personal liberties have emerged after a transitional period. Examples abound—South Korea, Chile, Spain, Brazil, Taiwan, Portugal, Argentina, the Philippines, and many others, including of course (though it took hundreds of years, because it was the first) Britain itself. In another generation, or sooner, China and Singapore will have bourgeois electorates capable of responsibly limiting governmental control; Mexico, well on the road to economic progress, is showing signs of cleaning up its one-party corruption; Indonesia has reached the point where capitalism creates the forces to overthrow tyranny; and Poland, Hungary, and the Czech Republic have already turned the corner by concentrating on market solutions. Nelson Mandela has the unenviable task of making South Africa rich before it can be just; if he can succeed, much of Africa, now sunk in the double disaster of controlled economies and political repression, may follow. But his nation will not be just until it is rich.

Henry V, then, is a remote prototype of a new conception of sovereignty, as the protector of property rights and the guardian of the free market *and only thus* the bringer of personal and political liberty. But we have not yet dealt with what is perhaps the most painful part of his story, one that, however, is an essential part of his ritual myth of relegitimation. What is to be done with Falstaff? Falstaff has provided the boar's head that is temporarily inscribed on Hal's coin instead of the head of the usurper. But that bestial inscription must itself be defaced in order that "Harry-as-representative-of-the-people" can be stamped on it instead. The crown of the king of the May must in turn be usurped; the rule of natural man, the animal-headed biped, must itself be brought to a bloody and sacrificial end—or rather, it must be transformed into the regime of the legitimate monarch.

"Banish plump Jack, and banish all the world" (II.iv.484). These were the words by which Falstaff, in the first part of *Henry IV,* had presented Hal's problem. Hal had faced it squarely, saying to himself, "I do, I will." But when it comes to it, the act is painful. The newly crowned Henry V, on his coronation procession, encounters the fat old man. Falstaff calls out to him: "My king! My Jove! I speak to thee, my heart!" Generations of critics have been chilled by Henry's reply:

> I know thee not, old man. Fall to thy prayers.
> How ill white hairs becomes a fool and jester! . . .
> Presume not that I am the thing I was.
> (*2 Henry IV,* V.v.46)

And so follows, in *Henry V,* the pathos of Falstaff's death. "The king has killed his heart," says Mistress Quickly, unconsciously suggesting that the sacrifice involves the traditional cutting out of the victim's heart (II.i.89). In one of the most moving of all epitaphs, she indignantly denies that Falstaff has gone to hell and insists that "He's in Arthur's bosom, if ever man went to Arthur's bosom" (II.iii.9). Arthur's bosom, not that of Abraham or Jehovah or even Christ. Falstaff has gone to a third place, neither heaven nor hell; perhaps it is the old elfland, where the small folk still weave their dances under the green hill. Arthur is of course the legendary and archetypal king of England, standing for a national continuity that is pre-Christian and deeply identified with the fertility of the soil and the turning of the seasons— a continuity that has been Christianized, but that keeps its ancient festivals beneath the surface. Shakespeare underlines this interpretation when Henry V condemns Bardolph, Falstaff's old companion, to death for looting a church. The Hanged Man is another ancient symbol of the sacrificed nature god (who will miraculously resurrect himself in the coming spring). The result of the human sacrifice with which Henry begins his reign is not the disappearance of the mythic energies that Falstaff embodies, but their incorporation into the new king himself. The legitimacy of the monarchy is refounded upon this sacrifice, and the charisma of the king is restored because of its demonstrated and tragic cost.

There follows victory over a foreign enemy, and a fertile marriage. *Henry V* concludes with Henry's successful wooing of Katherine, the daughter of the king of France, and their decision to beget a son together who will inherit both kingdoms. So the final symbol of the solution to the problem of the legitimation of value is a marriage, which is explicitly a bond of love and property. As Henry puts it: "Kate, when France is mine and I am yours, then yours is France, and you are mine" (V.ii.177). Like *A Midsummer Night's Dream,* this great cycle of history plays ends with a royal wedding, the "blessed bond of board and bed."

The Well-Struck Coin

In economic terms, the royal marriage is equivalent to the effective bonding of the metal and the inscription of a coin of the realm. In *A Midsummer Night's Dream* we saw how the inscription by itself is not enough to make a seal or coin genuine; the material must cooperate and will refuse a stamp that denies its nature. In *Henry IV* we found out the corollary: it is not enough to have good metal if the stamp is illegitimate, and the stamp can only be legitimated by sacrifice.

Just how pressing this issue was for Shakespeare may be understood in the light of the trial of Christopher Marlowe. Marlowe was Shakespeare's friend, fellow poet, and brother dramatist. He was one of the only contemporaries that Shakespeare ever directly referred to in his plays—in *As You Like It,* written shortly after Marlowe's death in 1593, Shakespeare addresses him sadly as "dead shepherd" (III.v.81). At the time of Marlowe's murder in a tavern brawl, Marlowe was on trial for his life, on charges of treason and heresy. Some scholars believe he was killed to prevent him from revealing sensitive material in open court, for Marlowe had been a secret agent in the employ of Francis Walsingham, the queen's spymaster. But the interesting thing for our purposes was that one of the charges against Marlowe was that he had, in his cups, claimed that he, Marlowe, had as good a right to strike coins as the queen did. This claim is entirely consistent with Marlowe's whole wild, doomed, speculative adventure. Many in his time identified Marlowe with his most celebrated creation, Dr. Faustus, the brilliant scholar who sells his soul to the devil in exchange for knowledge and power—and Marlowe himself, who had a taste for publicity, did little to dispel the impression. Like others of the circle of Walter Raleigh, the "School of Night," Marlowe was thought to consort with supernatural powers and nature spirits; and at the same time he was associated with the origins of modern science, for the School of Night included physicists, explorers, mathematicians, chemists, astronomers, and the man who was perhaps the first inventor of the telescope, that same Thomas Hariot whom we have encountered already. As a spy, Marlowe existed between the legal and moral systems of nations, in a state of nature, prior to the covenants of sovereignty.

In claiming that he could mint coins if he pleased, Marlowe was asserting the arbitrariness of legitimacy, and claiming that the universe would accept whatever inscription an artist might give it. It is the claim of the hubristic artist, very familiar in our own time, that denies the original and given, and challenges any transcendent source of meaning. Today such critical movements as Deconstruction and Foucauldian discourse analysis deny even to the author the privilege of the originating presence, the role of the giver of what is given; instead the critic, as the final interpreter, is left holding the field with the unchallenged claim to be the final inscriber, the mint of all meaning.

This reduction to absurdity, which now holds the discipline of literary study in a state of paralysis, was not unforeseen by Marlowe himself, though he was unable to resist the imaginative excitement of his devil's bargain. In *Doctor Faustus* the result of Faust's transaction with Mephistophilis is not a grand voyage of discovery but a grotesque and pointless farce, filled with images of dismemberment, fragmentation, deconstruction, sterility, and hallucination. The one thing that Mephistophilis refuses to Faustus when Faustus demands it is a true and fertile marriage, though Faustus can of course have any whore he wishes, even Helen of Troy. (She will of course, being in an Elizabethan play, be acted by a boy.) Because he was a homosexual, Marlowe's insight here is especially poignant.

Shakespeare shared his friend's hubris and delight in the newly discovered powers of the Renaissance artist, as is clear from the great speeches of Prospero in *The Tempest* that celebrate his "so potent art" (V.i.50). But Shakespeare also had the wisdom to see that Marlowe's death was of a piece with Marlowe's chosen life of debauchery, blasphemy, wit, and defiance. There is more than a trace of Marlowe's character in the portrait of Falstaff. Just as Hal must banish fat Jack, so Shakespeare must finally reject the claims of his dead friend Kit Marlowe. The reason should now be clear. To put it in economic terms, an economy in which counterfeiting is legitimate is one in which no coin has value. In *A Midsummer Night's Dream* and the plays that tell the story of the accession of Henry V, Shakespeare shows where Marlowe was wrong and establishes a basis for a new kind of economy, one that recognizes the limits of both economic "fundamentals" and the financial instruments and bonds with which we attempt to control them. Shakespeare provides in poetic terms a guide to the sacrificial mechanism by which the "derivatives" of social authority and political charisma can be tied back to the fundamentals of natural increase and identifies the criteria for legitimate minting.

We live today at a time in American history when there is a similar questioning of legitimacy, a similar debate over the nature of our coinage. A few years ago, the Congress and the president, locked in philosophical conflict over the national debt, brought the federal government to a standstill. Today a president whose sign might well be a boar's head rules a country of great wealth that is losing faith in its government. What might a writer in today's America make of Shakespeare's solutions? America clearly needs a mythic history that will identify it as a nation and enable it to contain in one picture both its historic crimes of dispossession, genocide, and enslavement, and also its grand and unprecedented human achievements in political freedom, economic prosperity, technological progress, and cultural creativity. Such a writer might perhaps imagine some great fiction, in which the full mystery of the American land is concentrated into a larger-than-life character; in which a future hero or heroine has the task of legitimating the American Dream; in which a tragic sacrifice takes place; in which the old debts of our society, which can never be paid off, are anchored by the sacrifice in the substance of reality itself and the open-endedness of the future; and in which a new unity, including the mythic powers of the old regime and the justice of the new, are recombined in a marriage and a heroic act of coinage.

7

"thou owest god a death"

Debt, Time, and the Parable of the Talents

Talents

In the Gospel of Matthew, 25:14–30, Jesus tells a remarkable parable. The kingdom of heaven, he says, is like a wealthy man who goes traveling and lends his three servants money (reckoned in weights of specie called talents) until his return. The servant that gets five talents uses the money to trade and doubles the money to ten, which he gives to his master on his return. The servant that gets two talents also doubles the money, to four, and renders it to his master. The wealthy man praises these two servants and promotes them, effectively making them partners in his firm. The third servant buries his talent in the ground and repays it unrisked and unenhanced, explaining that he was afraid that the master, who has a hard reputation of reaping where he has not sown, would blame him if he lost the money in a risky venture. The master condemns him and orders the one talent to be taken away and given to the servant with ten talents, explaining angrily that the one-talent servant should at least have "put [the] money to the exchangers"—played the financial market—so that he could have given it back with usury (interest). "For unto every one that hath shall be given," Jesus concludes, ". . . but from him that hath not shall be taken away even that which he hath."

This disturbing story is traditionally taken to be about our duty to develop the natural capabilities given us by God, that it is not enough to sit on one's bodily and mental gifts, preserving them for the final audit of death; we are expected to risk them in the world, make something of ourselves, and have something to show for our lives. This metaphorical interpretation, which comfortably internalizes and defuses the problematic financial and interpersonal implications of the story, is no doubt partially correct. Indeed, the word "talent," which had always meant a physical weight (with metaphorical extensions in the senses of counterweight, tax, charge, cost, punishment, retaliation, and money denominations) has now come in English to mean exclusively a special ability or psychological gift, because of the weight of this interpretation of the parable. But the parable also has a more direct and less palatable meaning, concerning the morality of commerce, whose implications are the more fascinating and far-reaching for having been muffled through so many centuries of prejudice against business.

The fundamental structure of the parable is that we start out in debt, having taken out a loan (from God, from the physical world, from nature, from our ancestors, from our parents, from our nation), and that it is not enough that we repay the principal; we are justly being charged interest as well. In other words, we are expected to reimburse the lender for the time during which we have the use of the loan; the value we have been given is not the value of the money but the value of the money *times* the amount of time we have the manage of it. What this means is that we have to run just to stand still; it is up to us to increase the value of what we have been lent, by at least the interest rate, and preferably by more still. The master has bought a bond in the servant's enterprise, which must be redeemed when it expires at a face value higher than what the master paid for it.

The parable adds, however, that if we, the servant, can show a sufficiently favorable return on the investment, that is, if we treat the bondholder as a shareholder in our business and pay him not just the stipulated interest but also the dividend accorded to a part owner, the original bond may be exchanged at its expiry for a share in the *lender's* enterprise—the servant is made a stockholder in the master's firm. Thus the use of time becomes the key issue; time must be cultivated and enriched at a faster rate than the interest on the loan; if we can do so, treating our creditor as we would a shareholder, we can ourselves be transformed from a debtor into an owner, so that we and our former creditor now own stock in each other's businesses. By the proper use of time—"use" in the financial sense—the bond we owed can become a unit of profitable stock that we own, and the interest we once paid over the passage of time now becomes due to us.

An old, rather blasphemous song from the sixties made fun of the shady economics of fundamentalist and evangelical religion:

> Jesus puts his money in the First National Bank,
> Jesus puts his money in the First National Bank,
> Jesus puts his money in the First National Bank,
> Jesus saves.

But the connection between saving as the accumulation of money at interest and saving as spiritual salvation is not an altogether frivolous or coincidental one. Words that have the same sound but unconnected meanings tend to drift apart; but "save" remains resolutely ambiguous, because its different meanings amplify rather than suppress each other.

Jesus' parable is a kind of gloss on the story of Jacob and Laban, another story of saving and salvation, which Shylock quotes in *The Merchant of Venice*. In the story Jacob serves as the ranch manager for his uncle and father-in-law, Laban, who is, like the master in Jesus' parable, a hard man who reaps where he does not sow. Jacob is so expert and creative in his work that he makes Laban a rich man, and despite the fact that Laban keeps changing the rules of his employment, Jacob ends up with both of Laban's daughters and huge flocks and herds of his own. He serves seven years for Laban's elder daughter, Leah, seven years for the younger daughter, Rachel, and six years for his share of Laban's flocks and herds. Jacob's peculiar expertise seems to be in animal breeding: he mates the most vigorous stock in his uncle's herds and improves the breeds. His knowledge of stock breeding is symbolized by the rather mysterious procedure of setting up a peeled branch before the herds when they come to drink; this peeled branch, the staff of Jacob, is interpreted in the Zohar as being the same as the rod of Moses, the staff that can change into a snake and back. It is also connected with the institution of circumcision, the process by which a Hebrew male was enabled to give birth to himself a second time and be reborn in the spirit. The staff of Moses is said in ancient Jewish folk tradition to have been given to him by the angel Metatron, who is the messenger spirit between God and human beings. The staff was originally a branch of the Tree of Life, from which Metatron plucked it when the world was young. Sometimes the staff itself is called Metatron; like Ningizzida, the Mesopotamian messenger god, who is depicted alternatively as a caduceus or in human form with two snakes coming out of his shoulders, the god and his symbol are confused. Metatron's rod is thus one version of the magic staff shared by many circum-Mediterranean and Asian religions, and is a direct analogue of the caduceus of Hermes/Mercury. As we have already seen, the caduceus is an exact diagram of the double-helix DNA molecule. Jacob is evidently an ancient expert in recombinant DNA! Jacob's genetic expertise, the story insists, is taught to him by God, who also promises to bless Jacob himself with a multitude of descendants.

Thus among other things the story is about what one might call traditional evolutionary theory. Success is defined as reproductive success; Jacob is the fittest in these terms. He himself sires twelve sons by various women. He prospers by acting as a selective force on his herds, accelerating their evolution by what in modern terms we would call genetic engineering. What the story says about God is that God is the spirit of evolution and the true guide for what will survive into the future. But God too reaps where he does not sow: a rentier, so to speak, an owner of the means of production who gives employment to his workers. God, like Laban, is a kind of friendly adversary whose demands for repayment create the economic discipline and stimulate the technical ingenuity that ensure prosperity, and whose arbitrary tests warrant the survivor as the rightful heir to the future. The Bible story hammers this point home by having Jacob wrestle all night with a man (usually interpreted as an angel) who actually turns out to have been God himself. Jacob suffers a torn sinew in his groin from this battle, but gets in recompense a divine blessing, and a new name: Israel, that is, the position of ancestor to the whole nation. Jacob, the great saver, is saved.

Let us return to Jesus' version of the story. The master expects a return on his money equivalent to what a competent money manager could get by playing the financial markets over the period of time the master is away. The interest rate represents the cost of time. In present-day scientific terms the cost of time is the increase of entropy, or thermodynamic disorder. The increase of entropy shows up in human life in the process of aging—including the onset of menopause, which is a key element in the Jacob and Laban story and in the whole related cycle of stories in Genesis. As Shakespeare describes it so movingly in the Sonnets, we, and the physical world around us, wear out over time. The order that we inherit is a loan, which not only must be repaid, but also carries with it a finance charge; the repayment is death, and the finance charge is aging. But two of the servants in the story manage to beat the entropic market rate. Jesus says that they do it through trade, which means that if he has the Jacob and Laban story in mind, which he surely must, Jesus equates trade with the process of evolutionary husbandry practiced by Jacob. In other parables of production, such as that of the sower, Jesus explicitly outlines the process of natural selection that enables one seed to bring forth a hundredfold while another brings forth only fortyfold and another none at all. Thus trade, or productive business, is the continuation of the natural process of creative evolution, and it is one way in which we can use the investment loan of our lives and the available resources of nature to beat the interest rate of entropy.

These economics coincide closely with certain leading ideas in contemporary cosmological physics. The universe is subject to the increase of thermodynamic disorder over time; the demands of Laban and of the master in the parable cannot be denied. But other processes are at work. The enormous pressure within the dense primal fireball causes it to expand. As the universe expands, it cools, according to Boyle's Law. The cooling process itself triggers spontaneous symmetry breaking, as when crystals suddenly form in a supersaturated cooling solution, or frost flowers blossom on a winter windowpane—as predicted by Josiah Gibbs's free energy formula. Crystals and frost may seem very symmetrical, but they are much less so, forming along specific planes and axes as they do, than the omnidirectional symmetry of the liquid or vapor that gave them birth. That symmetry breaking can give rise to higher levels of order, embodied in more and more complex molecular forms whose asymmetries paradoxically provide a whole new field of opportunities for new kinds of symmetry to emerge. These forms must in turn compete with one another for survival and thus further elaborate themselves, until in at least one place in the universe they generated the amazing variety of living organisms, including Jacob's rams and ewes, and Jacob himself. Thus the evolutionary view of the universe corresponds nicely with the biblical conception that life is a debt to be repaid with interest, but also an investment, which if properly used can yield a return superior to the interest rate.

These implications were quite clear to Shakespeare, who adopts the basic structure of the parable of the talents in his theory of debt and interest. We have already looked at Sonnet 11, where Shakespeare identifies economic and evolutionary profit:

> Let those whom Nature hath not made for store,
> Harsh, featureless, and rude, barrenly perish.
> Look whom she best endowed, she gave the more;
> Which bounteous gift thou shouldst in bounty cherish.
> She carved thee for her seal, and meant thereby
> Thou shouldst print more, not let that copy die.

In *Timon of Athens* Shakespeare works out the terrible consequences of failing to put one's literal talents—of gold or silver—to use. *The Merchant of Venice* shows Antonio, the classic entrepreneur, risking his talents on the high seas for high stakes; Bassanio in turn uses the three thousand ducats he borrows from Antonio as "a sprat to catch a mackerel," a modest investment ventured at risk to gain a big reward, in just the entrepreneurial spirit of the first and second servants in the parable; and the reward he seeks is the right to sire Portia's children. In *A Funeral Elegy,* a poem recently proved by the scholar Donald Foster to have been composed by Shakespeare, we find a concise expression of the theme:

> Then in a book where every work is writ
> Shall this man's actions be revealed, to show
> The gainful fruit of well-employed wit,
> Which paid to Heaven the debt that it did owe.

The theme of debt and repayment is clearest of all in the *Henry IV* plays, where there is a fascinating contrast between what one might call the "loan management" strategies of Falstaff and Prince Hal.

Debt and Death: Falstaff's Version

Just before the Battle of Shrewsbury Falstaff confides with disarming honesty to Prince Hal that he wishes it were bedtime and that all were well. This is a wonderfully direct expression of the feeling we all have about great challenges, tests, and dangers; we would like to leap over the time of trial and instantly put it into the past, where the uncertainty would be removed and the stress of action stilled. Hal's reply to Falstaff answers the deep assumptions Falstaff is making rather than the explicit content of what he says: "Why, thou owest God a death" (V.i.126). Falstaff immediately picks up on Hal's meaning in his own fashion, which is by means of the pun between "death" and "debt": " 'Tis not due yet," says Falstaff. "I would be loath to pay him before his day." In Elizabethan English debt and death would have been much closer in sound than they are today, and their connection was a stock theme of the pulpit. Christ was the redeemer in the financial sense, the repayer of a bond; his sacrifice pays the ransom owed by humankind to its diabolical captor; he buys us out of the prison of death to which we condemned ourselves by the Fall; he becomes the pledge or pawn of our collective salvation. The poetry of the Battle of Shrewsbury is saturated with images of payment, loan, redemption, and the cost of time: this is Prince Hal on the subject:

> In both your armies there is many a soul
> Shall pay full dearly for this encounter . . .
> (V.i.83)

And this is Harry Hotspur:

> O gentlemen, the time of life is short!
> To spend that shortness basely were too long . . .
> (V.ii.81)

And now Falstaff, punning on "shot," meaning both the bill for an evening's drinking and a bullet, and on "score" as an account and as a blow:

Though I could scape shot-free at London, I fear the shot here. Here's no scoring but upon the pate.
(V.iii.30)

Falstaff, claiming falsely to have killed Percy:

> I have paid Percy, I have made him sure.
> (V.iii.47)

Prince Hal again:

> It is the Prince of Wales that threatens thee,
> Who never promiseth but he means to pay.
> (V.iv.40)

Hotspur in his dying speech, using the metaphors of "titles" (sealed documents of legitimate ownership) and "survey" (the legal assessment of real property lines in the settlement of a debt) to lament the loss of his honors:

> O Harry, thou hast robbed me of my youth!
> I better brook the loss of brittle life

Than those proud titles thou hast won of me.
They wound my thoughts worse than thy sword my flesh.
But thoughts, the slaves of life, and life, time's fool,
And time, that takes survey of all the world,
Must have a stop.
(V.iv.75)

Falstaff, again, describing what Douglas would have done to him had he not feigned death:

that hot termagant Scot had paid me scot and lot too.
(V.iv.111)

"Scot and lot" were parish taxes, the interest that the village makes us pay on our property, the municipal equivalent of the increase that the master expects on his talents. Later in his life, in 1605, Shakespeare invested a large sum (440 pounds, very roughly equivalent to $440,000 in contemporary money) in "a lease of tithes," in the vicinity of Stratford, whereby the lender could draw the (mostly agricultural) income otherwise due to the parish. The arrangement was like a modern municipal bond. Thus Shakespeare himself was to become a master of the vineyard, receiving taxes rather than paying them.

Falstaff's wish that he could be in bed and the battle over is unrealistic precisely because it ignores the cost of time. In the first place, what makes time the medium of human existence is precisely that time must be gone through, experienced, with all its open-ended uncertainty; we cannot abolish an uncomfortable piece of it. In the second place, time, as Hotspur says, has inevitable endings. Falstaff would like to delay the repayment of the debt of time indefinitely. As he says later of his borrowing habits: "I can get no remedy against this consumption of the purse [he is thinking of consumption as the wasting disease that we now know as tuberculosis]. Borrowing only lingers and lingers it out, but the disease is incurable" (2 *Henry IV,* I.ii.239). Falstaff's solution to the problem of debt is ingenious; just keep borrowing, and your creditors will not be able to afford your going bankrupt and will keep you afloat.

As we saw in the previous chapter, Falstaff is being prepared as a sacrifice, to redeem the legitimacy of the English crown. Part of that preparation is, strangely, the accumulation of his indebtedness. It is as if he were taking on the sins of the whole nation, like a scapegoat; and at the same time as if his consumption of the good things of the earth—"consumption" in its other sense, Falstaff being the consummate consumer!—makes him the fattest of beasts and thus the fittest and most acceptable for sacrifice, in the deep and terrible mythic economy of the play. When Falstaff has amassed enough debt to England in the form of money, food, and goods, he crosses a threshold at which he must now pay with his vitality, his grand richness of being, his fertile warmth: "Now I, to comfort him," says Mistress Quickly of the dying Falstaff,

> bid him 'a should not think of God; I hoped there was no need to trouble himself with any such thoughts yet. So 'a bade me lay more clothes on his feet. I put my hand into the bed, and felt them, and they were as cold as any stone. Then I felt to his knees, and so upward, and upward, and all was as cold as any stone. (*Henry V,* II.iii.19)

Falstaff is in the last stages of consumption, and what is consuming him is the earth and stone of England itself, taking back its loan.

But strangely, it gets back a greater vital heat in the end than it spent on his riotous living; for in Falstaff England has forever its own grand image of the boon companion, the irreverent wit, the enjoyer of life, Father Christmas, the king of the May, the fat and jolly old man who makes us laugh. His genius was to transform thermodynamic energy (in the form of fat capons, eggs and butter, gold, and vast quantities of sherris-sack) into informational energy (in the form of wit, anecdotes, and a mythic national story). The fact that he is objectively a wicked man, who lies congenitally, robs strangers, cheats his friends, drinks to excess, fornicates at every opportunity, abuses for profit his official position as an army recruiter, deliberately leads his ragamuffin troops into a position where they will be wiped out by gunfire in order to draw their pay, and falsely takes credit for Hal's victory over Hotspur does not make his sacrifice any less painful. We do not live in a correct world whose moral budget is in balance, but in a tragicomic world of debt, incomplete transactions, and mixed feelings.

The biblical master on his return might at first glance condemn Falstaff even more roundly than he did the servant who returned the single talent; Falstaff, after all, has spent *his* talent and borrowed and spent several more. But in his own way Falstaff does put what he borrowed from the master to good use. He certainly does not bury his talents, but risks them in trade; and the issue is whether what he has to show for them at the audit of his death is an acceptable form of profit. At least he earns a place in "Arthur's bosom"— though not, as we have noted, in God's or Abraham's—by investing his talents in mirth and wit and storytelling. Arthur, the old god of England, reckons things in his own way, it seems; and perhaps there is a place in the lake island of Avalon, the resting place of the merry English kings, for the greatest jester in the world, even if his services are expensive.

Debt and Death: Prince Hal's Version

Prince Hal's strategy of debt management is rather different from Falstaff's. Hal "never promises but he means to pay." From the very beginning he has planned a spectacular dividend on the risky investment England has made in him:

> So when this loose behavior I throw off
> And pay the debt I never promisèd,

> By how much better than my word I am,
> By so much shall I falsify men's hopes,
> And like bright metal on a sullen ground,
> My reformation, glitt'ring o'er my fault,
> Shall show more goodly and attract more eyes
> Than that which hath no foil to set it off.
> I'll so offend to make offense a skill,
> Redeeming time when men least think I will.
> (I.ii.205)

"Redeeming time" comes from the epistle of Paul to the Ephesians (5:1 ff.), a passage worth quoting at length in this context, as it is Paul's own gloss on how one should invest the loan of life that Christ refers to in the parable of the talents:

1 Be ye therefore followers of God, as dear children:
2 And walk in love, as Christ also hath loved us, and hath given himself for us an offering and a sacrifice to God for a sweet-smelling savour.
3 But fornication, and all uncleanness, or covetousness, let it not be once named among you, as becometh saints;
4 Neither filthiness, nor foolish talking, nor jesting, which are not convenient: but rather giving of thanks.
5 For this ye know, that no whoremonger, nor unclean person, nor covetous man, who is an idolater, hath any inheritance in the kingdom of Christ and of God. . . .
18 And be not drunk with wine, wherein is excess; but be filled with the Spirit. . . .
13 But all things that are reproved are made manifest by the light: for whatsoever doth make manifest is light.
14 Wherefore he saith, Awake thou that sleepest, and arise from the dead, and Christ shall give thee light.
15 See then that ye walk circumspectly, not as fools, but as wise,
16 Redeeming the time, because the days are evil.

I have altered the sequence of these verses slightly to make a point. What Paul is condemning is exactly what Falstaff is, and what Hal chooses as his surrogate father. The Boar's Head gang are referred to directly as "Ephesians . . . of the old church"—that is, those whom Paul condemned (2 *Henry IV*, II.ii.149). Paul wants us to use the loan of life by transforming it into spiritual goods—into what he calls light, which, in good agreement with today's information science, he correctly identifies with information ("whatsoever doth make manifest is light"). If we do so we will share, as in the story of Jacob and in the parable of the talents, in the "inheritance" of "God." This is the meaning of "redeeming time" for Paul.

But Prince Hal and Shakespeare give the idea a further twist. For Paul, the redeeming sacrifice is Christ. But for Hal, the sacrifice is going to be Falstaff, and with Falstaff Hal's own youth, his personal existence as a private human being, his pleasure, even his old name. Hal is to become a "new man," to be reborn of the spirit as Paul puts it; but Shakespeare seems to have figured out a way to keep what is good and valuable and fertile about Falstaff, what is dear to the bosom of Arthur as well as what is dear to the bosom of Abraham. Or perhaps we could put it thus: Jesus himself was the companion of publicans and sinners, and the friend of the Magdalen; he might even have kept company with the likes of Falstaff. Jesus tells the parable of the prodigal son, who spends his inheritance and comes back penniless, yet who is welcomed and rewarded by his loving father, much to the annoyance of his good brother. Perhaps Christ is wiser here than Paul, and perhaps Shakespeare has perceived this fact and provided Hal with a deeper solution to the problem than the puritanical one outlined in Paul's epistle. But how can the parable of the talents be reconciled with that of the prodigal? The answer must be that the prodigal son has, somehow, amassed certain invisible goods that constitute an acceptable return on the investment of his father. Perhaps he has made a sacrifice—of his youthful independence, of his riotous ways?—that makes him shine more brightly in his father's affections than the dutiful son who has, after all, rendered back only what he has been given.

Luckily Hal gives us another example of his methods of self-redemption, in how he deals with his rival Hotspur. In *1 Henry IV*, III. ii, the prince has a most unpleasant interview with his coldly furious father, Henry IV. Henry repeats his wish that Hal had been exchanged with Harry Percy, the Hotspur, in the cradle, and calls Hal his "nearest and dearest enemy." Hal replies:

> I will redeem all this on Percy's head
> And, in the closing of some glorious day,
> Be bold to tell you that I am your son,
> When I will wear a garment all of blood,
> And stain my favors in a bloody mask,
> Which, washed away, shall scour my shame with it. . . .
> Percy is but my factor, good my lord,
> To engross up glorious deeds on my behalf;
> And I will call him to so strict account
> That he shall render every glory up,
> Yea, even the slightest worship of his time,
> Or I will tear the reckoning from his heart. . . .
> If not, the end of life cancels all bands. . .
> (132)

Hotspur, then, is the sacrifice of *Henry IV, Part One*, as Falstaff is the sacrifice of *Henry IV, Part Two*. The point is that Hal is not proposing to eliminate what Hotspur is, but to appropriate it for himself. Harry Hotspur is a rebel; if Hal is going to appropriate what Hotspur is, that will logically include Hotspur's great gifts and talents of rebellion! Hal will become the better qualified for his eventual legitimating usurpation of the throne from his usurping father. Hotspur is Hal's "factor," his agent or servant or broker, who will increase Hal's loaned talents through the risky trade of war; and Hal will be the master who demands a reckoning. The sacrificing priest takes on the characteristics both of the victim and of the god to whom he sacrifices; Hal takes on the heroic rebellious qualities of Hotspur together with the legitimacy of the British royal line.

And the strategy of the much greater sacrifice, of Falstaff, is much the same. Hal does not reject the vital warmth, the merry wit, the insight, and the pleasures of Falstaff; he incorporates them into himself. This is the key move, which Paul cannot make in Ephesians, where we are called on to simply reject the joys of wine, jesting, and licentiousness. When Hal sees Falstaff counterfeiting death on the battlefield, the moment is emblematic: the prince stands between his two sacrifices, the dead Hotspur and the apparently dead Falstaff. He grieves for his friend:

> What, old acquaintance? Could not all this flesh
> Keep in a little life? Poor Jack, farewell!
> I could have better spared a better man.
> O, I should have a heavy miss of thee
> If I were much in love with vanity.
> Death hath not struck so fat a deer today,
> Though many dearer, in this bloody fray.
> Emboweled will I see thee by-and-by;
> Till then in blood by noble Percy lie.
> (V.iv.100)

The pun on "deer," "dear" (beloved), and "dear" (expensive) sums up the whole mythic transaction. Like Henry IV, Falstaff is a counterfeit and must eventually be melted down. But Falstaff's time has not yet come. In a comic resurrection after Hal has exited, Falstaff "*riseth up*," as the stage direction puts it, and unintentionally describes what will, symbolically, happen to him in *Henry V.*

> Emboweled? If thou embowel me today, I'll give you leave to powder
> me and eat me too tomorrow. 'Sblood, 'twas time to counterfeit . . .
> (V.iv.109)

Death, as Hal has said to his father, "cancels all bands [bonds]"; but Hal has found a way to turn the deaths of others into shares of the kingdom, to incorporate Hotspur's valor and Falstaff's merriment into his own new conception of kingship. Harry le Roy will need both qualities on the battlefield of Agincourt: the first to endure the terrors of war, the second to hearten and inspire his troops, and in the long run to make possible the enfranchisement

Friar Lawrence scolds poor Romeo in the language of finance, adding to the charge that he is an unwise investor the further charge that he is like an improperly formed contract seal, that he has the shape of a man but the inconstant substance of wax—an idea with which we are already familiar in *A Midsummer Night's Dream* and the *Henry IV* plays:

> Fie, fie, thou shamest thy shape, thy love, thy wit,
> Which, like a usurer, abound'st in all,
> And usest none in that true use indeed
> Which should bedeck thy shape, thy love, thy wit.
> Thy noble shape is but a form of wax,
> Digressing from the valor of a man . . .
> (III.iii.122)

It seems, then, that we are caught in a double bind. According to the parable of the talents, we are not only in debt, but are more so every day by compound interest; yet if we rush to invest our resources, even if the investment is the highest-yield portfolio, faithful and devoted love, we are in terrible danger of losing everything in our own personal crash. Yet there is an investment policy that will generally pay off, and Shakespeare explores it in his last plays, especially *The Tempest*.

Sexual Delay as Investment Strategy

In *The Tempest* Prospero is faced, as a father, as the rightful duke of Milan, and as a wizard, with the responsibility of arranging the fortunes of the next generation in a more prosperous and auspicious way than those of his own generation. His very name suggests two ideas, both crucially related to Shakespeare's fundamental economic ideas: prosperity and hope for the future ("spero" means "I hope" in Latin, and "pro" is a prefix implying a future event). By his charms Prospero creates a storm and a shipwreck, which deliver to his magic island his former enemies, including his usurping brother. His plan is to take back his dukedom, but more important, to marry his daughter Miranda to Ferdinand, the heir to another of his former enemies, the king of Naples. Amity will be restored and old wrongs righted.

The plan depends crucially, then, on the success of the love match between Ferdinand and Miranda. It is not too difficult for Prospero to get these two beautiful and innocent young people to meet and fall in love. Nature is on his side. But the trick is to turn the natural reproductive intoxication into a truly human respect and friendship. He does this in two ways. The first is by pretending to deny Ferdinand's suit and taking on the role of the stern father. He lays upon Ferdinand the burdens that Laban laid on Jacob, that Jehovah laid on Adam in punishment of his disobedience in eating of the tree of knowledge. Prospero makes him labor, subjects him to shame, and forbids the free expression of love between the young people.

This has the effect of forcing them to disobey Prospero and thus assert their own will in sacrificial service to their love; more important still, it forces them to collude together, establishing their relationship on a basis of collaborative planning and work rather than just mutual enjoyment.

This done, Prospero reveals his deception and his true motive, which was to test the lovers and make them prove their commitment. But now he arranges a second test, more subtle than the first, and as unknown to them. He provides for them an exquisite, rather old-fashioned entertainment, a masque of spirits performing a poetic allegory of faithful love, in order to help them pass the time. He sits them down together in front of it—two young people so desperately in love they can barely keep their hands off each other—with this injunction to Ferdinand:

> If thou dost break her virgin-knot before
> All sanctimonious ceremonies may
> With full and holy rite be minist'red,
> No sweet aspersion shall the heavens let fall
> To make this contract grow; but barren hate,
> Sour-eyed disdain, and discord shall bestrew
> The union of your bed with weeds so loathly
> That you shall hate it both. Therefore take heed,
> As Hymen's lamps shall light you.
> (IV.i.15)

The key to avoiding time's destructive effects on love is resistance to the immediate gratification of desire. In this passage the destructiveness of time is symbolized by the weeds that will choke the garden of the lovers' bed, and the smoke that will choke the flame of Hymen's torch. The weeds may remind us of the "garden economics" of the Sonnets, where "lilies that fester smell far worse than weeds" (94), and Hamlet's description of the sensualities of corrupted Denmark: " 'tis an unweeded garden / That grows to seed. Things rank and gross in nature / Possess it merely" (I.ii.135). As for Hymen's lamps, it was believed that if the torches of the bridal ceremony burned clear, it would be a good omen for the marriage, but if they smoked, it boded ill. "There lives within the very flame of love / A kind of wick or snuff that will abate it," says Claudius, who, as the murdering usurper in *Hamlet,* has given himself over entirely to the world of power and entropic decay (IV.vii.114). Prospero, then, is using the postponement of desire as the means to weed the garden, to trim the flame of love so that it does not smoke, to defeat the process of increasing entropy by the use of its own weapons.

The series of ordeals and tests imposed by the wizard forces the lovers to repeat the evolutionary struggle through which the whole human race had to pass in the achievement of the higher moral virtues of love, honesty, self-control, insight into others, and acceptance of death. The tests imply the establishment of a mode of sexuality beyond the prehuman norm of mutual

rape, the evolutionary replacement of lust by marriage. They involve especially the capacity to remain silent: not to blurt out unthinkingly what is in
one's head but to observe, restrain oneself, wait, think, reflect. Freedom consists in an internal feedback loop, which can only be established if the immediate connection between stimulus and response, sense perception and expression, is temporarily broken. Freedom is an enlargement of the present
moment. Only in this way may an interval be made between irrevocable past
and predetermined future, an interval or delay in which a whole universe of
intention and creative decision can be opened up.

Prospero's masque of spirits reinforces the message of sexual delay. Prospero self-deprecatingly describes his masque as a mere vanity of his art, a
pastime, to while away the time before the nuptials. But like his modesty,
which implies a capacity for silence, the masque's function of postponement
is of fundamental importance. The gods of carnal desire, Venus and Cupid,
are kept back from the lovers, "Whose vows are, that no bed-right shall be
paid / Till Hymen's torch be lighted" (IV.i.96). Prospero, observing that Miranda and Ferdinand have started to kiss each other as they watch the play,
warns them:

> Do not give dalliance
> Too much the rein; the strongest oaths are straw
> To th' fire i' th' blood.
> (IV.i.51)

But the point is emphatically not that sex is dirty or any such nonsense.
What is dirty is the destruction of the interval of the present, and the bestial
unfreedom that is the result. That interval, properly taken, is not a frustra-
tion but a delight. Ferdinand comments on the masque:

> This is a most majestic vision, and
> Harmonious charmingly . . .
>   . . . Let me live here ever!
> So rare a wond'red father and a wise
> Makes this place Paradise.
> (IV.i.118)

Ferdinand's sudden insight is that there is a deliciousness in this time of waiting and anticipation, the ultimate and perhaps perverse human pleasure;
somehow the eros of the awaited moment bleeds into the rest of life, making
it precious, memorable, magical. This time is protected from any future pain
or grief by the sweet security of the consummation that is to come, which
serves to create a walled garden, an interior space that is infinitely cosy and
yet also mysterious, holy, even terrifying, steeped as it is in the strange perfume of the nuptial ordeal. Anyone who has seen the frescoes of Villa of the
Mysteries in Pompeii, where against a background of glowing dark red the
golden figures of the gods prepare a young girl for her wedding night, will

recognize what I mean. It is a time that is in and out of time, "When I shall think or Phoebus' steeds are foundered / Or Night kept chained below," as Ferdinand puts it (IV.i.30).

In our own era this sense of the sacred madness of delayed sex has been lost or reduced, written off as repression or brushed aside in the rush to instant gratification. The role of authority in controlling sexual activity has been almost universally condemned as religious mind control or political oppression; but perhaps we need gourmet chefs of love, like Prospero, to linger sexual anticipation out, to make it a cordon-bleu experience rather than a brutal gobbling of the fleshly hamburger. Even Mae West conceded that she liked a man who took his time. Sex is transubstantiated into love by poetically and ethically managed delay.

The Magic Island

Sex at the right moment, then, is the embodied version of paradise. Shakespeare gives us two poetic landscapes in the masque, one of a lovely shivery virgin potential, and one of gorgeous married fertility, the miracle of new growth and creation:

> Thy turfy mountains, where live nibbling sheep,
> And flat meads thatched with stover, them to keep;
> Thy banks with pionèd and twillèd brims,
> Which spongy April at thy hest betrims
> To make cold nymphs chaste crowns; and thy broom groves,
> Whose shadow the dismissèd bachelor loves,
> Being lasslorn; thy pole-clipt vineyard;
> And thy sea-marge, sterile and rocky-hard . . . .
> (IV.i.62)

This fresh, virginal landscape will be transformed into the rich harvest land of married love:

> Earth's increase, foison plenty,
> Barns and garners never empty,
> Vines with clust'ring bunches growing,
> Plants with goodly burden bowing;
> Spring come to you at the farthest
> In the very end of harvest.
> (IV.i.110)

But it is not only the lovers within the play who are sitting through a masque of spirits and undergoing certain tests of their emergent humanity. We, the audience, are too. The play itself is like the magic island, on which we are held captive by a magician, who is Shakespeare. This mythical place is in fact an archetype, which appears again and again in human stories and fairy tales—Eden, the Happy Hunting Grounds, Arcadia, the Islands of the Hesperides, the Chinese myth of the Western Mountain, the Celtic Island of the Blest, the Mesopotamian Dilmun, the Arthurian Avalon; it is the halls of Sarastro in *The Magic Flute,* Tolkien's Middle-Earth, Narnia, Oz. The magic land is as bright and fresh as a dream, as a rainbow; both dream and rainbow are part of its imagery. It is in brilliant Technicolor, where ordinary life is in shades of gray. It is the land in Prospero's masque, with its turfy mountains, its nibbling sheep, its crisp brooks, unshrubbed down and bosky acres, and its blue rainbow. It is an arcadian and pastoral place, cut off or islanded from the real world.

In the magic island different versions of reality can be tried out. As a land of dream it represents the alternative psychological spaces of the person, not bound by the convention of a single awake rational self. A political playground, it can serve as a *Gedankenexperiment*—a thought experiment—where various utopias can be tried out, including Gonzalo's naturalistic anarchy, Prospero's magical philosopher kingdom, the miniature mob dictatorship of Caliban, Trinculo, and Stephano. As an artistic space, the island is itself a theater, a picture frame, a field of musical thematic motifs. In another sense it is a sort of Disneyland, carnival, or circus. As in Aristophanes' Cloudcuckooland we are on holiday there and do not need to take things too seriously; though what we do there is the most serious thing in our lives, to find out the meaning of life. It is a test bed, limbeck, or laboratory for new ideas alchemical, psychological, social, scientific, and philosophical.

The magic land is also a fairyland, that is, a place intermediate in nature between heaven and hell. According to an old legend the fairies were originally angels neutral in the war between the hosts of Satan and St. Michael, who were cast out of heaven when Satan was defeated; they did not fall all the way to hell but settled in the middle air about the Earth, and offer a third way to the human seeker. When in the old Scots ballad Thomas the Rhymer sees a beautiful lady on a horse by the crossroads of the Eildon Tree, he asks her if she is the queen of heaven. She replies that she is not, but that she is the queen of fairyland, and that if he kisses her she will possess his body. Of course he does kiss her; she makes him get up on the horse behind her and they ride off through strange lands until they come to a place where three ways lead off from their path. One is the broad and easy road down to hell; one is the steep and rocky path up to heaven; but the third, which they take, is a bonny path that winds about the ferny brae. It is the road to fair elfland. That open-ended, helically winding, evolutionary third path, that yellow brick road, distinct from the dead ends of heaven and hell, is the way that Prospero points out to the prince and Miranda, and is the future of the human race.

The topology of the magic island is rather peculiar, and until the recent discovery of fractal geometry there existed no way of clearly describing it. It exists in the world but is cut off from it by a finite boundary, often spherical or circular ("the great globe itself" is Prospero's term, punning between the planet Earth and the Globe Theater, which would indeed "dissolve" [IV.i.153], as Prospero prophesied, in a fire two years after the first performance of *The Tempest*). The dome of the just pagans in Dante's *Inferno*, bounded on the outside but spacious and lit by its own light on the inside, is a precursor of this place. The cave of the dragon men in Blake's memorable fancy of the printing house in Hell is another version. Within the dome of the magic land there is an infinite inner space, much like mathematical Koch curves, the space-filling arabesques of Peano, or the infinitely recursive patterns of the Mandelbrot Set. The magic island is thus a symbol of a putative human capacity to create or discover a "Paradise within thee, happier far," as Milton puts it (*Paradise Lost,* XII.587), unlimited by our external constraints of space, time, and death, an informational universe that is boundlessly deep and generative, and that resists and reverses the tendency of the world to decay and run down. In another sense yet the magic land is both the land of the ever-living and the land of the dead. The implication is that it is a place where we cannot stay; we must leave it, as Prospero and his friends must leave the island, and return to real life. We discover the open-endedness of the world on the island but must return to Earth, where death is still to come, in order to pursue it.

Inheriting the Vineyard (Before the Reading of the Will?)

After the masque is over, Prospero sets one more test for the lovers: he leaves them alone together in his cave. It is a huge risk he is taking, but he has enough faith in them now to permit it. In the last scene of the play he will draw aside the curtain of his cell to reveal them to the assembled gentry on the island; much to his relief, we might imagine, they are not making the beast with two backs, but playing chess.

Deferral of desire itself creates a new pocket of time, complete with new tenses and verbal modes such as the conditionals, optatives, and subjunctives, within which new kinds of magic, and a dense new interplay of information—the poetry of life—can emerge. When Prospero draws aside the curtain of his cell to reveal the young lovers playing chess, they have entered a world of interpersonal complexity, one in which the natural physical strength of the male is cancelled and compulsion thus irrelevant; one in which one can cheat without wickedness, and be intimate without collapsing the delicate structure and dignity of personhood. Of course in marriage the miracle is accomplished, and we can be both beast and spirit; but we must first learn to be spirit and not beast. To learn how to make the game of life real, we must first learn how to make reality into a game.

Prospero's masque of spirits is just a pastime, in one sense—a delightful show to distract the lovers from their passionate desires. But in another sense it is a symbol of that delay between desire and fulfillment, initial conditions and final heat-death, debt and payment, which holds open our brief window of time between the two eternities that lie before the origin and after the end of the world. If the sexual and mortal debt is paid off at once, then life ceases; life, and its intensification in consciousness, is a sort of postponing, a litigation, an equivocation, a staving-off by interest payments, of the day of reckoning. For Ferdinand, under the tutelage of Prospero, that interim between the arousal of desire and its consummation becomes a paradise.

Thus Shakespeare has revised the parable of the talents; the steward need not wait until the return of the master and the final audit of death, but can enter into possession of the vineyard—to mix the metaphor—through what in financial terms might be called a coup in the futures market. Essentially the lovers are using as security (or pledge, or pawn) the assurance that they will possess each other, in order to invest in a future sexual happiness and take the profit now in the form of their delight in such games as masque watching and chess. Thus their lent capital of potential physical experience, which is due to the master with interest as part of their biological endowment, can remain untouched while its earning power is employed to the maximum. Had Romeo and Juliet a wise and severe mentor like Prospero, rather than the permissive one they have in Friar Lawrence, their tragedy might not have occurred. (But then, of course, they might not have left us the huge inheritance of their moving story.)

Prospero, however, has not cheated death; the final audit will still come, both for him and for his daughter and son-in-law. Will he still be able to face the master's reckoning? Does the steward have the right to use not only the master's five talents but also the master's credit as well, anticipating the future reward of his efforts and using them as security for larger investments? Is there even something impious about the magic by which he created his earthly paradise? The question applies with added force to Shakespeare himself. We his audience, sitting at a great performance of a Shakespeare play, might not wish ourselves any place but there, even if that place were in the presence of God among choirs of angels. If the angel of death should summon us to heaven and the beatific vision of God as we sit watching act III of a really good performance of *The Tempest*, might we not be tempted to ask him to come back in forty-five minutes? Should not the wizard who arranged the spectacle be condemned, like Marlowe's Faust, to eternal damnation? Marlowe claimed that his right to strike coins was as good as the queen's and stood condemned for it; may an earthly wizard mint with impunity such delightful currency as the divine sovereign's?

This is the reason that Prospero casts away the sources of his magic powers, his book and staff, and frees his familiar spirit Ariel, when their good work is done; it is also the reason for the fear and trembling evident in his last speech to the audience:

Now my charms are all o'erthrown,
And what strength I have's mine own,
Which is most faint. Now 'tis true
I must be here confined by you,
Or sent to Naples. Let me not,
Since I have my dukedom got
And pardoned the deceiver, dwell
In this bare island by your spell;
But release me from my bands
With the help of your good hands.
Gentle breath of yours my sails
Must fill, or else my project fails,
Which was to please. Now I want
Spirits to enforce, art to enchant;
And my ending is despair
Unless I be relieved by prayer,
Which pierces so that it assaults
Mercy itself and frees all faults.
As you from crimes would pardoned be,
Let your indulgence set me free.
(Epilogue, 1)

Many of the themes we have already heard come together here. Prospero has pardoned the deceiver; if Prospero/Shakespeare forgives *his* deceivers, can he not hope for pardon for his own deceptions and counterfeitings? He prays to be released from his "bands"—his bonds. He calls upon Mercy, to mitigate the justice that might condemn his overreaching. He asks for the hands of his paying audience, both in applause and prayer. And he craves indulgence, that is, a special exemption from the pains of purgatory that could be bought with good deeds. Indulgences were a part of the old Roman Catholic ritual system that the Elizabethan Protestant church had usurped—indeed, the Reformation began when Luther objected to their abuse. Shakespeare's theater partly mimicked and replaced that old ritual; underlying the great art of the English Renaissance there is always an anxiety whether their new, humanly devised religious system is really acceptable in the eyes of God. Is there an indulgence for such a sin?

The problem is similar to the one that faces Prince Hal: how to legitimate a justifiable but sacrilegious usurpation. In both the *Henry IV* plays and in *The Tempest*, the answer is by a further twist of the strategy pursued by the profiteering servants in the parable of the talents and by the entrepreneur Jacob in Genesis. By sacrificial identification and renunciation Hal turns Falstaff's (and, in a different way, Hotspur's) profligate spending into a method of accumulating legitimate capital for his sovereignty. By sexual postponement and artistic futures-magic Prospero turns unconsummated desire into paradise. Render unto Caesar what is Caesar's, and unto God what is God's, said Jesus; and Shakespeare adds, with fear and trembling, unto the poet-magician what is the poet-magician's, as long as he does not think himself exempt from the claims of God and Caesar.

The work of the poet-magician is to create a postponement in the trajectory of time toward its eventual heat death and to generate a new space there, to be filled with good things. Nature, we know now, is itself full of such delaying games, which so complicate the deterministic fall of the universe toward final stasis that an infinite but bounded fractal hierarchy can emerge within the temporal interim that is opened up. The creative process of emergence through feedback by which the world is thus complicated is the foundation of Shakespeare's economics of abundance and profit. But this idea, which Shakespeare explores most deeply in *Antony and Cleopatra*, will require another chapter.

8

"BOUNTY . . . THAT GREW THE MORE FOR REAPING"

Why Creation Enters into Bonds

The Laboratory of Creation

At the core of Shakespeare's economics, as we have seen, is a radical vision of the world as spontaneously generating order, structure, and value in a continual self-metamorphosis. The notion of natural profit makes possible a world in which the zero of balanced accounts can yield a near-infinite return, in which market values and higher human values can be integrated with each other, in which mercy and gifts can coexist with justice and wages, in which coinage can meaningfully mediate between us and our world, and in which it becomes possible to beat the interest rate of thermodynamic decay charged on the debt of mortal existence. But though Shakespeare has in poetic and dramatic terms proved that natural profit and true human gift giving *do* happen, in the plays we have looked at he has only outlined and hinted at *how* they happen. *Antony and Cleopatra* takes up the challenge of explanation, in a way that constitutes a remarkably precise scientific analysis.

Antony and Cleopatra is a sort of thought experiment, in which the object of study—how emergent structures and values are created—is isolated and disentangled from other possible factors, so as to be examined in itself. Shakespeare is constrained by the logic of his investigation to purify of any extraneous causes the natural creative process and the bonds and gifts that are its human extension, revealing their essential mechanisms. This purification or subtraction is not the same thing as the attempt by Immanuel Kant and many other moralists to purify human actions from self-interest and thus from the deterministic material motives that might in their view discredit the ethical status of such actions. Shakespeare recognizes that our participation in the universe's generative process is essentially impure, adulterated, and compromised. What he is trying to do is to see that impurity purely, so to speak, to seek its source. He is not trying to separate it from its natural expressions in the market, in marriage, in successful political policy, or in the Judeo-Christian and Romano-Greek moral traditions, but rather to see what it was before those expressions of it gave it form.

Shakespeare chooses for his grand fable of value a social world largely outside the calculations of the marketplace. His imagined Mediterranean world is one in which possession is determined by contestation, gift, or negotiation, not by market pricing. Furthermore, his characters—the triumvirs of Rome, the empress of Egypt, and their chief followers and rivals—are the richest people in the world, governed to the extent that they are governed at all by the code of royal honor rather than the ethics of business practice, and beyond any possible need of commerce or labor for material gain. If a market of a kind emerges from such a state of affairs, that shows how natural the market is; but Shakespeare's concern here is with what it emerges from.

Shakespeare must also ensure that the source of creative energy he is seeking is not something else in disguise. Freud was not the first observer of human nature to notice that if we suppress some natural appetite or drive, it will often reappear in some other form. The moral rules governing sexuality have often been regarded as ways to sublimate sexual energy to the service of artistic or social goals. Indeed, Shakespeare could be said to be partly in agreement with this view in his treatment of Ferdinand, Miranda, and many other courting couples in his plays. But here his question is not about how to redirect and use the creative impulse, but what it is in itself. Thus he gives us a story of two people who have thrown over the sexual traces and live in open violation of the codes of marriage and sexual self-restraint. "Nay, but this dotage of our general's / O'erflows the measure," begins the play. Even if their lack of control results in disaster—as it indeed does—we will see the unbanked furnace blazing and know its heat in its very waste.

To fulfill his purpose Shakespeare must also isolate his subject from any prudential considerations—that is, his hero and heroine must fail. The creative delight must be savored for itself, not for any success or gain that it might produce. The genre of tragedy is here put to a special use, to strip away the quiet satisfactions of victory and security from the central core of the creative drive. As events develop, it becomes clear to both Antony and Cleopatra that their interests are not being served by their association with each other. "These strong Egyptian fetters I must break," Antony vows unavailingly to himself (I.ii.117). Cleopatra is shrewd enough to consider doing a deal with Caesar to sell her lover out. But Shakespeare cannot give his lovers the conventional satisfactions of tragic self-destruction either. There is a sort of prudence in assuring oneself a niche in the tragic faithful lovers' hall of fame. This prudence, too, must not be allowed to muddy the waters. Cleopatra knows that she will be represented after her death as a strumpet, some "squeaking Cleopatra" will "boy" her greatness "i' th' posture of a whore" (V.ii.220). The "quick comedians," including Shakespeare himself, will stage her, just as she fears. Neither Antony nor Cleopatra is motivated by saintly self-sacrifice or the grand romantic gesture, though they end up with death scenes even more moving and effective in their own strange way. The one thing both are faithful to is the incandescent edge of creative activity, and this is what the play is about.

Shakespeare must also isolate the action of the play from any religious or ethical system that might legitimately claim its participants and thus serve as a basis of praise or blame. If there is a divine reward that the participants know will requite their actions, or a divine after-death punishment that will settle the score, the enterprise of discovery will be lost. In the old Taoist system of China, the Tao itself is prior to Yin and Yang, prior to good and evil. It is that Tao that Shakespeare is after, that fountain of being that Melville described as joyous, heartless immensities. We find it in the Old Testament in the Jehovah who tempts Job, who creates Leviathan, and who dances upon the mountaintops at the dawn of the world; but this God has been overlain with millennia of a deity who is much more responsible and ethically praiseworthy. In this play, we might say, he is unearthed, and his avatar is, blasphemously, Cleopatra. Thus Shakespeare sets his fable just before the dawn of the Christian era, before the Christian principles of his audience could fairly be expected to apply to his hero and heroine. "That Herod's head I'll have," Cleopatra observes lazily one day (III.iii.4); her casualness with the name and her complete unawareness of the gigantic resonances of her words with the fate of the Baptist usher the audience into a pagan world where their religious preconceptions must be put aside. Shakespeare is doing something that Federico Fellini tried to do in his *Satyricon*: to imagine a pagan world, to remove a whole class of moral categories and poetic imagery that Christianity created.

But Shakespeare must engineer a further removal from the cultural and religious world of his audience. Elizabethans, like ourselves, were the heirs of the pagan Greco-Roman system of virtue, restraint, and reason as well as of the Judeo-Christian system of redemption, humility, and love. Shakespeare includes the Greco-Roman framework of judgment in the play, but takes his lovers out of it and plunges them into another, stranger place where even these rules do not apply. He invents an Egypt of endless fertility, luxury, desire, and unrestraint, that finds Roman orderliness faintly ridiculous. Cleopatra's historically Greek roots are erased, and she is given a more ancient, genial, cynical, sensual wisdom that is applauded by her own holy priests. Certainly the uptight, upstart new civilizations of the West will, with their greater discipline and political enthusiasm, overwhelm the old regime of the Nile; but they will have done so at the cost of truncating their own sources of pleasure, innocence, and joy. Or at least this is what Cleopatra would have us believe, and who could argue with such a lady? Antony is convinced, at least:

> Let Rome in Tiber melt, and the wide arch
> Of the ranged empire fall! Here is my space.
> Kingdoms are clay: our dungy earth alike
> Feeds beasts as man. The nobleness of life
> Is to do thus . . .
> (I.i.33)

—whereupon he kisses her. The Rome of *Antony and Cleopatra,* moreover, is not the idealistic and high-minded Rome of the Republic, but the sophisticated, theologically skeptical, politics-ridden, world-weary imperial Rome that Shakespeare would have been familiar with from the works of Plutarch, Martial, Juvenal, and his favorite authors, Ovid and Lucretius. If something strange and new and beautiful is to come to birth in such a world, it cannot be by dint of religious self-sacrifice or moral aspiration or the redirection of repressed desires.

In turning toward the classical pagan past in search of a space for new invention, Shakespeare was very much a Renaissance writer. Renaissance thought tended to seek out the neutral spaces in between established pairs of opposites. Artists took the line between the great dualities—thought and deed, good and evil, true and false, abstract and concrete, sacred and secular—and used that line itself as a spacious theater of invention. They sought a third reality, transcending the existing categories. Between Christian Europe and the pagan Indies they found America. Between good and evil they found play. Between work and prayer they found poetry. Between truth and falsehood they found fiction, magic, and science. Between the merely serious and the merely comic appeared the Renaissance pastoral. The world was repopulated with what C. S. Lewis calls theologically neutral spirits, and between angels and devils there appeared much that was not dreamed of in the old philosophy. This was also the birth time of modern science. Bacon and Descartes outlined for us that whole area of objective, morally and epistemologically colorless "fact"—that fictive space that became, two hundred years later, the only apparent domain for a respectable thinker.

The "new heaven, new earth" (I.i.17) of Antony, like More's Utopia or John Donne's "new-found land" (Elegy 19: "To His Mistress Going to Bed"), was not bound by the old laws or describable by the old categories: it was a neutral space, a noplace where experiment isn't harmful. One cannot afford experiment, or science itself, in a place where, if the experiment fails, the world of the experimenter is destroyed. Utopia is neither truth nor falsehood: it is fiction, the line or space that separates them. Morally *Utopia* cannot be called a good book or a bad book. The author takes no stand on whether the lessons to be learned are edifying or heretical; there are not necessarily any lessons to be learned. The only sin one could be accused of in reading the book would be the neglect of duties more important. The book is playful, it exists in the world between work and prayer. The beauty of Donne's mistress is that her body is not bound by the old dualities of good and evil, profane eros and sacred caritas—it is the place where he can pursue *amor,* that intense, spiritual-erotic-romantic love celebrated by Michelangelo, Spenser, Sidney, Shakespeare. Perhaps the greatest discovery of the Renaissance was a new kind of fiction. We have already examined the fictional space discovered by Brunelleschi in 1420 when he invented perspective, the space that divides the subject of the painting from its surface and its literal existence from its figurative one. An analogous artistic space was the "metrical fiction" discovered by the English sonneteers—the ability to vary the rhythm of a poem while keeping the verse form intact—a technique that enabled them to operate in a rhythmic space between strict meter and the rhythm of speech, and therefore to adopt poetic voices that were not necessarily their own.

Language, the Word, is the neutral space that lies between thought and action. For the new religion of Protestantism this meant the primacy of the Word of God, and the abolition of all other mediators between the human and the divine. The Word, though, can separate Man from God at the same time as it enables them to speak to each other. For humanists the new emphasis on language was embodied in their fascinated attention to the golden ages of classical literature: it expressed itself philosophically in a new interest in rhetoric as opposed to logic, on one hand, and grammar, on the other. In its most extreme form—for instance, in the thought of the linguistic philosopher Peter Ramus—humanism violently rejected Aristotelian logic and insisted that the value of an idea was primarily its accessibility, expressibility, and convincingness, not its adherence to certain abstract forms. Only after the hearers had comprehended an argument emotionally, and understood it clearly, could they decide on its truth or falsehood; and by that time it would be too late: they would already have been convinced. The great language building of the sixteenth century all over Europe, in which monarchs and poets cooperated in expanding and refining the national languages, is related to this change of emphasis. To expand the language is to expand the thinkable; it is a heady project. We can see this spirit in Sidney's *Defense of Poetry,* where he contrasts the work of the poet with that of any professional who is bound to nature as it is:

> Only the poet, disdaining to be tied to any such subjection, lifted up with the vigour of his own invention, doth grow in effect another Nature, in making things either better than Nature bringeth forth, or quite anew, forms such as never were in Nature, as the Heroes, Demigods, Cyclops, Chimaeras, Furies, and such like [how like Shakespeare's Antony this sounds!]; so as he goeth hand in hand with Nature, not enclosed within the narrow warrant of her gifts, but freely ranging only within the zodiac of his own wit. . . . Her world is brazen, the poets only deliver a golden.

For the great Elizabethans artistic invention took its place at the summit of human capacities. Invention for Sidney

> is not wholly imaginative, as we are wont to say by them that build castles in the air, but so far substantially it worketh, not only to make a Cyrus,

which had been but a particular excellency, as Nature might have done, but to bestow a Cyrus upon the world to make many Cyruses, if they will learn aright why and how that maker made him.

Neither let it be deemed too saucy a comparison to balance the highest point of man's wit with the efficacy of nature. . . . But these arguments will by few be understood, and by fewer granted. . . .

It is perhaps hard for us to recapture that huge artistic hubris. They believed that though incapable of miracle, we may be capable of magic. Magic could make a man author of himself.

But with this hubris went a profound sense of insecurity, alienation, and crisis. If one explored beyond the known world, there was the danger of falling off the edge. In many respects the opening of the neutral space created the gigantic rift that separates modern persons from their psychic home. The genesis of the Renaissance adult ego cut off child from parents, the dependent from the comforter. Renaissance language separated thought from action, so we have Hamlet ("a neutral to his will and matter" [II.ii.488]) trapped within his own marvelous discourse. Renaissance phenomenology separated perceiver from perceived: perspective at once creates a separate observer and a vanishing point. The great social bond between lord and peasant broke down with the collapse of feudalism and the enclosure of land for bourgeois commercial purposes. The cold Word of God took the place of the Eucharist: instead of communion there was the loneliness of the individual conscience. The great mediators—the sacraments, the Blessed Virgin, the liturgy, the Latin that one did not need to understand, for it was an incantation—were swept away. The Earth itself, no longer at the center of the universe, pursued its lonely way somewhere between center and periphery in neutral ground.

The gap between the old opposites was now filled by art. Renaissance art was, on one hand, a splendidly, assertively healthy growth and, on the other, a lovely iridescent scar tissue that filled the wounds of medieval culture. Just as scar tissue is specially liable to cancerous growths, so Renaissance art always had a tendency to proliferate wildly into disorder, excessive and drunken forms—witness Elizabethan melodrama, Tudor architecture, euphuism, Renaissance epic, and so on.

Anthony and Cleopatra is a consciously Renaissance play. Like its great predecessors it creates a neutral space, a new world, "new heaven, new earth." It is primarily in the rhetoric of the play that this neutral space is generated; it is an area uncontrolled by the normal rules of linear logic, inference, morality, or political consequence; in it the central realities of love, self-awareness, creativity, and freedom are explored. This space is, however, doomed both by the outside world of history and by its own abandonment of form; and we can see the play as a convincing symbol of the close of the English Renaissance. Its self-consciousness is itself perhaps a sign that the era is coming to an end, and the cooler, drier airs of neoclassicism are blowing through the culture.

Shakespeare chose for his play a time in the history of the world that he sensed was comparable in importance to his own time: the change from the Roman Republic to the Roman Empire, the shifting of the center of world culture from Greece to Rome (Plutarch was Greek, Octavius Roman), the decision of Europe to develop westward rather than eastward, the time of the birth of Christ (Jesus was born thirty years after the death of Antony), the waning years of the pre-Christian world. But Shakespeare sensed the forces that were gathering to suppress and control the chaotic liberties of his fictional universe. They are summed up in Octavius and his sister. Spenser, Sidney, Marlowe, Shakespeare, the Donne of the love poetry, would give way to Jonson, the Donne of the Holy Sonnets, Milton, and finally Dryden and Pope. Control and artistic austerity would triumph over abundance and deliquescence. And this process was taking place in Shakespeare's own art. In *Antony and Cleopatra* the poetry is so overwhelming that it almost overcomes itself. Shakespeare can do anything in verse now. If he can do anything, he can do everything, and to do everything is to do nothing. In the plays written after *Antony and Cleopatra* poetry is never quite so wildly given its head. When it occurs, it is, so to speak, in quotation marks, and Shakespeare never lets us forget that it is all only art, a play, an entertainment. By poetry of course I mean here that rapturous and limitless creativity, which flourishes so luxuriantly in *Antony and Cleopatra*—a creativity that expresses itself in nature, in the lovers' human imagination, and in the peculiar self-reflectiveness of the language of the play.

Bounty: Spontaneous Generation in Things and Persons

Antony and Cleopatra is packed with images of natural self-creation. Although Shakespeare's ultimate goal is the source of human imagination, he refuses, for reasons we are already familiar with, to divide humans from the rest of nature with respect to creativity and even freedom. As we have seen in the Sonnets and *The Winter's Tale,* the artificial is but a continuation of the natural, and nature is made better by no means, but nature makes that means. In *Lear* the love bond that we share with other animals can outdo the illusion of unconditional love, and in *The Merchant of Venice* the soul cannot be detached from the body. So the Egypt of Shakespeare's great experiment is not only a place of cultural creativity but also a fecund womb of physical and biological diversity. The river Nile is the central symbol of this overflowing natural foison.

> The higher Nilus swells,
> The more it promises; as it ebbs, the seedsman
> Upon the slime and ooze scatters his grain,
> And shortly comes to harvest.
> (II.vii.21)

But the Nile, according to some in the play, does not merely nurture existing life; it is capable of spontaneously generating new life. Lepidus, drunk, owlishly buttonholes Antony:

LEPIDUS: Y'have strange serpents there.

ANTONY: Ay, Lepidus.

LEPIDUS: Your serpent of Egypt is bred now of your mud
by the operation of your sun: so is your crocodile.

ANTONY: They are so.
(II.vii.25)

Now it is clear that Shakespeare is a little skeptical of the popular medieval and Renaissance belief in the spontaneous generation of life. Lepidus' drunken rambling sounds like the credulity of the uninformed, and Antony, who despises Lepidus and considers him a source of amusement, may very well be agreeing with him just to put him on. But Shakespeare is half-inclined to think as Lepidus does. Images of spontaneous generation, ferment, seeding, and fertility recur often in the play, as in this delightfully dissipated exchange among Cleopatra's handmaidens Iras and Charmian and the palm reader that their friend Alexas has brought in for their entertainment:

CHARMIAN: Prithee, how many boys and wenches must I have?

SOOTHSAYER: If every of your wishes had a womb,
And fertile every wish, a million.

CHARMIAN: Out, fool! I forgive thee for a witch.

ALEXAS: You think none but your sheets are privy to your wishes.

CHARMIAN: Nay, come, tell Iras hers . . .

IRAS: There's a palm presages chastity, if nothing else.

CHARMIAN: E'en as the o'erflowing Nilus presageth famine.
(I.ii.38)

If spontaneous generation is a popular superstition, it is one that raises a really major philosophical question: how did life arise in the first place? Even the biblical account gives to the *prima materia* of the world, to that chaos over which hovers the Holy Ghost, the essential capacity of fecundity; and the emergence of life is the result of cooperation between God and the elements. As we have already seen in chapter 3, the *prima materia* of contemporary physics, the quantum vacuum, is capable of spawning whole new universes. Alchemy maintained that the correct combination of elements might trigger the emergence of life. Although the Dutch spectacle maker Zacharias Janssen had developed the principles of the microscope by 1590, it was not until after Shakespeare's death that Anton van Leeuwenhoek first observed microscopic organisms and thus revealed that life need not be visible to the naked eye to exist and be capable of visible results. Indeed, it was only in this century that the mystery of plant seeds, which appear to be dead in all respects, began to yield to DNA research. How *did* life arise in the first place?

This play, like *A Midsummer Night's Dream* with its similar obsession with the creative ferment of nature, is full of minute observations of iterative physical processes. It pays special attention to the turbulent flow of liquids that so fascinated Leonardo da Vinci. One example is the "vagabond flag upon the stream," which

> Goes to and back, lackeying the varying tide,
> To rot itself with motion.
> (I.iv.45)

What Shakespeare has noticed here is a classic physical feedback system. The rush or reed is caught in the current of the stream. It swings toward the bank, is then out of the current, and its natural resilience pulls it upright, where it is then able to reassert its lean into the current, and again it is pulled under and back, into calmer water; so again it rises out of the stream, and so on. Meanwhile variations in the current—its turbulent nonlinear dynamics, contemporary physicists would say—add a further element of unpredictability to the rhythm of the process. If a computerized camera were to record it, and the periodicity and amplitude of the reed's swings precisely measured and plotted on a graph, the Lorenz Attractor would emerge, a beautiful butterfly-shaped form whose shape is unmistakable yet never complete, for new fractal depth would be revealed at each iteration. Of course Shakespeare did not have cameras and computers. But the human eye and ear are deeply attuned to such processes and, as I have shown in my book *Beauty: The Value of Values*, the classical human arts are deeply based on the presence of these systems in nature and cultural practice. "Sometime we see a cloud that's dragonish," says Antony (IV.xiv.2), anticipating the language of Benoit Mandelbrot, the great mathematician who discovered fractal shapes and called them "dragons," citing cloud structure as a prime example. The point is that "damped, driven, nonlinear dynamical systems," as these phenomena are called, have a complex, self-organizing behavior much more elaborate than the simple inputs of energy they require. Something new, not given in the initial conditions, emerges out of the very process; their next behavior is the result of an impossibly complicated interaction of all their own previous behaviors, and thus they are in some very elementary fashion autonomous. They create the rules that govern them, and the creation process is too complex to be predicted by its inputs from the environment. This description should bear a striking resemblance to the psychological behavior of the two principal characters in *Antony and Cleopatra*, and it is this parallel that has caught Shakespeare's curiosity.

Did life itself, then, emerge as an inconceivably rich combination of such "dissipative systems," as Ilya Prigogine calls them? Present-day evolutionary biologists are almost unanimous in agreeing that it did, and if my analysis of Shakespeare's imagery is accurate, he must have intuited it too. According to Prigogine, the order of dissipative systems is not thermodynamic order in itself, but rather that second-order kind of order I have already discussed in the second chapter, which feeds upon the flow of increasing thermodynamic disorder but is able to maintain itself at least temporarily against that flow, and even to elaborate itself meanwhile. Both Prigogine and Shakespeare know that such a system can "rot itself with motion"; but they also know that whenever a steep gradient exists between order and chaos, a current of flowing energy can be set up that can supply the nourishment for its renewal. And as both Shakespeare and Prigogine recognize, the "far-from-equilibrium" situations that encourage such gradients and flows will always arise out of any open system. The quantum vacuum we looked at in the context of Cordelia's "nothing" is only the most primal and extreme example of such open systems.

In *Antony and Cleopatra* the flow of energy is provided by the Nile. It is out of the mud of the Nile, where water, earth, the fire of the sun, and the fresh air intermingle, that new life is said to be engendered. That new life is in the terms of Shakespeare's time the basest and simplest kind: crawling creatures, worms, insects, and especially snakes. This vision of natural fertility can be definitely unpretty; Cleopatra in her wrath lays this curse on her country:

> Melt Egypt into Nile, and kindly creatures
> Turn all to serpents! . . .
> So half my Egypt were submerged and made
> A cistern for scaled snakes!
> (II.v.78, 94)

By "kindly creatures" she means creatures produced by normal reproduction, as opposed to spontaneous generation. But is Cleopatra herself a "kindly creature"? The poetry suggests not. Antony calls his lover his "serpent of old Nile" (I.v.25); plainly Shakespeare visualized her wearing the uraeus, the snake crown of the Pharaohs, and he may have known that its root, the Egyptian word "uro" (which is also the root of the Ouroboros, the world-encircling snake that eats its own tail) means "asp." Of course Cleopatra commits suicide with an asp, so the instrument of her death is both the sign of her queenship and the major symbol for the Nile's powers of spontaneous generation.

As we have already seen, the snake or serpent is also part of the caduceus, the snaky rod of Mercury, which is in turn symbolic of life itself. Thus Cleopatra concentrates in herself Shakespeare's deepest understanding of that protean, multitudinous, inventive, dying yet undying mantle of living tissue that envelops this planet.

> Age cannot wither her, nor custom stale
> Her infinite variety; other women cloy
> The appetites they feed, but she makes hungry
> Where most she satisfies; for vilest things
> Become themselves in her, that the holy priests
> Bless her when she is riggish.
> (II.ii.237)

The word "become," "becoming" epitomizes her:

> Whom everything becomes—to chide, to laugh,
> To weep; whose every passion fully strives
> To make itself, in thee, fair and admired.
> (I.i.49)

> . . . my becomings kill me when they do not
> Eye well to you.
> (I.iii.96)

"Becoming" combines two contradictory senses: fitting, proper, dignified; and transformation, metamorphosis, evolution. She is a "breather," not a statue like her rival Octavia, who "shows a body rather than a life," and is of a "holy, cold, and still conversation" (III.iii.23, II.vi.122). Like the "terrene moon," Cleopatra is changeable, and waxes and wanes by the month (III.xiii.153); as the snake changes her outer, so she, as a woman, changes her inner skin and renews her fertility. She is associated with the most feminine words in the Indo-European linguistic heritage: "woman," "womb," "whore," "queen," "wench," "witch," whose roots also give us gyn- and Guinevere. She epitomizes the ancient Mediterranean and Mesopotamian snake-and-moon goddesses: Ashtoreth, Innanna, Ishtar, Aphrodite, Venus. The hubris of Cleopatra—at no point does she refer to any deity, including that of the Hebrews, with more than a sense of fellow feeling or even mild contempt—her presumption in daring to create herself, her assumption of complete freedom, her refusal to let any other power on earth judge her actions—all these would be hallmarks of a spiritual rebellion against God if she were living in a Christian system. There is even something satanic about Cleopatra. She has magical powers, she is a "charm," a "witch," a "spell"; Charmian at her suicide exclaims, "O eastern star!" and the names of that star include not only Venus but also Lucifer (IV.xii.16, IV.xii.47, IV.xii.30, V.ii.308).

But the moment we try to pin Cleopatra down, she escapes. The holy priests bless her when she is "riggish." The snare in which she catches Antony is a "strong toil of grace" (V.ii.347); the imagery of the Madonna and of martyrdom surrounds her death as densely as that of rebellion and damnation. Antony calls her "this great fairy" (IV.viii.12); like the queen of

Faerie in the Ballad of True Thomas she is a force neither of heaven nor hell, but of the energy field that precedes both. Cleopatra is a developed version of Titania in *A Midsummer Night's Dream,* the divine lady who wraps herself in the enameled skin of a snake. In fairyland there are no moral judgments, and the laws are the laws of beauty and psychology. The rules of empirical logic, which assert that you can't get something for nothing, don't seem to apply to her: she "makes a show'r of rain as well as Jove" (I.i.151). Cleopatra enables Shakespeare to perform artistic impossibilities in his play. Without her the fragmented plot, sprawled over half the world and a period of years, the extravagant language, the cast of thousands, the inconsistency of many of the major characters, and the gross theatricality of many of the big scenes would cause the play to collapse. But she carries it.

Perhaps the finest description of living matter as revealed by the science of biology can be found in Thomas Mann's *Magic Mountain*. It remains as true today in its broad outlines as when it was written a lifetime ago.

> What then was life? It was warmth, the warmth generated by a form-preserving instability, a fever of matter, which accompanied the process of ceaseless decay and repair of albumen molecules that were too impossibly complicated, too impossibly ingenious in structure. It was the existence of the actually impossible-to-exist, of a half-sweet, half-painful balancing, or scarcely balancing, in this restricted and feverish process of decay and renewal, upon the point of existence. It was not matter and it was not spirit, but something between the two, a phenomenon conveyed by matter, like the rainbow on the waterfall, and like the flame. Yet why not material—it was sentient to the point of desire and disgust, the shamelessness of matter become sensible of itself, the incontinent form of being. It was a secret and ardent stirring in the frozen chastity of the universal; it was a stolen and voluptuous impurity of sucking and secreting; an exhalation of carbonic acid gas and material impurities of mysterious origin and composition. It was a pullulation, an unfolding, a form-building (made possible by the overbalancing of its instability, yet controlled by the laws of growth inherent within it), of something brewed out of water, albumen, salt and fats, which was called flesh, and which became form, beauty, a lofty image, and yet all the time the essence of sensuality and desire. For this form and beauty were not spirit-borne; nor, like the form and beauty of sculpture, conveyed by a neutral and spirit-consumed substance, which could in all purity make beauty perceptible to the senses. Rather was it conveyed and shaped by the somehow awakened voluptuousness of matter, of the organic, dying-living substance itself, the reeking flesh.

> (Thomas Mann, *The Magic Mountain,* trans. H. T. Lowe-Porter [New York: Knopf, 1975], pp. 275–276.)

Mann's images, of warmth, fever, decay, slime, the intricate (or "intrinsicate") knot of life, of impossibility, sweetness, balance and continually corrected overbalance, fluidity, incontinence, sexual desire, sucking and secreting, breath, fermentation, form, beauty, life as opposed to sculpture, voluptuousness, the "reeking flesh" itself—all these Shakespeare uses in his description of Cleopatra. Cleopatra, then, is an independent source of new reality, like the Nile that engenders life; not exactly an Unmoved Mover, since she is moved by every little thing that happens to her, and is "sentient to the point of desire and disgust," but a shaper of surprises, a transformer of chaotic raw material into beautiful and unexpected form.

This quality is also central to her lover, Antony, in whom it is given a name: bounty. In Cleopatra's great elegy for Antony after his suicide, she compares him to the heavenly fires that give life to the world:

> His face was as the heav'ns, and therein stuck
> A sun and moon, which kept their course and lighted
> The little O, th' earth. . . .

Antony, then, is not a net taker of the world's energies, but a net giver; and as in *King Lear,* he is what makes the "little O" of the zero a fertile source rather than an absence. Cleopatra continues her evocation of the endless circle of productiveness:

> . . . His legs bestrid the ocean: his reared arm
> Crested the world: his voice was propertied
> As all the tunèd spheres, and that to friends;
> But when he meant to quail and shake the orb,
> He was as rattling thunder. For his bounty,
> There was no winter in't: an autumn 'twas
> That grew the more by reaping. . . .
> (V.ii.79)

What Cleopatra claims for Antony in her magnificent elegy for him is that his generosity is not achieved at the cost of a diminution of value elsewhere; Antony is not a zero-sum game, his creativity is not accompanied by the entropy of a winter and does not wear out from being used. Antony's bounty is such that for the only time in all of literature, a man is killed by sheer generosity alone. Enobarbus, Antony's friend, has deserted him and gone over to Antony's enemy Octavius. Antony does not reproach Enobarbus, but sends after him all the treasure that he had abandoned in his desertion, together with a huge gift of his own. Enobarbus, to do him credit, cannot shake off the burden of this gigantic magnanimity; his heart stops, and he dies that night under the moon. Enobarbus is not a fool; he is quite as capable as we are of seeing through an empty gesture. But he has been struck by something superhuman—as one soldier puts it, "Your emperor / Continues still a Jove" (IV.vi.28). Even at his weakest and most self-indulgent Antony can still make his most cynical followers weep—and even we, "asses," are "onion-eyed" (IV.ii.35). This is the quality we know as charisma. His vitality is such that he can keep going even after his defeats, cannot commit a clean suicide, lives two more scenes after inflicting his own death wound. Cleopatra continues:

> . . . His delights
> Were dolphinlike, they showed his back above
> The element they lived in.
> (V.ii.88)

This is the tender observation of the lover, who finds a sweet pathos in
Antony's abandonment to his passionate pleasure. Cleopatra is associated
with the sea goddess Thetis; she is the element he lives in. "Die when thou
hast lived," she says to him in his last moments, his head cradled in her lap
(IV.xv.38). The motion of the dolphin plunging in and out of the sea is thus
intensely sexual, and Cleopatra is talking about that moment in sexual climax which leaps beyond, is thrown beyond pleasure into another world.
"Hyperbolein," from which we get "hyperbole," is Greek for "to throw beyond." But the image is also a metaphysical statement. The dolphin was for
medieval and Renaissance natural philosophy the highest and noblest member of the class of fishes, and thus shared in the characteristics of the next
higher category in the Great Chain of Being. This for them explained its
warm-bloodedness and recognizable moral intelligence. Antony thus transcends the category human as the dolphin transcends the category fish. He
shows what we would call emergent properties, the higher integration and
warm-blooded self-feeling of a more evolved being. Octavius is a cold fish by
comparison. In another passage Cleopatra imagines the "tawny-finned
fishes" she "betrays" when she goes angling to be "each one an Antony,"
and when she draws them up she will cry in triumph, "Ah, ha! y' are
caught!" (II.v.11) So it is Cleopatra herself that has drawn Antony up into
the higher world. She continues her praise of his bounty:

> . . . In his livery
> Walked crowns and crownets: realms and islands were
> As plates dropped from his pocket. . . .
> (V.ii.90)

Again, the imagery of roundness, this time associated with "plates," that is,
silver coins signifying value. Finally she demands:

> Think you there was or might be such a man
> As this I dreamt of?

DOLABELLA: Gentle madam, no.

CLEOPATRA: You lie, up to the hearing of the gods.
But if there be nor ever were one such,
It's past the size of dreaming; nature wants stuff
To vie strange forms with fancy, yet t' imagine
An Antony were nature's piece 'gainst fancy,
Condemning shadows quite.
(V.ii.93)

What she means is that nature's creativity cannot match human fancy (because human fancy already has the raw material, the "stuff" of nature to work with, while nature must make her own stuff); but if nature were to imagine an Antony, which indeed she must have done, that Antony would be nature's masterpiece ("piece"), defeating utterly the mere shadows of human artistic fancy. It is a bewildering idea, this contest of imaginations, and its logical form, turning back reflexively upon itself, is one we must look at more closely later on.

The core problem of the play is the relationship between Antony and Cleopatra: for their bounty, their generativeness, takes place chiefly in the context of their love. Whatever mysterious process it is that they share with the creative forces of nature cannot be only internal to the person; it must also be something that happens between persons. But can it be love if it is virtually devoid of the moral characteristics we traditionally associate with love—constancy, faithfulness, dependability, trust, truthfulness, mutual support? After all, both history and Shakespeare's treatment of it agree that Antony and Cleopatra betrayed each other, lied to each other, and deserted each other in their hour of need. When we first see Antony in the arms of Cleopatra, he is married to another woman and planning behind Cleopatra's back to return to Rome to look after his political interests. After Fulvia's death he doesn't marry Cleopatra but Octavia; and even when he returns to Cleopatra, he does not level with her about his military fortunes and becomes so angry with her that he is ready to kill her. Cleopatra for her part is utterly untrustworthy, manipulating Antony mercilessly, abandoning him in the middle of a battle, sending him lying messages about her death that indeed lead him to suicide, plotting a deal with Octavius behind Antony's back, and even flirting with Octavius' messenger. Nor was she a spring chicken when Antony came upon her, having already efficiently used her sex to exploit no less a personage than Julius Caesar. If bonds are essential to love, as so many of the other plays and poems of Shakespeare imply, surely Antony and Cleopatra must have broken them all. Certainly, by the end of the play Antony will have reinvented traditional masculine discipline in a new form, Cleopatra will have found her own strange version of "marble" constancy, and touchingly, she will enter her suicide with words that are almost those of a bourgeois marriage: "husband, I come." But their task is to generate those forms and constraints on their own, without what would be for them a slavish acceptance of precept. Loving according to one's bond cannot be taken for granted: it must be discovered.

The first words between the lovers in the play meet this problem head-on.

CLEOPATRA: If it be love indeed, tell me how much.

ANTONY: There's beggary in the love that can be reckoned.

CLEOPATRA: I'll set a bourn how far to be beloved.

ANTONY: Then must thou needs find out new heaven, new earth.
(I.i.14)

Quite casually, almost by accident, Antony and Cleopatra are spinning out immortal poetry. We do not experience the actual human drama *through* the convention of verse, as for instance we perceive the psychological conflict in an opera through the utterly unrealistic medium of music; rather, we see two people talking to each other and, astonishingly, it is poetry. They are being spontaneous, but not in the sense given that word by the romantic poets—unself-conscious, sincere. They are surrounded by followers, attendants, ambassadors, are aware of their own magnificence and exploiting to the full their unique license to be intimate in public. But their "play-acting" of the roles of the great lovers *within* the play abolishes for a moment the theatrical medium: their reality is theatrical; therefore, our theater seems for a moment real. The bonds of theater are thus being broken, rather as we saw them broken in the scene on the cliffs of Dover in *King Lear.*

Antony and Cleopatra are answering each other, and each answer generates an answer from the other. They have created, so to speak, a dyadic nonlinear feedback system that is unpredictable and can thus emerge across the threshold, or "bourn," of the existing order into another plane of being. To cross that frontier is, it seems, to break the bonds of all established rules—here, the Roman code of marital decorum and military self-discipline. They cease to be earthbound. The conversation between them has built up enough power by its gathering oscillation from one to the other that it finally takes off with the words "new heaven, new earth."

The phrase "heaven and earth" and its variants are Shakespeare's own code for the grand boundary of the world—the present moment that divides the known past from the unknown future, that demarcates the realm of life and the "undiscovered country" of death "from whose bourn," as Hamlet puts it, "no traveler returns" (*Hamlet*, III.i.79). This strange boundary-land is the dwelling place not only of lunatics and lovers, as Theseus points out in *A Midsummer Night's Dream,* but also of the poet, whose eye

> Doth glance from heaven to earth, from earth to heaven;
> And as imagination bodies forth
> The forms of things unknown, the poet's pen
> Turns them to shapes, and gives to airy nothing
> A local habitation and a name.
> (V.i.13)

In the conversation of Antony and Cleopatra what we see is a spontaneously self-generating system in action. It is unpredictable and self-organizing, and can surprise both participants. The threshold crossing of "heaven and earth" is the result. We experience this state as a special intensity of time, a special attention to the present moment, in which we seem to have a greater subjective presence but also a greater sensitivity to the world:

Now for the love of Love and her soft hours,
Let's not confound the time with conference harsh.
There's not a minute of our lives should stretch
Without some pleasure now.
(I.i.44)

Eternity was in our lips and eyes,
Bliss in our brows' bent, none our parts so poor
But was a race of heaven; they are so still . . .
(I.iii.35)

The world of Antony and Cleopatra creates a kind of present in the past, in contrast to the Roman history in which it is embedded. When we are switched rapidly from Rome to Alexandria and back, we feel a curious sense of anachronism. Though Egypt is the more ancient civilization, it feels more present to us. Antony and Cleopatra stand out of history, "stand up peerless," full of surprises (I.i.40), almost able to make us disbelieve the historical account of Antony's defeat by Octavius (Shakespeare actually causes the result of the conflict to be much longer in doubt than it is in his source for the story, Plutarch's *Lives*). The relationship between the lovers and their historical world is the same as the relationship between Shakespeare's play (live, in the present, full of suspense) and the historical account (over and done with, a foregone conclusion). It is the difference between lived time and recorded time. The problem of any historical dramatist, which is to be true to the dead facts and to make a live play on stage at the same time, is thus brilliantly solved—by making the problem into the central theme. This solution makes possible such total aesthetic triumphs as the passage describing Cleopatra in her barge, where Shakespeare transforms Plutarch's historical description into a thing of magic and wonder, changing only a few words from the original. Here is Plutarch, in the translation by Sir Thomas North that Shakespeare used:

Therefore when she was sent unto by divers letters, both from Antonius himself and also from his friends, she made so light of it and mocked Antonius so much that she disdained to set forward otherwise but to take her barge in the river of Cydnus, the poop whereof was of gold, the sails of purple, and the oars of silver, which kept stroke in rowing after the sound of the music of flutes, hautboys, cithers, viols, and such other instruments as they played upon in the barge. And now for the person of herself: She was laid under a pavilion of cloth-of-gold of tissue, appareled and attired like the goddess Venus commonly drawn in picture; and hard by her, on either hand of her, pretty fair boys, appareled as painters do set forth god Cupid, with little fans in their hands with the which they fanned wind upon her. Her ladies and gentlewomen also, the fairest of them, were appareled like the nymphs Nereides (which are the mermaids of the waters) and like the Graces, some steering the helm, others tending the tackle and ropes of the barge, out of the which there came a wonderful passing sweet savor of perfumes that perfumed the wharf's side, pestered with innumerable multitudes of people. Some of them followed the barge all along the river's side, others also ran out of the city to see her coming in, so that in the end there ran such multitudes of people one after another to see her that Antonius was left post-alone in the market place in his imperial seat to give audience.

("The Life of Marcus Antonius," in Sir Thomas North, *The Lives of the Noble Grecians and Romans by that eminent historiographer and philosopher, Plutarch of Chaeronea*)

And here is Shakespeare:

> The barge she sat in, like a burnished throne,
> Burned on the water: the poop was beaten gold;
> Purple the sails, and so perfumèd that
> The winds were lovesick with them; the oars were silver,
> Which to the tune of flutes kept stroke and made
> The water which they beat to follow faster,
> As amorous of their strokes. For her own person,
> It beggared all description: she did lie
> In her pavilion, cloth-of-gold of tissue,
> O'erpicturing that Venus where we see
> The fancy outwork nature; on each side her
> Stood pretty dimpled boys, like smiling Cupids,
> With divers-colored fans, whose wind did seem
> To glow the delicate cheeks which they did cool,
> And what they undid did. . . .
> Her gentlewomen, like the Nereides,
> So many mermaids, tended her i' th' eyes,
> And made their bends adornings. At the helm
> A seeming mermaid steers: the silken tackle
> Swell with the touches of those flower-soft hands,
> That yarely frame the office. From the barge
> A strange invisible perfume hits the sense
> Of the adjacent wharfs. The city cast
> Her people out upon her; and Antony,
> Enthroned i' th' marketplace, did sit alone,
> Whistling to th' air; which, but for vacancy,
> Had gone to gaze on Cleopatra too,
> And made a gap in nature.
> (II.ii.193)

If we look at the changes Shakespeare makes we can see, with uncanny intimacy, the mind of this great subtle gentle genius at work. There are five ways in which he has systematically transformed Plutarch so as to make this passage the shimmering glowing mystery that it is. The first, of course, is by putting it into the easy sinuous blank verse of his mature period, giving it a subtle insistent rhythm that links all the words together in a musical, rather than just a grammatical fashion; the words feed back upon each other in a way that is beyond prose or free verse. (Enobarbus, the character who speaks this passage in the play, usually speaks in prose, so Shakespeare's choice of verse here is quite marked.) The second transformation Shakespeare makes in Plutarch is the faceting and texturing and filtering of the simple matte colors of Plutarch, so that the gold becomes beaten gold, the fans become divers-colored, the boys are dimpled, the perfume becomes strange in its invisibility. The third change, and perhaps the most striking, is to make the movements and actions of the scene feed back upon themselves, so that they seem iterated, reverberant, strangely self-referential: the water that the oars beat follows faster, the wind of the fans glows the cheeks that they cool, the city casts its own people out upon itself, and so on. Most odd of all is the reflexivity of the passage describing Cleopatra as like a Venus in a painting. Since Roman art—already an imitation of Greek art—there had been at least two more iterations of the classical tradition: the Italian Renaissance, imitating the ancient Romans, and the English, imitating the Italians; and now Shakespeare adds a bewildering contest between art and nature: Cleopatra makes a better picture than those works of fancy that surpass ("outwork") nature. Is she art or nature?—we have seen the same reflexive emulation in the passage about Antony as "nature's piece 'gainst fancy." The fourth change in Plutarch is the way Shakespeare has given to "inanimate" nature a consciousness and sensitivity reminiscent of an older imagined universe, where every natural object was inhabited by a spirit, a feeling, and a will of its own: the water is amorous of the strokes of the oars, the winds are lovesick with the odor of the sails, the ship's tackle becomes engorged and erectile with the touch of the mermaids' hands, the wharves sense the perfume, the air itself yearns to go look at Cleopatra.

The fifth—the deepest and strangest—change Shakespeare makes in Plutarch is one that would be inexplicable if we had not already looked at *King Lear's* paradoxes of nothingness, the zero, and creation. At the end of each of the two main segments of the speech there is a phrase of reflexive negation: "what they undid, did" and "made a gap in nature." The fans of the cupids do what they undo, they inflame what they cool, and what they cool is Cleopatra. The air is dragged toward Cleopatra as to a vacuum; it is only the possibility of a paradoxical "vacancy" (nature, according to Renaissance science, abhors a vacuum) that prevents the air from being sucked in toward her. The implication is that Cleopatra represents—*is*—one of those spaces or opportunities for nature to do new things that are described by today's chaos theory. She is, in mathematical terms, an endless unrepeating space-filling algorithm; in physical terms, she is a universe-spawning quantum vacuum. Her "infinite variety" is fractally deep. And in this odd description of her all the other changes Shakespeare makes in Plutarch make sense. His verse provides the language of the speech with the feedback connections needed to make it nonlinear. That nonlinearity gives what is associated with her the faceted, textured, filtered qualities Benoit Mandelbrot attributes to fractal phenomena: they are "grainy, hydralike, in between, pimply, pocky, ramified, sea-weedy, strange, tangled, tortuous, wiggly, wispy, wrinkled." Objects with these qualities "take on a life of their own," they are active and sensitive in surprising ways.

All these strange phenomena take place in the charged field between Antony, enthroned in the marketplace, and Cleopatra, sitting in her barge. Love can constitute a field that generates its partners rather than vice versa. What *Antony and Cleopatra* have discovered between them is literally, in the cant phrase, bigger than both of them. Without it he is an aging failed general, she is an aging spoiled courtesan. If *Antony and Cleopatra* were mimed throughout, or rewritten by Hollywood scriptwriters, that is all we would see. For in Shakespeare's play the spontaneously self-generating system of love is immanent in—*is*—the language of the play.

The Language of the Ouroboros: Hyperbole, Climax, Reflexivity, Tautology, Paradox

The rhetorical style of *Antony and Cleopatra* is what Jacobeans called "Asiatismus"—a kind of writing full of figures and metaphors, a style opposed to the more severe "Attic" rhetoric. Cicero distinguishes two types of Asianism: the "subtle-sententious" and the "grandiloquent-impetuous." The Romans in the play tend toward the cooler Atticism; the Egyptians are unfailingly subtle, sententious, grandiloquent, and impetuous. As it happens, Asianism in rhetoric was at the time the play was written (1607) going out of fashion, and the austere Attic or Senecan style was in the ascendant. Octavius' characteristic style is the successful style of the new post-Renaissance world.

Let us look at four rhetorical figures in the play, all characteristic of "Asiatismus" or Asian rhetoric: hyperbole, climax, self-reflective figures including tautology, and paradox. In the greatest speeches of the play many of these figures are combined together.

Hyperbole in this play hardly needs illustration. Almost every scene dealing with Cleopatra and Antony contains it in riotous abundance:

> His legs bestrid the ocean; his reared arm
> Crested the world: his voice was propertied
> As all the tunèd spheres . . .

A peculiarly strong form of hyperbole in the play occurs five times: "love of Love," "man of men," "captain's captain," "king of kings," "lord of lords." This figure contains a variety of operations, all of which are central to the play's meaning: transcendence, superlativeness, the extraction of a quintes-

sence, and the emergence of the absolutely concrete. It is also a reflexive figure, like so many in the play: the subject referring back to itself, requiring no
comparison, complete in itself. Cleopatra threatens to give Charmian bloody
teeth if she "with Caesar paragon again" her "man of men" (I.v.71). You
cannot explain the less contingent by the more contingent. You cannot measure the superlative with the comparative. Infinite virtue cannot be counted.

Hyperbole is also used sarcastically and ironically, to describe falsity and
weakness. There is a hint of this when Enobarbus describes Cleopatra as
dying "twenty times upon far poorer moment" (I.ii.143)—but Cleopatra,
even when she is acting a part, is always absolutely 100% genuine as well:
"she makes a shower of rain as well as Jove." The irony is heavier when
Enobarbus hyperbolically parodies Lepidus—

> Hoo! Hearts, tongues, figures, scribes, bards, poets, cannot
> Think, speak, cast, write, sing, number—hoo! —
> His love to Antony.
> (III.ii.16)

—and hyperbolically deflates Antony's hyperbolical rhetoric: "Now he'll
outstare the lightning" (III.xiii.195).

Another characteristic figure in *Antony and Cleopatra* is climax (grada-
tio, auxesis, ascendus, methalemsis) and a variant of it, a kind of "heaping
up" figure (accumulatio, congeries). The evolutionary progression in the following example is typical:

> Kingdoms are clay: our dungy earth alike
> Feeds beasts as man: the nobleness of life
> Is to do thus . . .

Clay, dung, earth, feeds, beasts, man, nobleness of life: the series passes
through all the levels of creation and explodes, like Cleopatra's dolphin, out
of its element: speech is replaced by Antony's great public kiss; the rhetoric
has become concrete; and the world of comparison has given way to the un-
measurable, the least contingent, the "peerless." Most of the great encomi-
ums of the play (in other words, most of the great speeches, for this is a play
of and about praise) are climactic or cumulative in form, and conclude with
a hyperbolical leap at the end of the series.

But climax also has its opposite in the play: a sort of progressive reductio
ad absurdum, reduction to absurdity:

> O, let him marry a woman that cannot go, sweet Isis, I beseech thee,
> and let her die too, and give him a worse, and let worse follow worse
> till the worst of all follow him laughing to his grave, fiftyfold a cuckold!
> (I.ii.64)

dox. Once an event has happened, it was always inevitable; if it was inevitable there is nothing its victim can do to escape, and all his attempts merely bring him closer to his doom. History is the discipline by which we convince ourselves that what did happen had to happen.

The self-strangling metaphors suggest also a certain psychological condition, well known to those who compete in games of skill: as when the natural golf swing or tennis stroke is ruined by excessive self-consciousness. It is a crippling syndrome; the consciousness of one's consciousness as the cause of failure becomes in turn the maiming consciousness of which we are maimingly conscious. It is an infinite regress that for once richly deserves the name "regress." The psychological mechanism is the same in some forms of sexual impotence and insomnia. When this mechanism is at work in a game that combines luck and skill, its workings are almost indistinguishable from bad luck to the loser. A poker player on a losing streak, conscious that he is on a losing streak and conscious of that consciousness as a bias to the game, always suffers horribly bad luck. This is exactly what happens to Antony in his games of dice and cockfighting with Caesar. Antony's handicap is his limitless self-consciousness, taught him by Cleopatra. Enormous sexual potency as well as sexual impotence can result from this feedback of awareness, and the line between them is very thin. Images of both are strongly associated with Antony: his reared arm crests the world, his virtue (manhood) is infinite; but he "cannot hold this visible shape," and "the soldier's pole is fall'n" (IV.xiv.14, IV.xv.65).

All the great tropes that we have seen in the play suggest highly self-aware thought processes. Climax expresses the cumulativeness of mental feedback; hyperbole its curious power to be always one step further than one's assessment of it, since the assessing itself must then be assessed. Reflexive figures express the self-referential qualities of self-awareness; and paradoxical figures express the polarities between which the mind oscillates and also its potential for self-paralysis. The reductio ad absurdum figure suggests the odd way in which the mind can run itself into an impossible situation that can only "purge itself" by some "desperate change."

Creation and Control

It must now be clear what is the central mechanism of creation in *Antony and Cleopatra*. Shakespeare has isolated it by means of the peculiar historical setting and story of his play, and has turned the magnifying glass of his poetry on the operations of the creative process in physical and biological systems, in the psychology of creative individuals, in the relationship of his larger-than-life lovers, and in the microstructure and microprocess of language itself. The key mechanism is essentially the same, though it has many names: nonlinearity, feedback, sensitivity, reflexivity, self-reference; nonlinearity at the logical and mathematical level, feedback at the level of simple physical systems, sensitivity at the level of complex ecological systems with many players, reflexivity at the level of human consciousness, self-reference at the level of language. It is only recently that the grand synthesis of chaos and complexity theory has made possible the gathering of all these phenomena under one conceptual umbrella, and thus we do not yet have a single uncontested term for the general principle. But we can state it roughly as follows: new things emerge in the universe through the iterative process of old things (including even the originary nothing itself) affecting and being affected by themselves and each other. This is as true for persons as for turbulent flow systems, for fractal geometry as for interpersonal dynamics, for the structures of language as for the operations of the marketplace.

Put baldly this way, the principle seems oversimple—too abstract to use and common sense anyway. But when we follow up its implications, we get a useful set of distinguishing characteristics or landmarks that will tell us when we are on the right creative track. One is that the elements of our system are free to communicate with each other—that is, they possess a common language and expressive medium and are not isolated from one another, and at the same time the constraints of that language do not erect barriers between the elements. Another is that the process goes on by itself and does not always have to be jogged. Another is the emergence of strange attractors, beautiful global forms, out of the apparently random results of repetitive iteration. Yet another is that articulated order does not decrease in such a creative system, as it would if it were based on linear dynamics, but increases. One hard-to-define characteristic is the kind of shape it produces—branchy, self-similar (its details resemble its macrostructure, with continuous variations), rhythmic, deep, multidimensional, rich yet simple, and aesthetically satisfying.

The great advantage of the feedback principle shows up when we think of the errors we make when we try alternative explanations for creativity. If we wait for the advent of a boundless *outside* source of creation, we may neglect the humble growth that goes on in and around us, out of the fertile nothing here and now, when we participate in it. If we mistrust self-awareness and insist that creativity must always be unconscious of itself, we will miss the point where the iterative reflections of mental feedback begin to sketch out the new shape of a strange attractor, where the feedback process becomes so complex as to forget its own origins, where thought turns into mystical contemplation, and the self-mirrorings extend out into an infinite new country. If we believe that new things only happen by means of the linear application of power, our efforts will founder in thermodynamic decay amid the wreckage of what we have destroyed to fuel and clear the way for our actions. If we believe that no new creation *can* happen, we become parasites upon those who continue to take the risk of inner self-transformation and outer interaction. If we get too quickly bored by the repetitiveness of the iterations by which the feedback proceeds and reject a mimetic tradition because of its apparent stagnation and lack of novelty, we may cut off the creative process before it has had its chance to crystallize out into an emergent new structure. And if in panic or disgust at the apparent lawlessness of the creative process, we try to apply inappropriate constraints and bonds to it, which interrupt its interactions and development rather than provide a more sensitive medium of communication, we may abort it altogether. It is this last point that bears most directly on our present theme.

For indeed, *Antony and Cleopatra* tackles more directly and frankly than any other play the problems associated with bonds. We have already seen in *A Midsummer Night's Dream* the sterile and deadly consequences of trying to impress an inappropriate stamp on the wax of human nature and the rebellion that such bonds inspire. This was a brief glance, forgotten in the happy ending. But in *Antony and Cleopatra* there is everywhere a sense of the agonizing constriction and chafing of simple-minded bonds, prohibitions, and restraints, especially when the expedient political morality of the Romans attempts to curb what it takes to be the wild voluptuousness of the Egyptians. The Romans counter the excesses of random fertility and productiveness with an ethic based on negativity, control, restraint, and the cutting off of extraneous possibilities. The characteristic images are of coldness, hardness, and tight bindings, which evoke the feeling of wearing armor. One must "pull oneself together" rather than "let oneself go." In the Alps, still a disciplined Roman, not yet corrupted by Cleopatra, Antony was like a stag in the snow, feeding on the bark of trees; his eyes glowed like "plated Mars," his "great fights" "burst the buckles on his breast" (I.i.4). The league between Antony and Caesar is a "band," a "knot," a "hoop," that "knits" or "cements" them together; Octavia is like a "statue," "still," "cold," and "holy"; a man should control himself as he controls his horse, and the neigh of a curbed horse is used to symbolize restraint; the "squares" of war and the "square" of moderation, the golden rule, imply a squareness and uptightness in the Roman worldview that are reminiscent of the hippie idiom. Above all, the Roman gods are invoked as principles of control (not forces of creativity)—a kind of moral body armor that a man puts on to make his flesh insensitive. But these images of control become images of strangulation, freezing, tearing, and grinding, as the "band" between Antony and Octavius becomes a halter and a noose. The two surviving triumvirs are like teeth that fruitlessly grind each other. The tender flesh is torn by steel. The state crushes the creativity that it is supposed to nurture.

But it is not merely the restraints of the Romans, however unimaginative and "square," but the boundlessness—the bondlessness—of the lovers that brings about their downfall. They do, after all, commit suicide, and their deaths are full of the imagery of dissolution, of the loss of structure, of melting. Instead of fighting on land, where his strengths are, Antony insists on fighting at sea; indeed, he wishes he could fight in the fire and the air too. This attempt to transcend "the element he lives in" culminates in the scene of his suicide, whose poetry evokes a strange dissolving of the solid world into vapor:

> Sometime we see a cloud that's dragonish,
> A vapor sometime like a bear or lion,

> A towered citadel, a pendant rock,
> A forkèd mountain, or blue promontory . . .

All this is like the painted backdrop of a stage, tiny, gaudy, hypnotic—but here revealed for what it is—

> With trees upon't that nod unto the world
> And mock our eyes with air. Thou hast seen these signs;
> Thy are black vesper's pageants.

Indeed, Antony's pageantry is being dissolved, since it was, after all, no more than a cloud, an optical illusion, the castles in the air of his rhetoric, the miraculous meaningful air of language.

> . . . now thy captain is
> Even such a body: here I am Antony,
> Yet cannot hold this visible shape, my knave.

Antony prepares to take off his costume—the costume of the Roman general, the armor of self-control, the external shape of his character.

> Unarm, Eros. The long day's task is done,
> And we must sleep.
> (IV.xiv.2–36)

The noble Roman warrior would not ask his armorer to kill him, as Antony now does; Eros is more under control than Antony and neatly dispatches himself rather than have to kill his master. Certainly a traditional hero would not botch his suicide; Antony, however, does not get his sword in right and survives another two scenes. The constraints and conventions of the theater have collapsed. There follows one of the most awkward and potentially ludicrous pieces of stage business in Shakespeare—the hauling of Antony aloft into Cleopatra's monument. Antony even begins his last speech too early—"I am dying, Egypt, dying"—and has to wait until they have got him up before he can start again (IV.xv.18, 41). He asks for wine to clear his throat. Cleopatra's lament for him after he is gone reinforces the theme of melting, dissolution, the collapse of restraints and boundaries:

> The crown o' th' earth doth melt. My lord!
> O, withered is the garland of the war,
> The soldier's pole is fall'n: young boys and girls
> Are level now with men. The odds is gone,
> And there is nothing left remarkable
> Beneath the visiting moon.
> (IV.xv.63)

But in his last moments Antony's Roman rhetoric recovers its martial splendor. Perhaps Antony is only "acting out" a grand suicide scene for which he is unqualified by his newfound self-consciousness and reflexive sensibility—the old uncomplicated Antony would make a better heroic actor!—but nevertheless on his deathbed he rediscovers the need for bonds and the keeping of contracts. He becomes a dying husband, rather than a failed lover; he earns back the title of hero, but in a new way, not as the one who is unconscious of pain and death, but as the one who carries his consciousness through to the end.

> The miserable change now at my end
> Lament nor sorrow at, but please your thoughts
> In feeding them with those my former fortunes,
> Wherein I lived; the greatest prince o' th' world,
> The noblest; and do now not basely die,
> Not cowardly put off my helmet to
> My countryman . . .
> (IV.xv.51)

Unarmed, he somehow still wears the poetic helmet of his bond, but it is a reinvented one. He is, in his own epitaph, "a Roman, by a Roman / Valiantly vanquished." The language is both reflexive and self-conscious, and at the same time simple and grand. Somehow between them Antony and Cleopatra have rescued this scene; and Cleopatra, having found her poetic voice, now takes complete control of the play, a grip that will not weaken until the last scene is over.

This strange recovery of bonds and legitimate titles is even clearer in the death of Cleopatra than in that of Antony. Although the images of melting and dissolution do not go away—"I am fire, and air; my other elements / I give to baser life" (V.ii.289)—they are joined with a new emergent structure of commitment:

> Husband, I come:
> Now to that name my courage prove my title!
> (V.ii.287)

She has recovered the notion of bond—literally, in the "band" of "husband"—and claims title, legal possession, through the sacrificial means with which we are familiar in the Henry plays. Blood is the sealing wax that legitimates the contract. In her last words the imagery of melting combines strangely with the devotion of motherhood, as she takes the snake to her bosom:

> Peace, peace!
> Dost thou not see my baby at my breast,
> That sucks the nurse asleep? . . .
> As sweet as balm, as soft as air, as gentle . . .
> (V.ii.308)

She dies in her full queenly regalia, crown, robe, and all, asserting her sovereignty and the bonds that bind her to her people and to Antony.

In these last scenes there is an episode that has scandalized Shakespeare's critics: Cleopatra, part prisoner of the victorious Romans, lies to Caesar's accountants about the extent of her wealth, holding secret the bulk of her treasure so as to keep at her disposal the power to give imperial gifts. How can she think of possessions at a time like this? But the attempt to stay ahead of the game is entirely in her indomitable spirit, it is delightfully comic, and more— it shows that she knows the worth of money, the concentrated and universalized fertility of human gratitude, obligation, incentive, bond. It is something, as Jane Austen says, to be "mistress of Pemberley," and diamonds are a girl's best friend. Uptight Octavius, when her ruse is revealed, claims that he is above haggling: "Caesar's no merchant, to make prize with you / Of things that merchants sold" (V.ii.183). He is unaware of his own implied insult— that Cleopatra *is* a merchant, even a whore. This insult—or rather the priggishness that would make it one if Octavius had the sensitivity to see the implication—makes Cleopatra livid with fury and cements her resolution to frustrate his plans by suicide: "He words me, girls, he words me, that I should not / Be noble to myself!" (V.ii.191). Shakespeare allows the question to arise whether Cleopatra would have considered suicide if she had been able to avoid the indignity of being exhibited in Octavius' triumphal procession as a trophy, a belonging of his. The point here, though, is that Cleopatra does achieve a magnificent suicide. This is far more interesting than some abstract, disinterested Kantian decision to do the Right Thing. Who will blame Cleopatra if some of her motivations are not of the purest?—especially since her very principle is impurity, the inclusion and communication of all possible motions in a turbulence that issues in beautiful emergent form. She achieves, as a breather, the perfection of sculptural shape that Octavia, her rival, could only reach through bloodless stoicism and insensitivity:

> My resolution's placed, and I have nothing
> Of woman in me: now from head to foot
> I am marble-constant: now the fleeting moon
> No planet is of mine.
> (V.ii.238)

This emergent form can be found in the very vocabulary of Cleopatra's final scene. The sounds of the words, energized by such an immense linguistic force field, fall naturally into certain patterns; the language was just waiting for this inevitable form to crop up in it. The word "aspic," with its vowels "a" and "i," and the consonants "s," "p," and "c," is the key: "juice," "Egypt's," "grape," "moist," "lip," "Iras," "last," "lips," "aspic," "stroke," "as a lover's pinch," "proves me base," "spend that kiss," "intrinsicate," "poor venomous fool, / Be angry, and dispatch," "speak," "ass unpolicied," "peace," "sucks the nurse asleep," "as sweet as balm, as soft as air," "A lass unparalleled" (V.ii.280–316).

Thus the result of Shakespeare's grand experiment, his search for the inner mechanism of creativity and economic production, yields a further fruit. Indeed, the feedback processes and reflexivity that creation requires must be liberated by the breaking of existing ossified structures, the bounteous abandonment of economic prudence, and the apparent drowning of being in process. But the outcome of the self-organizing processes that result is new coherent form, new titles of possession, new being. The martial heroism of Antony and the marble-constancy of Cleopatra in their deaths arise spontaneously out of the brew of their claimed freedom; they are not artificial rules imposed from outside. The bonds that they rediscover, of husband and hero, queen and wife, are now proven to be necessary consequences and appropriate expressions of the creative turbulence.

A Philosophical Coda

We may even add a further, metaphysical thought.

In Antony and Cleopatra rhetoric claims for itself, and indeed possesses, concrete force (the dramatist, of course, is at liberty to assign greater or lesser concreteness to whatever elements in his play he chooses: this is part of the amazing freedom of art). The rhetoric of Antony's reply to the desertion of Enobarbus has real killing force. The rhetoric of Cleopatra in her death scene is able to fell Iras as if poleaxed.

In this play the distinction between how you find out and what you find out—between epistemology and ontology, between sensation and reality, between rhetoric and action—this great distinction breaks down, in a way that constitutes a further twist upon Shakespeare's great insights about the productive zero in *King Lear*. In the world outside the theater, it is our philosophical fashion to preserve the distinction; the distinction itself is a useful part of our rhetoric. Similarly, we are comfortable with a mimetic theory of meaning, since some idea of reference, mimesis, or representation is useful to keep these two faces of reality apart. In some respects, indeed, Shakespeare makes that extratheatrical world triumph in the play: Caesar remarks on the fact that the ground has not in fact convulsed with earthquakes at the death of Antony. But Cleopatra explains:

> . . . young boys and girls
> Are level now with men. The odds is gone,
> And there is nothing left remarkable
> Beneath the visiting moon.

The death of Antony *was* the earthquake.

The concreteness of rhetoric is apparent in another sense as well. The poetry that Antony and Cleopatra exchange is Shakespeare's theatrical convention to represent their sexual intercourse. The rhetorical medium of the play is the love between its protagonists.

It is therefore not surprising that of all Shakespeare's plays *Antony and Cleopatra* should have the largest number of messengers and scenes in which messengers are important. A messenger and his message are the natural symbols of knowing and what is known, of epistemology and ontology, rhetoric and reality. Cleopatra characteristically confuses them at all times. When Alexas arrives with the orient pearl Antony has kissed, she says to him:

> . . . coming from him, that great med'cine hath
> With his tinct gilded thee.
> (I.v.36)

The passage where she physically attacks the bearer of the news of Antony's marriage is justly famous. We exclaim that Cleopatra is wrong, that she is totally unjust; but her performance in this scene is actually an uncanny piece of psychological self-preparation and autotherapy. By the end of the scene we realize that she has received this crushing news without being crushed, that she has preserved all her weapons intact, that the encounter has actually toned up her emotional muscles for the battles to come. In the next scene in which we see her, she is both pumping the messenger for information on her rival and at the same time turning his replies into what she wants emotionally to hear. She is in splendid trim and there is no doubt she will get Antony back. In what sense, then, was she wrong in confusing the messenger with the message? By doing so she is able to alter the message so that she is capable of dealing with it and deflecting its consequences. By her response she actually changes the nature of the event at a range of over a thousand miles, since an event is, after all, the sum of its consequences.

Antony, when under the influence of "Roman" thoughts, tends to separate messenger from message: "Speak to me home, mince not the general tongue" (I.ii.106); but under Cleopatra's influence he treats the bringers of unpleasant news much as she does. The classical example is the whipping of Thidias. One of the most poignant signs of Antony's decline is his use of the schoolmaster as an ambassador, where once he was able to send kings as errand boys. The concrete force of Antony's rhetoric seems to be fading, though as the death of Enobarbus shows, it still has its impact. Ironically enough, it was the Thidias episode that persuaded Enobarbus to leave Antony. Antony's voice, which can be as "loud as Mars," "like all the tuned spheres," or like "rattling thunder," is one of his most prominent characteristics. Again, it is described as having concrete force. Many of the descriptions of Antony and Cleopatra sound like directions to impossibly ideal actors. Clearly Shakespeare must have realized that these protagonists are unplayable, if one is to do them justice. This difficulty is itself put to emotional use by the dramatist. The actor is a sort of messenger, his part the message; the pathos of Antony and Cleopatra is partly that their roles must be performed by lesser human beings—by the stage actors, by themselves.

In deliberately confusing ontology and epistemology, Shakespeare is making a philosophical point of great importance: that physical objects have being only to the extent that they feel and and are felt by other physical objects; that to be sensitive and sensible to other objects is to have being. For centuries material determinists have insisted on the deadness, the essential lack of internal spontaneous process, of self-awareness and self-motivation, in the fundamental matter of the universe. We now know, from Richard Westfall's fine biography of Newton, that the reason natural philosophers of the Enlightenment insisted on the deadness and inert passivity of material nature was in order to concede to God a necessary role in giving it all life and animation, so that the divine would not be a fifth wheel in the world. Not daring to see God as immanent in the universe, and preferring to keep him outside it where he could, so to speak, be kept an eye on, they tried to make physicality as incomplete as possible in respect of all the properties attributed to soul, consciousness, reflectiveness, initiative, originality, so that he would still have something important to do.

Partly because of their purely arbitrary distinctions between substance and accidents, the natural philosophers never sufficiently recognized how great a problem it was for their view—of the physical universe as insensitive and devoid of internal process—that matter has properties. That is, particles, atoms, and molecules are not totally transparent; they interrupt the forces that encounter them in such a way as to make them perceptible to humans and other animals. The light must be broken, scattered, transformed, absorbed, refracted, for us to see things at all: and it is only what is seeable—perceptible, in more general terms—that can be of any concern to science. If matter had no internal process, light would come to us utterly unaltered by the matter it had encountered, and thus the matter would be invisible. Further, it is only where matter resists the complete logical explication of its internal process, where it interrupts the linear flow of rational consequence and we are forced to establish a constant, a given, that we have any fixed point that might justify a claim for its actual existence. It is the irreducibility of the fundamental constants—the speed of light, the gravitational constant, the electron volt constant, Planck's constant, pi—their darkness and opacity to any further reductive explanation, their mathematical irrationality, their idiosyncratic characterization of the fundamental relations of physical objects—that gives them their foundational role in our understanding of reality.

As we now know, simply taking up space is a complex performance for matter, and its other qualities, of mass, charge, parity, and so on, are the maintained achievements of its internal process. Its external communicative process is more remarkable still, of course—crystals, plants, animals, we ourselves, are the emergent forms that such communication makes possible. Thus the universe postulated by the material determinists, lacking that mysterious inner negotiation and external sensitivity that make matter observable, would be completely invisible—and of course untouchable, unsmellable, inaudible, and tasteless as well. Since science relies essentially on observation, science would be impossible in such a universe. It is only to the extent that the universe and the things in it have some analogue to inner metabolism and outer sociability—only, that is, the extent to which they are alive—that they can be said to be at all. Being is not given, but the achievement of the universe's continuous originating inventiveness, its life and growth.

A large part of this liveness, this internal reflexivity, of ordinary matter is devoted necessarily to making more or less crude representations of the rest of the universe. Butterfly chrysalises often combine two or three levels of representation, aimed at various possible predators: the appearance of a dead leaf for the stupidest ones, a spot of color denoting poison for the cleverer ones that have spotted the disguise—and sometimes the false appearance of a chrysalis of a truly poisonous species, saving the metabolic expense of manufacturing real poison. Vines pestered with butterflies will grow leaves that look like butterflies, on the correct theory that butterflies will not lay eggs on what they think are fellow butterflies. But these are simple forms of representation and imitation compared to what one finds among higher animals. The greylag goose expresses its love for its mate by pointedly making a mimed attack on an absent, counterfactual goose, in a "triumph ceremony" that is a fine analogy of human theater. Courting bowerbirds build elaborate useless bowers as representations of their excellent nest-building genes. But the need to represent and depict goes all the way down to the most primitive entities in the universe. An atom must find ways of translating the impact of incoming energy into terms that it can absorb without flying apart; indeed, all the atoms that exist are the ones that didn't fly apart. Atoms do this by adjusting the disposition of the electrons in the harmonic series of electron shells that makes up their outer skin; and they relieve the pressure of such impacts by giving off photons of their own, whose unique signature can be picked up by a spectrograph. Those spectral emanations are in fact representations of their environment, in terms that are unique to the element that produces them.

A former student of mine, the designer and architect Jack Rees, has suggested in unpublished work that it is no coincidence that the great physicists—Newton, Einstein, and so on—tended to make their discoveries in mechanics simultaneously with their discoveries in optics. Perhaps, he suggests, optics and mechanics are at base the same thing. That is, objects in the universe exist (have mechanical properties) only in and through the fact that they express themselves and experience the expressive activity of other objects (they see and are seen). All exchanges of information are conducted by the photons of light or by particles that can be translated into photons. And mechanical processes are fundamentally exchanges of information. Certainly the basic principle of all physical science is that it must be based on observation—that is, it assumes that an object has reality only to the extent that it is observable, even if indirectly. Scientific reality is observability. At the same time the only way that anything can be observed is by its effect on other things; thus for scientific reality we need not only a world of observable objects but also a world of observing objects, that is, objects that can register by their response the presence of other objects. The power of the observer in the constitution of fundamental reality has been confirmed again and again by quantum physics, and is already a feature of our electronic technology. We can generalize this idea to the proposition that every thing exists if and only if, and to the extent that, it represents other things and is represented by them—that is, it expresses itself in such a way as to to be intelligibly recognized as what it is, and it registers and records its fellow beings in such a way as to make *their* existence concrete.

Thus representation is a fundamental feature of reality, not just a superficial freak of civilized mimicry. The universe was only a "buzzing, booming confusion," as William James put it, at the first moment of the Big Bang. Since then it has been painting and sculpting itself with greater and greater precision, evolving complex chemistry, plants, and animals to do it more effectively, and achieving thereby a denser and denser reality and concreteness, the more sensory modalities it has brought into play.

It is significant that at the very beginning of Western material science, in the age of Bacon and Descartes, Shakespeare should have given us a play that founds being upon creativity rather than the reverse. It has taken us four hundred years, through some of the most brilliant intellectual achievements of the human race, to reach a scientific view of the world that confirms his insight; in which we can now see the particles of matter, no less than living organisms or conscious brained beings, as feedback processes with some measure of autonomy, self-determination, unpredictable historical identity, and reciprocal communication with the rest of the universe. One way of putting this is in the language of another former student of mine, the Belgian philosopher Koen dePryck. He says that the world we live in is an onto-epistemological universe—that is, it only exists to the extent that its participants know and experience themselves and each other, and it is only knowable to the extent that all its inhabitants have an individual inexplicable existence. Everything experiences itself and each other into being. Thus if, in the terms we have explored in *King Lear,* everything *can* come from nothing, the mechanism by which it does so is the mutual "observing-into-being" that is the central theme of *Antony and Cleopatra.*

Putting this thought in economic terms, we may even say that the universe is a market, a system of communication and exchange, in which value—that is, being—is built through internal and external feedback processes. It is a network of bonds, a "fair chain of love," as Chaucer put it, and the warrant of being is what Dante called "the love that moves the sun and the other stars." The currency of the market is codified and abstracted obligation—debt—which is the economic version of gratitude and love in the moral sphere. Money is love incarnated as best it can be in physical property relations. But art is also the incarnation in crude physical terms of values that are the result of far more subtle and complex (though no less physical) neural and social processes. A great painting or sculpture must endure its material enactment in paint or stone, as love and gratitude must endure theirs in bequests, wages, gifts, and payments. As modernist critics of the market have rightly pointed out, markets are based on reproducibility, representation, and image. Thus an artist seeking to create truly authentic art—art that has the concrete reality and presence of other objects in the universe—should not avoid or seek to undermine the methods of the market, which are themselves a developed and concentrated version of the universal process of natural evolution. Rather, such an artist should, as his or her predecessors did in Florence, Amsterdam, and Paris, include the turbulence of market feedback in the work of art, especially the turbulence that results when an object both *is* and *represents,* and thus has both a face value and an intrinsic value. The intrinsic value of an object, say one made of gold or precious stone, is itself fossilized face value, for as we have noted, the properties of an object—its color, ductility, crystalline structure, or refractive capacities—are *already* the way it represents the rest of the world and declares its own meaning; it has being to the extent that it has meaning.

9

"ᴅᴇᴀʀ Lɪfe ʀᴇᴅᴇᴇᴍs yᴏᴜ"

The Economics of Resurrection

The Statue Comes to Life

In the last scenes of *The Winter's Tale* Shakespeare presents us with an extraordinary episode whose meaning is still being debated. Leontes, king of Sicily, has completed sixteen years of penance for a monstrous crime. He had falsely suspected his wife, Hermione, and his best friend, Polixenes, of having an adulterous affair. His tyrannous pursuit of this obsession had resulted in the apparent deaths of his entire family—his faithful wife, Hermione, his little boy, Mamillius, and his nameless newborn daughter, who had seemingly perished at sea or been abandoned to her death on a remote seacoast. In the final scenes of the play the lost daughter, with the appropriate name Perdita, returns unharmed; and more marvelous still, Leontes' friend Paulina shows him a statue of his dead wife, whose amazing artistic verisimilitude is confirmed when she moves, steps down from the pedestal, and warmly embraces her astonished husband. Of course there is an explanation—she had not really died and had been kept secretly in Paulina's house. But Shakespeare did not find this episode in any of his sources—it is his own invention—and he keeps it deadly secret until the last scene. He even deliberately misleads us by having another character see a vision of Hermione's ghost in a dream, a piece of theatrical legerdemain he never practices anywhere else. He is deliberately setting up a theatrical miracle, the equivalent in the art of drama to the magical feat of Pygmalion in sculpture, whose statue of Galatea, according to the myth, turned into a living woman.

It is appropriate that we should conclude our close examination of Shakespeare's plays where we began it, in *The Winter's Tale*—one of the two plays (*The Tempest* is the other) in which Shakespeare summed up the art of his life. In its final scene all the economic themes we have looked at come together in a single grand yet subtle equation: the continuity of natural and human creation and the naturalness of profit; the divine fertility of the zero; the inseparability of personal and property rights; the constructive tension of justice and mercy; the sacrificial union of nominal inscribed value and given intrinsic value; the parable of the talents and the transformation of debt into ownership; and the iterative and reflexive sources of bounty. Above all, at the end of *The Winter's Tale* the bonds that are the common root both of the market and of moral relationships receive their most fully rounded explanation.

Nature and Art Revisited

In chapter 2 we looked closely at the conversation between Perdita, the shepherdess-princess, and Polixenes, her lover's royal father, about the naturalness of the "carnations and streaked gillyvors" she refuses to plant in her garden. Perdita's objections to their artificiality and her implicit separation of natural value from human economic value are gently refuted in the passage, or rather her right and proper reverence for "great creating Nature" is extended to human art and productiveness as well. Her reluctance to continue her relationship with a prince of the blood, despite her love for him, is related to this laudable but overnarrow construal of the value of the hereditary and natural, over the contrived and intended. The fact that she turns out to be a real princess is both a confirmation of her argument and a denial of it. It is a confirmation in that the genuineness and nobility of her feeling is vouched for by her royal blood. But it is a denial in that human social and cultural arrangements—"good breeding" through generations of aristocratic inheritance—can make their way into and mix themselves indissolubly with natural genetic descent, and thus Perdita herself is a sort of gillyvor, a refined and cultivated hybrid. But as Perdita reminds us, the selfsame sun that shines on the king's court "hides not his visage from our cottage, but / Looks on alike" (IV.iv.447). The implication is that we are all descended from the same stock—as the old peasant rhyme went, "When Adam delved and Eve span, / Who was then the gentleman?"

Leontes will only have an heir, says the Delphic oracle, when what is lost is found again. If Hermione and his children are dead, this means that he must marry again, but can only do so when what is lost is found. Thus the return of Perdita—the name means literally "what is lost"—is intimately connected with the possibility of Leontes' remarriage. In fact he is going to remarry his own wife, apparently returned from the dead, and "what is lost" is his heir herself; but in the deep logic of the play, the return of the queen is conditional upon the return of her daughter the princess. The first three acts

of the play recount the tragic and horrifying consequences of Leontes' jealous fury, as a fable of the corruption of conscious reason, social order, and
political authority. As in *A Midsummer Night's Dream,* so here: when the
conventional rule of law goes wrong, the only answer is a temporary escape
into arcadia, the natural subtext and precursor of the city. The fourth act of
The Winter's Tale is thus a delicious pastoral of springtime after winter, of
natural creation after civilized sterilization. In this final act, however, Shakespeare must reunite not only a broken family and a shattered theatrical plot
but also the estranged halves of what should be a philosophical unity—that
is, nature and art. Only if the shepherdess comes back into the court can the
statue come to life. Perdita's springtime breathes natural vitality back into
the dead stone of ossified social order, and the mother is reborn through her
daughter. The statue, then, is the exact symbolic reciprocal of the gillyvors—
they are nature cultivated, the statue is culture animated by natural life.

Further, the play itself is a kind of gillyvor, a kind of statue come to life.
The dead lines of its text must be animated by the live breath of actors in
each new generation, else the play dies. At the same time the theater is a
crude living form of entertainment that remains clownish and ignorant unless it is cultivated, as Shakespeare cultivates it, with poetry and the self-
reflection of high art. When the two come together, what results is riches beyond all measure. This last act of *The Winter's Tale* is saturated with images
of immense wealth and inexhaustible treasure, so much so that in the "blos-
soms of their fortune" the newly rich rustics cannot even get the word
"prosperous" right, "being in so preposterous estate as we are," as the old
shepherd puts it (V.ii.127,150).

Shakespeare insists on the artificiality both of the statue and of the theatrical medium in which it comes to life. He emphasizes the identity of the
sculptor, Julio Romano, who was in fact a real artist, an Italian Renaissance
painter whose name would have sounded vaguely familiar to his audience;
the anachronism (the period in which the play is set was over a thousand
years earlier) is quite deliberate, drawing attention to the contemporaneity
of everything that is happening on this magical stage. Further, he keeps re-
minding us that it is all a play, a story: "as if / The scene you play were
mine"; "I see the play so lies / That I must bear a part"; "This news, which is
called true, is so like an old tale that the verity of it is in strong suspicion";
even the messenger who brings the news of Perdita's arrival is a poet
(IV.iv.595, 658, V.ii.29, V.i.101). These reminders to us of the contrivance of
the thing are not like the arch and knowing editorializing of postmodern
artists and writers, whose intent is to debunk the cultural conventions of the
arts. Rather, they are designed for the opposite effect: to make us realize that
the action on stage includes the audience. When we see a play, we are all
here together in this peculiarly shaped big room, involved in a fairly major
exchange of real economic resources, doing something rather bizarre and
practically useless, agreeing to propositions that are explicitly counter to
fact. And what this ritual actually does is bring dead things to life, and make
the thoughts and feelings of absent or nonexistent persons flow in the brain

cells of those present. What a serious, holy, and dreadful thing it is we do when we communally engage in a fiction! When we do so, we are doing no more nor less than what a seed does when it springs up into a living plant, or what an embryonic cell does when it elaborates itself into an adult animal or human being.

I have taken part in performances of this play when the presence of one extra player was suddenly felt by everyone in the cast, as if the drape covering the statue would reveal not the actress playing Hermione but Shakespeare himself, brought back from the dead in this live performance. It is no more miraculous that the brains of a group of human beings should contain their own personalities than that they should contain, distributed, the soul of a dead poet. The statue scene has about it a strange, still, alchemical sanctity, a breathless poetry that for me vibrates the more after a hundred readings, since I first wrote about it thirty-five years ago:

> prepare
> To see the life as lively mocked, as ever
> Still sleep mocked death . . .
> (V.iii.18)

> What was he that did make it? See, my lord,
> Would you not deem it breathed? And that those veins
> Did verily bear blood? . . .
> The fixure of her eye has motion in't,
> As we are mocked with art.
> (V.iii.63)

But again, is it not just as miraculous that the eyes of real people should move by their own volition, and that what enters them should be seen by a living soul? It is magic either way, but "an art / Lawful as eating" (V.iii.110).

PAULINA: Either forbear,
Quit presently the chapel, or resolve you
For more amazement. If you can behold it,
I'll make the statue move indeed, descend,
And take you by the hand—but then you'll think,
Which I protest against, I am assisted
By wicked powers.

LEONTES: What you can make her do,
I am content to look on; what to speak,
I am content to hear; for 'tis as easy
To make her speak, as move.

PAULINA: It is required
You do awake your faith; then, all stand still.

Or those that think it is unlawful business
I am about, let them depart.

LEONTES: Proceed.
No foot shall stir.

PAULINA: Music, awake her: strike.
'Tis time; descend; be stone no more; approach;
Strike all that look upon with marvel: come;
I'll fill your grave up. Stir; nay, come away;
Bequeath to death your numbness, for from him
Dear life redeems you.
(V.iii.85)

The Productive Zero Revisited

We are in the same territory here as we were in the cliff-top scene in *King Lear,* when the disguised Edgar tells his father, Gloucester, that marvelous lying truth: "Thy life's a miracle." A despairing king experiences an apparently miraculous return from the dead and undergoes an epiphanic realization that life truly is a miracle, a realization that is not undermined by the fact that the miracle is a benign deception. This is the deepest symbol of the moral meaning of Shakespeare's plays; it is also the purest paradigm of economic activity, for it creates the highest value out of the humblest ingredients. In *King Lear* nothingness itself—the zero—is seen as a productive womb of being and value; in *The Winter's Tale* this idea is elaborated in the storm scene at the turning point of the play.

At the end of the tragic third act Antigonus is sent to get rid of King Leontes' baby daughter (later named Perdita), whom Leontes falsely believes to be a bastard conceived in adultery. Antigonus, acting under his royal master's orders though deeply unwilling, abandons the baby on the shore, wrapped in beautiful swaddling clothes and accompanied with rich treasures of gold and jewels. Immediately afterward Antigonus is killed by a bear, and the ship on which he traveled is wrecked by a sudden storm and goes down with all hands. The child is then found by a pair of shepherds, a father and a son, with all the mannerisms of traditional pastoral rustics. They assume that the foundling has been stolen and returned by the fairies, and that her riches are "fairy gold." They resolve to bring her up as their own. Stated baldly, the plotting of this episode is fantastic and improbable, like the libretto of a melodramatic opera, or an old romance. But Shakespeare makes no attempt to remedy the eccentricity of his material: instead he exaggerates it. The stage direction *"Exit, pursued by a bear"* (III.iii.57) is quite consciously comic, and the younger shepherd's account of how "the bear tore out his shoulder bone" is both gruesome and curiously funny. When the shepherd describes the sinking of the ship, he says that "the sea flapdragoned it" (III.iii.96): to flapdragon is to swallow down a flaming delicacy,

such as a sweet or raisin, floating on burning brandy, a practice associated
with the comic feats of wild young drunkards. It is a graphic image, but one
quite at odds with the tragic decorum of the first three acts of the play.
Somehow tragedy has been turned into farce. Worse still, the whole action is
taking place on the seacoast of Bohemia, which is and was known to be a
landlocked country with no coast. The place might as well be called Noplace; it is a sort of magic island, like Thomas More's Utopia or Homer's
Ogygia or Aristophanes' Cloudcuckooland—or Oz, or Narnia, or Middle-
Earth, or Disney's Magic Kingdom.

What on earth is Shakespeare up to? I believe that he is representing dra-
matically the chaos of both destruction and creation, out of which all new
things come. The old shepherd says to the younger: "Now bless thyself; thou
met'st with things dying, I with things new born" (III.iii.110). There is a
natural chaos, a tempest, at the border of earth and sea, life and death, the
animal and the human. It is an artistic and literary chaos, too—Shakespeare
has violently mixed the moods of horror, sadness, laughter, and disbelief,
and the literary genres of tragedy, pastoral, comedy, and grotesque farce.
There is something prelinguistic, unsayable, about this creative space, which
Shakespeare somehow manages to express by mixing his language so
strangely. Out of this chaos come the events that lead to the miracle at the
end of the play, the revival of the statue; but the next thing we see on stage is
Father Time himself, who delivers a mysterious speech.

> I that please some, try all, both joy and terror
> Of good and bad; that makes and unfolds error,
> Now take upon me, in the name of Time,
> To use my wings. Impute it not a crime
> To me, or my swift passage, that I slide
> O'er sixteen years, and leave the growth untried
> Of that wide gap, since it is in my pow'r
> To o'erthrow law, and in one self-born hour
> To plant, and o'erwhelm custom. Let me pass;
> The same I am, ere ancient'st order was
> Or what is now received. I witness to
> The times that brought them in; so shall I do
> To th' freshest things now reigning, and make stale
> The glistering of this present, as my tale
> Now seems to it. Your patience this allowing,
> I turn my glass, and give my scene such growing
> As you had slept between.
> (IV.i.1)

It was this speech that set me off on my own long journey of literary and
philosophical discovery. "One self-born hour" expresses the profound mystery of time, the creative zero out of which all things come. This is the Tao
that cannot be spoken, the mystery of Yahweh who cannot be named, the

Mayan shell or flower glyph, the dance of Shiva creator and destroyer, the unrepresentable countenance of Allah, the sound of one hand clapping— the "wooden O" of Shakespeare's theater, "the great globe itself" (*Henry V*, Prologue, 13; *The Tempest*, IV.i.153). It is in time that we must seek this mystery, in the secret heart of time, which some call eternity and seek to separate from time; but it is the very essence of time. The universe itself, with us in it, is like a beautiful baby found upon a shore after a tempest, with fairy gold about its feet.

Thus when the statue comes to life in the last scene, we are surely being reminded of the "things new born" and the "self-born hour" of the tempest episode and the speech of Father Time. The strangeness of cold inanimate stone turning into warm living flesh is not so strange after all, since it merely accelerates what the universe itself accomplished over its thirteen billion years of time, in this continued moment of the Big Bang: the explosion—or collapse—of the quantum vacuum into material being.

Person and Property Revisited

And we human beings are, miraculously, made of matter, and thus are part of an economic system. A statue in an art gallery is a piece of property, commissioned from an actual individual artist like Julio Romano for a fee, part of the economic system. In this play such a statue turns into a living woman. Part of the meaning of this symbol is that we are indeed property as well as persons; as we saw, *The Merchant of Venice* takes as its central subject all the knotty issues that come along with this fact. Those issues include eating itself (what, and with whom, does one eat, and how does common property legitimately become part of one's body, one's own?); the taking of interest on loans and profit in general (can money legitimately breed like a living thing?); the related issue of single-sex and both-sex love (what is the offspring—the profit, the interest—of single-sex love, and can it be combined with the offspring of both-sex love?); inheritance (what are the conditions under which property can descend to biological offspring?); tribal versus civic allegiance (are we more properly bound to our race and kin, or to the legal claims of our city?); employment and slavery (to what extent can a person be the property of another?); and marriage (in what sense do married people belong to each other?).

In *The Winter's Tale* there is a reprise of all these questions.

Eating and ownership

The unveiling of the statue is the climax of a dinner party at the house of Paulina: "Thither with all greediness of affection are they gone, and there they intend to sup," says one of the courtiers (V.ii.104): the occasion will be a sort of communion meal, a love feast. The art of turning the statue's dead matter into living flesh is indeed, as Paulina says, as "lawful as eating"; for that is what eating is after all. Having been deprived of ownership over herself by the king's tyranny sixteen years ago, Hermione now recovers that self-possession by a process analogous to that by which Locke's apple becomes part of, and thus a possession of, its eater. She can now, as mistress of herself, voluntarily reenter the contract of mutual ownership, which is marriage.

Interest and profit

When we look closer at the spiritually transcendent happy ending of the play, we notice that it can only take place if certain baser motives are enlisted into its service. Autolycus, the salesman and thief, the man of commerce who was "littered under Mercury" (IV.iii.25)—as we recall, he was born under a mercurial sign—is the key agent in revealing the truth and thus making possible the marriage of Florizel and Perdita, and the reuniting of Leontes and Hermione. Ironically, he is not in the least interested in honest dealing; as he admits, "Though I am not naturally honest, I am so sometimes by chance" (IV.iv.715). Autolycus is the spirit of the fairground. Medieval and Renaissance fairs were a sort of cross between the market, the theater, the circus, and the talk show—full of sharp practice and double-dealing, but the arena of the Invisible Hand that in the long run establishes "fair" prices and makes "fair," in the aesthetic sense, the plain life of ordinary folk. All Autolycus wants is to make a profit; and in pursuit of this goal he enormously enriches Perdita's step-relatives, whom he intends to con out of their money. "If I had a mind to be honest," he says,

> I see Fortune would not suffer me: she drops booties in my mouth. I am courted now with a double occasion—gold, and a means to do the prince, my master, good; which who knows how that may turn back to my advancement?
> (IV.iv.835)

The shepherds, who give Autolycus all they have in return for his useless advocacy with King Polixenes, end up making a splendid return on their investment when it is revealed that Perdita is Leontes' daughter. And this explicit praise of the profit motive is but the outer sign of the inner profit that Leontes gains from his marriage. "I might," he says, "Have taken treasure from her lips—" and Paulina breaks in: "And left them / More rich for what they yielded" (V.i.54).

Single-sex and both-sex love

As young men Leontes and Polixenes had been inseparable friends and loving companions. Leontes' unfounded suspicion that Polixenes had cuckolded him had, of course, estranged them from each other for sixteen years, suggesting that single-sex and both-sex loves cannot mix. But at the end of the play Polixenes and Leontes are reunited in friendship by the marriage of their children, in an echo of that reconciliation in *The Merchant of Venice* where Portia allows Antonio to give back to Bassanio, her husband, the wedding ring he had given away to save his friend.

Inheritance

Shakespeare faces this issue when Polixenes objects to the marriage of his son to a "shepherdess," who would then have property rights as a princess. Is Polixenes wrong or right to do this? Clearly it would be wrong to go to the lengths he contemplates—putting the bride and her family to torture and death. But there is a real issue whether marriage should include a prudent economic component, and should thus involve the advice and planning of the families and friends of the bride and groom, especially when, as here, large economic interests are involved. Perdita herself is deeply doubtful whether Florizel, the man she loves with all her soul, should so jeopardize both his own economic health and that of the kingdom to which he is heir by marrying her, a mere commoner. But he insists. In Shakespeare's time and for two hundred years afterward Polixenes would have been thought right in registering his disapproval of the union, though there would have been at the same time a countervailing sentiment, a fairy-tale Cinderella hope that the lovers might be united after all. From the beginning of the Romantic movement in the late eighteenth century until now, Polixenes would have been thought wrong, a tyrannous father. Now we are beginning to be ambivalent about the question. We have seen too many unwise marriages and liaisons fail, with disastrous consequences to children, families, friendships, and society as a whole.

The problem is indeed finessed—some might say, shirked—by Perdita's turning out to be a wealthy and highborn heiress; but perhaps it is a problem that ought to be finessed, if possible, rather than resolved on principle. Principles in such matters are instruments too blunt and heavy to leave the human situation unmangled when they are applied directly. Better to use them as guides in a more delicate process of approximation. Shakespeare brings off a similar finesse in *The Merchant of Venice* when Portia slightly cheats on her father's bequest by hinting to Bassanio that the right casket might rhyme with "fled," "head," and "nourishèd." More drastic is her twisting of the letter of the law so as to allow Antonio to escape the redemption of his bond with Shylock, and her use of his subsequent legal jeopardy to make him settle his fortune on his runaway daughter and her husband. Sometimes property relations and emotional bonds must be tweaked together by underhand means that leave unchallenged the rights of property owners and the irreducible historic and biological inequities between men and women, while gently subverting them; at the same time this tweaking allows us to keep a decent fiction that pure affection alone unites a family.

Tribal versus civic allegiance

The Winter's Tale does not directly deal with the relations between tribes, or what we call ethnic groups. But it reiterates the message of *The Merchant of Venice* (and *A Midsummer Night's Dream*) that the city cannot exist without a law higher than the claims of dynastic descent. Indeed, Shakespeare emphasizes the importance of this message by showing that it applies even to the head of state. Suppose Leontes had been right about his wife's infidelity, and therefore right to suspect her children of not being his, a suspicion that would cast doubt on the whole line of descent; it would still have been wrong for him to have her thrown pregnant into jail on the public charge of treason and to have his wife's baby daughter marooned on a desolate seacoast. Resistance to authority at this point becomes a duty. Paulina exhorts Leontes' courtiers, who know he is wrong but are reluctant to disobey him: "Fear you his tyrannous passion more, alas, / Than the queen's life?" (II.iii.28). Polixenes, too, comes close to being in violation of the law that makes him king when he threatens Perdita, her foster father, and foster brother with death for their supposed part in the projected marriage. Even if he is right, or half-right, in objecting to his son's marriage to a commoner, he should not subordinate the due process of law to his dynastic interests.

Employment

Perdita and Florizel, whose love appears to be as free of material interest as one could wish, are rescued from ruin and finally brought together by the agency of Autolycus. He has been hired—at an exorbitant fee—by the old shepherd and his son to act as their advocate with the enraged King Polixenes. He is also a one-time employee of the prince. As we have seen, Autolycus is an agent of the marketplace. This means that he is a vector of communication, a persuader and seducer, a channel of knowledge in a world whose parts would otherwise remain fixed in isolation, parochialism, mutual suspicion, and hostility. Employment, by giving an employer partial ownership of an employee, mediates between personal and property rights, and thus mediates between persons, since it is only in the material world that persons can come into contact with each other. It is thus the market, paradoxically, with its democratic flow of information, that reveals that Perdita is really a princess. The market is, among other things, a device that translates human work into economic value and vice versa, creating this liquidity of knowledge. Mercury the merchant is Mercury the messenger. There is a clear distinction between the market's contractual exchange and the absolute ownership that the kings in this play, when in their tyrannous passion, claim over their subjects. A person can voluntarily cede over property rights in himself to another, but only up to the point where the employer's rights of ownership begin to damage the voluntary nature of the employee's agreement to the contract. From this point on we move from the realm of the market into the realm of coercion—which, when it has no collective justification, is called crime, and when it has such justification is called the state; but the justification must itself be based on consent of the governed, and it was to establish this that we devised the market of the vote.

Marriage

The Winter's Tale is, among other things, a parable of the legitimate and illegitimate ways in which a husband and wife can belong to each other, and can endow each other with their worldly wealth. The young Leontes at the beginning of the play is plainly a classic example of the tyrannous husband who uses legal and political power to reduce his wife to a thing, a chattel. But the answer to this problem is not the one we have pursued in all good conscience for the last two hundred years: the disentanglement of the personal, emotional, and spiritual bond from the economic, legal, and contractual bond. That way, we have found, marriage is dephysicalized, denatured, and privatized out of existence. The reuniting of Leontes and Hermione makes it plain that, in Shakespeare's view, husband and wife contractually belong to each other, but that in true marriage there is no inequality between husband and wife. Leontes only gets Hermione back after sixteen years' penance for his tyrannous conduct toward her; but he does get her back, or rather, *she* gets *him* back on her terms, and Paulina makes sure that the restitution does take place. Paulina makes a joke of the reversal: "When she was young, you wooed her; now, in age, / Is she become the suitor?" (V.iii.108). Thus though the ownership is mutual and not one-sided, there is no doubt that the marriage bond is an economic as well as an emotional, spiritual, and biological one, and that it is precisely this combination, and the inner feedbacks their union makes possible, that gives marriage its power to create new value.

Justice and Mercy Revisited

The grace that inspires wonder is the central theme of *The Winter's Tale*. In an earlier scene of the play a messenger, Dion, is bringing an oracle from the god Apollo that will clear Hermione's name; "gracious be the issue!" he says, as he hurries back to the Sicilian court (III.i.22). Hermione's first words after her awakening from the dead are a blessing:

> You gods look down,
> And from your sacred vials pour your graces
> Upon my daughter's head!
> (V.iii.121)

This is an unmistakable echo of Portia's words in *The Merchant of Venice*:

> The quality of mercy is not strained;
> It droppeth as the gentle rain from heaven
> Upon the place beneath.

Both mercy and grace are imagined as a pure liquid poured down from above by beneficent powers. They are, perhaps, the same thing—mercy is grace given to us when we stand under just condemnation for our actions, grace is the mercy that is shown us before we act, that helps us do what is right when we might not otherwise have the strength to do so.

We have already looked at the connections among mercy, Mercury, commerce, and the market: mercy is not only a divine attribute but also a property of the noncoerciveness and tolerance of the marketplace, the lubricant that separates the hard surfaces of justice from one another and enables them to turn and hinge and do their job. Mercy is essential to business. Mercury is a liquid, not a solid; so is the market. Even before the institution of bankruptcy was created, which permits a debtor to commute his debts to so many cents on the dollar and mitigates the effect of a failed business on the principals of it, the great trading cities had already evolved an informal system whereby merchants of good character could be given a break during hard times. One essential element in such arrangements is the allowance of a "grace period" during which a debtor can liquidate assets and seek assistance from friends to raise the money. Indeed, the first scene of what is most likely Shakespeare's first play, *The Comedy of Errors,* deals with precisely this situation: Egeon, under sentence of death unless he can come up with a thousand marks—owing the state a death!—is mercifully given a day's grace to pay the fine, and this mercy results in the joyful reunion of broken families and a happy ending. (Shakespeare, by the way, moved the scene of this play from Epidamnus, where his source, Plautus, set it, to the merchant city Ephesus, which Paul addresses in the great epistle we looked at in chapter 7. This epistle contains his advice on "redeeming time." I owe this observation to my acute student and colleague Ronald Cantrell. Paulina, who presides over Leontes' penance and redemption in *The Winter's Tale,* surely gets her name—an odd one among the Roman and Greek names of most of the characters—from the great church father.)

The connection between the religious and financial meanings of "grace" is explicit in *The Winter's Tale.* The final scene begins with this exchange:

LEONTES: O grave and good Paulina, the great comfort
That I have had of thee!

PAULINA: What, sovereign sir,
I did not well, I meant well. All my services
You have paid home. But that you have vouchsafed,

With your crowned brother and these your contracted
Heirs of your kingdoms, my poor house to visit,
It is a surplus of your grace, which never
My life may last to answer.
(V.iii.1)

Thus the word grace, which will be central to Hermione's first speech after
her revival, has already been established in the general context of Leontes'
long penance, the "grace period" in which he has "paid" for his sins, and in
the immediate context of Paulina's repaying the grace Leontes and Polixenes
have done her by dining at her house. Grace, then, is a mysterious flow
among persons that constitutes us as social beings and is also a general gift
that rains down on us from the divine heavens. By its means the lethal judgments of the kings in this play are averted and reversed—Hermione is saved
from Leontes, Perdita from Polixenes; and by its means also Florizel and
Perdita, the heirs of the kingdoms, are "contracted" in marriage, thus unit-
ing two kingdoms, two economies, into one.

In this play the dependence of true justice upon mercy, or grace, is stated
most clearly of all. Justice requires evidence and proof; and justice must not
only be done, but it must be seen to be done. Thus justice is fundamentally
dependent upon the communication of information. In a world of time,
where there is a minimum period and rhythm for information to communicate itself throughout the system and be responded to by it, justice cannot
pretend to be instantaneous and timeless. King Leontes and King Polixenes
both jump to conclusions and try to stop the clock upon their judgments:
their justice thus becomes unjust. True justice requires that the economy of
the human and even the prehuman world has a chance to mull over the information it gets and to engage in the nonlinear feedback process, the commerce, out of which its fresh ideas can emerge. "I, that please some, try all,"
says Time, the chorus of this play. Time is the only final judge. There is indeed a need for speedy and expeditious judgment, but this need is in tension
against the need for mercy, for the provision of a grace period in which
things can work themselves out and find their own "market solutions."
Grace and mercy are the temporal space in which the creative process oper-
ates; Antony is caught in Cleopatra's "strong toil of grace." Grace and
mercy constitute an expanded present moment, like the magical delay in
paying the sexual debt in *The Tempest*; and that postponement, that ampler
present, that delay, is the only arena of human freedom.

Intrinsic and Nominal Value Revisited

The word that Shakespeare uses repeatedly to refer to the statue of
Hermione is "piece." The term has the meaning that it has in "masterpiece";
it implies an exceptional and unique work of art. But it also has another
meaning, as in Falstaff's characterization of Prince Hal as "a true piece of

gold." A gold piece is a coin that can be stamped out in many identical copies; the artist, Julio Romano, is admiringly called nature's ape, for being such an expert mimic or copyist, for inscribing upon the inert material of the statue the marks that make it valuable and give it a face and a denomination. Perdita, Hermione's daughter, is also given this word by the poet who brings the news of her arrival: "the most peerless piece of earth, I think, / That e'er the sun shone bright on" (V.i.94). There is a paradox in this phrase, too, since a piece of earth is an image of the utterly commonplace, whereas this one is "peerless," incomparable. The hereditary resemblance of both Florizel and Perdita to their parents is remarked upon: "Your mother . . . did print your royal father off, / Conceiving you" (V.i.124).

The statue come to life is, among many other things, Shakespeare's final statement of the relationship between intrinsic value and nominal value, between the unique, idiosyncratic material of a coin, a seal, a statue, a page of poetry, or a person, and the replicable, reprintable, standardized, and rationally disposable inscription that we give them. In *A Midsummer Night's Dream* we explored the predicament that results from the attempt to impose a paternal stamp upon refractory material, and its solution in the liquid world of the midnight forest. In the *Henry IV* plays we saw Prince Hal exchange the boar's head for the counterfeit king's head on his own "true piece of gold," and then sacrifice that boar to make his own head, as Harry the Fifth, stick to it when he comes to the throne. Here in *The Winter's Tale* all these ideas are summed up in the symbol of the statue—if one's statue did indeed come to life, like Pygmalion's, then one would know for sure that one had perfectly and fundamentally made one's carving stick upon one's material.

Of course we still have a way to go in our understanding of DNA and the process of cellular and fetal development, before we can literally achieve the miracle of Pygmalion and "Julio Romano," and turn dead matter into a living human being. And in any case this is not Shakespeare's point; Romano didn't actually make the statue. It is a miracle that, though impossible literally, is one that morally and psychologically we may achieve, if we go about it the right way. Through a kind of reifying jealousy we may turn other persons metaphorically into stone, "as smooth as monumental alabaster," as Othello puts it, murdering his wife under the grip of that same sin. We can so reduce them to a linear result or effect that they do not exist for us as living beings, and perhaps do not even exist for themselves if our actions are cruel enough. But to the extent that we can turn a living person to stone, to that extent we can bring one back to life. Othello says that he knows not "where is that Promethean heat / That can thy light relume" (V.ii.12). This play shows where. It is in a combination of sacrifice—Leontes' long penance—with imaginative creativity, in a communal ritual where each person keeps "his part / Performed in this wide gap of time," as the last words of the play put it. Like Edgar, who playacts the counterfactual drama of a just universe and merciful gods, we must perform these moral resurrections into being. And that performance is costly: it involves a payment, a sacrifice, the voluntary destruction of dear resources.

Shakespeare leaves us with an unforgettable experience of what the perfect melding of nominal and intrinsic meaning feels like when it has truly worked. It is the dawning realization on the part of both the audience and Leontes that this statue has all the characteristics of life. Leontes notices first its posture—something an artistic genius might capture, but at the same time idiosyncratic and individual—the endearing intangible habit of bearing that is instantly recognizable in a loved one. Next, it is the agedness of the statue:

> LEONTES: . . . But yet, Paulina,
> Hermione was not so much wrinkled, nothing
> So agèd as this seems.
>
> POLIXENES: Oh, not by much.
>
> PAULINA: So much the more our carver's excellence,
> Which lets go by some sixteen years, and makes her
> As she lived now.
> (V.iii.27)

It is time, then, that makes us alive rather than dead; motion and change, the very things that destroy us in the end, are also the sign that we exist. "The fixure of her eye has motion in't, / As we are mocked with art." "What fine chisel / Could ever yet cut breath?" Finally, Leontes takes her hand and cries out softly, "Oh, she's warm!" (V.iii.67–109). The most perfect coin of meaning is one that is as full of vitality and potential as what it stands for—indeed, that *becomes* what it stands for. What does this mean for a possible economics toward which we might aspire? A virtual, nominal, made world that is also a real living world as well? A kind of coinage that no longer indicates, but is, the goods and obligations whose exchange it mediates? To explore such questions I will need another chapter.

The Parable of the Talents Revisited

To say that the best representation of life, the best statue, would have to be as alive as its subject, brings us back to the economics of time, as we have explored it in the Sonnets, in the Falstaff and Hal plays, in *Romeo and Juliet,* and in *The Tempest.* We examined the peculiar process by which we transform our natural state of debt—of being contracted to repay a bond—into a state of ownership and partnership, tracing the idea through the story of Jacob and Laban, the parable of the talents, the parable of the Prodigal Son, and Paul's epistle to the Ephesians, and then showing how Shakespeare developed the biblical idea into the makings of a humanistic economics. Decay and aging are the interest we pay on the loan; "Beseech you, sir, / Remember," says young Florizel to old Leontes, "since you owed no more to Time / Than I do now" (V.i.218). But in *The Winter's Tale* time appears increasingly as the medium of supernatural profit as well as of natural loss. Leontes passes his final test by being prepared to embrace a statue because it shows signs of change and movement—by showing, psychologically, that he loves not the eternal and ideal image of his wife but her living, breathing reality. Cleopatra, too, was a "breather" rather than a statue. Thus the decay that the carver has given to Hermione's image is the very thing that triggers Leontes' spiritual redemption.

And indeed this scene is a redemption, in the economic as well as in the religious sense. "All my services," says Paulina to Leontes, "you have paid home" (V.iii.3). Cleomenes tells him:

> No fault could you make
> Which you have not redeemed; indeed paid down
> More penitence than done trespass.
> (V.i.2)

Like the good stewards, like Jacob, Leontes has put his loan to such good use that his profit has not only exceeded the debt of his life, but also the further debt he incurred with his tyrannous jealousy. The reward, provided by Paulina, the priestess of this Pauline ritual, is the "resurrection" of Hermione. Unlike Orpheus, who questioned the miracle of resurrection by looking back to see if his revived wife Eurydice was following him out of the land of the dead, Leontes gives himself over to absolute trust. And this is the result:

> Music, awake her: strike.
> 'Tis time; descend; be stone no more; approach;
> Strike all that look upon with marvel; come;
> I'll fill your grave up. Stir; nay, come away;
> Bequeath to death your numbness, for from him
> Dear life redeems you.
> (V.iii.98)

Hermione can pay off to death the full debt she owes him, by a posthumous bequest to him of her very numbness—the incapacity to feel pain enjoyed by the dead. Having paid in full, she has redeemed the bond that death held in her and is now a shareholder in "dear life"—a dear and valuable property indeed.

The ending of the play is also a redemption for Perdita and Florizel. For they too have been undergoing their own kind of test, their own stewardship. Despite the huge obstacles set in the way of their marriage and the seemingly endless time they must wait for consummation, can they remain chaste and not blow the great loan of their youth and beauty on a momentary spending spree? The play assures us that, like Miranda and Ferdinand, their "honor" is "not o'erthrown by" their "desires" (V.i.230). They too change from debtors to owners, in the most literal sense; by "honoring" their bond, they become the heirs to a double kingdom. And the intensity of their love, which flames up in the fourth act of the play into the very flowering of Spring, is the same "magic island," delimited by the postponement of desire, that is elaborated in *The Tempest*.

Bounty Revisited

We have already looked at the exchange between Leontes and Paulina regarding the kisses of man and wife:

LEONTES: I might have looked upon my wife's full eyes,
Have taken treasure from her lips—

PAULINA: And left them
More rich for what they yielded.

This idea recapitulates Cleopatra's description of Antony:

> For his bounty,
> There was no winter in't: an autumn 'twas
> That grew the more by reaping. . . .

And so we have returned full circle to the proposition with which Shakespeare, and we, began: that nature is an inexhaustible fountain of new value, and that human economic, moral, and artistic creation are properly the continuation of that productive process into new grounds of mental, emotional, and spiritual experience. The enactment of this assumption, in the most horrifying of Shakespeare's tragedies as well as in his warmest and most delightful comedy, is what still gives his audiences the peculiarly Shakespearean delight, that sense of fullness and richness, of the miraculousness of being.

Nature and culture are tied together by the sacrificial imprint of nominal value upon intrinsic value; and human beings are tied together with bonds that are always a subtle mixture of biological interdependence, emotional feeling, economic obligation, and spiritual commitment. When the bonds of human and natural communication are permitted to work themselves out in the free market, emergent forms of beauty and order arise out of the nonlinear chaos, drawn by the strange attractors of the next higher level of reflexive integration: thus is new value created. The resulting free flow of grace is fixed and given weight by the hard structures of justice; and the otherwise fixed and inflexible joints of justice are moistened and activated by the juice of mercy. By generating an evolutionary profit of love and art and technical craft upon the investment of our lives, we redeem the debt of time—or it is redeemed for us—and we become inheritors rather than debtors.

The most usual diagnosis of our ills, at least in the popular press, is psychological. The self is seen as the product of its emotional environment and history, and its pathologies are the effects of identifiable causes, such as traumatic early events, the oppressive structures of a dysfunctional family, and so on. Like the other explanations, this one has much real validity; but it also has its own problems. One is the very existence of people who have overcome the worst kind of circumstances to become loving and effective human beings. Another is the inherent implausibility of one-way cause and effect in human relationships; we all know that even in the most extreme cases there is always some kind of exchange going on when persons are in contact with each other, and thus the nature of the exchange and its nonlinear properties of feedback and self-adjustment must be taken into account, as well as the simple linear causes and effects of each action taken in isolation. Studies of hostage situations, for instance, show that the kidnapper and hostage influence each other's behavior and feelings in a nonlinear fashion, even though the imbalance of overt power between them is almost total. Good psychiatric theory and therapeutic practice, of course, take these nonlinear properties into account; but their goal is the health of the psyche, its ability to love and work, rather than the nature of the exchanges that make love and work possible. Much more damaging than any contact between human beings is isolation—the isolation of the neglected child, the isolation of an urban ghetto from the commerce of its city. Underclass boys and girls are only too glad to be exploited by drug merchants or random impregnators; at least they are then part of an exchange system. Even the most exploitative relationship involves some kind of two-way exchange, and such exchange is the very *essence* of humanity. Thus the heroic work of the mental health caregiver tends toward repair rather than the understanding and maintenance of psychic health, which depends on exchange.

All these approaches, however sophisticated, take as their paradigm the one-way application of power, both in their diagnosis and in their cure. More profound, in my opinion, is the approach of thinkers like James Hillman and Thomas Moore, who frankly seek to heal the soul and to do it in a nonlinear fashion. But their advice, it seems to me, has relevance only to people who have already achieved a certain level of emotional competence and—to put it delicately—economic engagement with other people. They own, owe, and are owed. Such persons can afford to stop and smell the roses; like aristocrats, they can refine the exchanges of life beyond the crassly materialistic. The deep participation in a healthy market is not the problem, but the prerequisite, for spiritual development; and a healthy market will always include at the lower end a frankly material component. Portia's sublime gift-exchange economy is founded upon the market exchange of Venice. Not that only the rich can save their souls! Participation in a market of human exchanges does not imply great wealth: the peasant bringing her apples and eggs to market is a true participant, while the idle heir to a fortune may well be an outsider. The psychoanalyst poet Frederick Feirstein makes a more candid acknowledgement of the human need for economic exchange.

For Feirstein the process of psychoanalysis is not so much an act of investigation and repair as it is a cooperative work of art, a play production or poem, in which value is created and paid for in economic terms.

So true psychic health depends on engagement in a market of human exchanges. Karl Marx was right in seeing economic relations as primary, as setting the stage for all other kinds of human activity, intellectual, moral, and artistic. Where he was wrong—and so wrong that it cost millions of human lives in the unnecessary revolutions he inspired—was in seeing property and market exchange as the obstacles to true human community, rather than the necessary preconditions for it. Ezra Pound, though his admiration for Marx and Lenin led him into the fascist anti-Semitism of his Mussolini period, said rightly that Marx did not understand money. But neither Marx nor Pound grasped the positive and beneficial aspects of usury, of the second-order financial effects that arise from the interactions of property, risk, time, depreciation, decay, productivity, and increase. They sought to detach the meaning of "bond" as a moral relationship between persons from "bond" as a financial instrument and to purge the latter by state action. But the word stubbornly refuses to be torn apart. And the same thing goes for all those other words we have looked at in this book—"trust," "goods," "save," "value," "means," "redeem," "redemption," "dear," "obligation," "interest," "honor," "company," "worth," "thrift," "use," "will," "partner," "deed," "fair," "owe," "ought," "risk," "royalty," "fortune," "venture," "grace," and so on. The words insist on the incarnation of their noble moral meanings in their base pecuniary ones. They recognize, so to speak, their own tragic embedding in a world of corruption and contingency. To Marx and Pound the fact that financial markets could be illegitimately manipulated was warrant enough to suggest their abolition or their planned control by the state; yet it is this very sensitivity of the market that makes it able to reflect and promote the deep moves a culture makes toward new knowledge, values, and creative work. As well abolish language—or reduce it to a state-controlled code—because we can so easily deceive and lie by means of it. Shakespeare and the framers of the U.S. Constitution were wiser, recognizing the need for legal regulation of markets, but in fear and trembling lest the market's miraculous communicative powers—and hence its creative powers—should thus be lost.

What my interpretation of Shakespeare seems to suggest is that the solution of many of our contemporary social, psychological, and moral ills may be rather simple. Perhaps we should seek the cure of the dysfunctional family first in its economic relations—is everybody in it justly exchanging goods and services with everyone else?—is this exchange one of grace and mercy, or is it frozen into a justice with no tolerance? Addiction, dependency, prejudice, depression, and so on, may be more deeply the results of a subconscious sense that the wares we are giving or receiving are too big or too small, that we are getting things too cheaply or too dearly, than of childhood traumas or chemical imbalances or political oppression. Baboons that have lost status—that is, that have fallen in arrears in the market of the troop's exchange of goods and services—have been shown to undergo a major change in the "dopa" group of neurotransmitters, followed by a collapse of the immune system, thus demonstrating one clear causal line from economic to psychological and physiological health. Perhaps the chief misfortune a person can suffer is not to be exploited by the market, but excluded from it. We gain our primary existential health by participation in the play, the drama itself; and one could only enter Shakespeare's theater of the world by paying one's "ordinary," that is, the price of the ticket, at the door.

One way of putting this notion of exchange is in terms of the meaning of money. Money is negative obligation. Shakespeare's complex and wise view of money helps us to see it once again in the light of its original use, that is, as a way of keeping track of mutual obligations within a community. In a small village, I can remember that Smith mended my roof last year and make sure I give her half of my crop of apples. I can even transfer the obligation, if I remember how Jones helped Smith with her weaving loom, by repairing Jones's wagon and thus cancelling Smith's debt to him. But in a bigger city I lose track of the web of transferred obligations; and thus we have money as a generalized and quantified measure of the obligations that unspecified others owe me and of the obligations I owe others. If I am short on money, it is because I have not fulfilled my obligations. If I am wealthy, it is because others are behindhand in their obligations to me. In the institution of the potlatch in various societies, notably the tribal cultures of New Guinea and the Pacific Northwest, we can clearly see the origins of financial wealth in the paradoxical practice of huge gift-giving ceremonies. The "big man" who gives away many gifts accumulates obligations throughout the community, which can then be exchanged for alliance in conflict, favorable marriages for one's kin, goods, and services. Even in contemporary macroeconomics we can see the same process at work. Japan, China, and Korea are potlatch economies, seeking by huge export largess to build up economic obligations in the world community. In this perspective, the desire to make money is nothing more than the desire to obligate others to oneself—and to obligate others is to serve them and give to them. In a strange way, to make money is in practice to love one's neighbor.

To own a large sum of money is actually to own nothing—especially if the money is in paper or electronic currency; rather, one is owed by everybody else the value of the goods and services one provided to accumulate the money. As long as there has been no cheating, a rich person is someone to whom other people are rightly obligated for past economic favors, and a poor person is someone to whom others are not economically obligated in strict justice. This description of the matter probably sounds extremely eccentric and counterintuitive; surely we are obligated to the poor, and not obligated to the rich! But our natural reaction, conditioned into us by centuries of piety both religious and political, must contend with the patent logic of obligation. One reason that we cannot grasp real obligation emotionally is that we have already discounted our first, almost unconscious, recognition of the fact that we are unlikely to be able to persuade a rich person to perform some service for us, because the rich person justly feels no sense of debt to us, while we automatically assume that a poor person is looking for services he can do for others and may thus be employable by us for work we want done. We do not feel the *emotion* of obligation to a rich person, because we have already accepted that we are in a *state* of obligation to that person. Given that state, if we are morally lazy about what we feel, we are inclined rather to resent the rich person's power over us than to feel gratitude for all the good things that person or his family must have done for others and ourselves to have earned the money. Likewise, our sense of moral obligation to the poor comes *after* we have tacitly accepted our position as potential employer of them, and with the same moral laziness we feel well disposed toward them because we know they cannot make just demands on us and should jump to repay the good things we have done that give us the advantage.

If the reader finds these reflections uncomfortable, so does the writer. For we have entered a region of embarrassment as shameful, perhaps, as sex— and in our century as suppressed and denied as sex was in the nineteenth. The psychopathologies of the 1990s may be as much the result of our repression of economic realities as those of the 1890s were of their repression of sexual ones; and we may need an economic Freud to disentangle our financial neuroses as the Victorians needed a psychological Freud for their reproductive ones. Perhaps that Freud has been with us all along, in the shape of Shakespeare.

However painful it may be, it is worth being healed. But does healing mean that we should learn to love the rich and despise the poor? Yes and no—yes to the first proposition, no to the second. Recognizing our position of obligation to the rich may help us to detach our objective evaluation of them as persons from the feelings of both resentment and unjustified awe that our indebtedness unconsciously inspires in us. We ought to love the rich, as we ought to love all human beings; we certainly should not hate them for being rich, and thus hate ourselves for any effort we might make to enrich ourselves by helping others. Likewise, to recognize the just indebtedness and obligation of the poor to ourselves is to detach and purify our proper feelings of love, respect, and compassion for them as human beings from the pleasant unconscious flattery of our hold over them as poor.

Poor people are offended most by the sentimentality and falseness of the well-to-do, especially when the well-to-do intend to place them still further in moral debt by predatory acts of philanthropy. The poor in traditional societies, when they either accept the economic order as basically just or have been kept in the dark about its injustices, generally do not want guilt-ridden offerings of public or private alms so much as the chance to equalize the position of debt by honest work and service, to reciprocate the gifts they have been given. Modern ideologies of the economic injustice of the market, despite the fact that they have been disproved in theory and have failed in practice, have created a resentful poor with historically new feelings of entitlement. The planet has groaned with wars and massacres for a century as a result, and the accumulated resentment has not gone away. The irony is that modern market economies are almost certainly much fairer than the feudal regimes they replaced, which were usually accepted as economically just by our peasant ancestors. When the poor reject their obligation to the rich and deny the "system" that creates that obligation, their apparently courageous and independent gesture is in fact a tragic self-severance from the market and from any human community that might help them out of their poverty; it is an amputation of themselves and their children from the exchange process that makes us human.

Shame and Beauty

Earlier I included in this analysis of the virtues of market exchange an important proviso: that there be no cheating. Of course this is an impossible condition; there is always cheating. But did the rich get rich by being better at cheating than the poor, or by colluding *not* to cheat and thus becoming more prosperous than those who went on believing in cheating as the only way to become wealthy, and who in the resulting war of each against all remained mired in poverty? Is there more cheating in the market than in the arrangements, maneuvers, and self-justifications of religion, the state, political parties, the military, the justice system, educational institutions, and any of the other organizations in which we put our (qualified) trust? Of course there should be the utmost vigilance in maintaining the fairness and truthfulness of the market; but in fact the market has self-adjusting mechanisms, such as competition and demand, that tend to redress abuses over time— mechanisms that are relatively lacking in the very institutions we might call on to oversee the market. The vote is actually a borrowing from the market, in that it sets electoral prices upon legislative wares; but the vote takes place only every few years, while the market is a continuous vote. Furthermore, we have a ready and easy-to-read index of how much cheating there must be going on in an economy: the rate of inflation. A low rate of inflation is the sign that a people at large, whatever they say about it, actually trust the fairness and truthfulness of the market that gives money its value—and the people at large are in the best position to know.

What is interesting is the psychology that makes us more suspicious of market cheating than of dishonesty in other spheres of action. Perhaps it is that we have painful repressed feelings about the worthiness of our own contribution to the market, our own dependence on material commerce to support and comfort our bodies. "I am ashamed," says Leontes, confronted by the statue in *The Winter's Tale*; "does not the stone rebuke me / For being more stone than it?" (V.iii.37). Leontes feels this shame—and owns up to feeling it, which is the hardest thing of all—for two connected reasons: the breaking of his contract with his wife and the realization of his own physical being. We are all, after all, made of minerals, and this materiality shamefully coexists with a conscience and with conscious feelings that must be ashamed of their base constituents. Our material existence makes us excruciatingly dependent on exchange with other people and thus vulnerable to the pang of shame if we feel that the gifts we have exchanged with others are too great or too small. To understand the healing that Shakespeare offers for our times, we need to understand shame far more deeply than we do; in what follows I summarize my own gleanings from such researchers on the subject as Thomas Scheff, James Hans, and Helen Lewis, collected together in my books *Beauty: The Value of Values and The Culture of Hope.*

If we look at the foundation myths of any culture, we will find some deeply shameful act at the origin of the human world. Take, for instance, the Eskimo story of Sedna and her father, Anguta. Sedna marries a dog against her father's wishes; the father kills her dog-husband; on the way back a storm rises and Anguta, to lighten the boat, throws his daughter overboard; she clings to the boat and he, to get rid of her, cuts off her fingers. Or the Shinto story of how the sun goddess Amaterasu was shamed by her bad brother, Susa-no-wo, who threw a flayed horse through the roof of her weaving hall. Her subsequent retirement to a cave deprived the world of sunlight—as did the shamed rage of Ceres in the myth of Persephone. Or consider the biblical story of the Fall, of the shame of Adam and Eve at their disobedience, their lies, and their nakedness; or Cain and Abel; or the shameful story of Christmas, of the infant god born between the two places of excrement, urine and feces, and laid in a manger among the brutes, because there was no room at the inn; or in the Greek tradition the shameful story of Cronus castrating his father, Uranus, with a sickle, and the generally incestuous provenance of the gods; or the shameful murder of the corn god in Amerindian mythology; or the various shameful acts of tabu murder and incest in Australian aboriginal creation myths.

These myths express the essential knot of our human predicament. The threads of that knot include the problematic coexistence of a reflective mind with a smelly, sexed, and partly autonomous body; the horror of death; the ambiguous relationship of human beings with the rest of nature; the incestuous paradoxes of kinship and parenthood; the crimes of our ancestors against the peoples or species they displaced; the capacity to lie given us by language; and the difficulty, obligation, and anxiety inherent in the socioeconomic acts of gift giving and dividing the fruits of the hunt. Our aboriginal human philosophy tended, with the intuitive economy of dualism, to divide the cultural from the natural. Today, in the light of evolutionary biology and cosmological science, we may be in a position to revise that ancient dichotomy. We recognize that to some extent other species share those reflexive paradoxes, and that our version of them is only an intensification— across certain crucial thresholds—of tensions inherent in the evolutionary process itself and belonging perhaps to the feedback nature of the universe as a whole. However, even if we do replace an absolute division between the human and the natural with a more continuous evolutionary gradient of increasing reflexivity, and even when we come to recognize nature as not just that which is given, but as the very process of accelerating evolution that transforms the given, we must still deal with a world in which greater and lesser levels of self-reference, feedback, intention, and freedom must somehow coexist.

And this coexistence is essentially shameful. We are ashamed about our sexuality, about how we came into the world, about how we did not at one time exist, either as a species or individually. We are thus ashamed of our parents, especially when adolescence forces on us a constant attention to the process of reproduction that originated us; and the reflexive appetite of the mind makes us at the same time seek out the nakedness of father Noah, the nakedness of mother Jocasta. We are ashamed at our bodies, which display an impure and inextricable mixture, a mutual *adulteration,* of the intentional and the instinctive. We are ashamed about eating, because, whatever we eat, we are assuming, upon the confessedly untrustworthy warrant of our own biased judgment, that we must be more valuable than what we destroy with our teeth and digestive juices. Hence we naturally find the end products of eating to be objects of disgust. We are at the top of the food chain and feel an anguished and unrepayable obligation to those beings that gave up their lives for us.

We are ashamed about our economic system, whereby we define ourselves as members in good standing of our community, and thus as human beings; we are never quite sure whether we have given the right gift, or given a gift when we should not have, or not given a gift when we should; and we are shamefully anxious about whether we have been given the right gift. We are ashamed at what we have made, whether because of uncertainty about its worthiness or because of the obligation we incurred to those parts of the world we destroyed to make our new contribution to it. The institution of money, by which we extend through time and space the reckoning-up of the balance of obligation for past gifts and so transcend the limitations of memory, is a basically shameful object of contemplation; we call lucre filthy and are always seeking ways to delegitimate our own economy, at least as it applies to ourselves. We are, finally, ashamed at our own feelings of shame, our own reflexiveness, our awareness of our awareness.

However, it is precisely in this whole area of experience—the reflective interaction at the deepest level with nature, with our origins, with our means of life, with our closest kin, with our community as an object of obligation, and with our very self-consciousness itself—that we encounter the beautiful. Thus in ways that are bearable to us because their story-nature insulates us from their direct personal application without denaturing their meaning, our myths conduct us into the realms of shame where the hot blush of consciousness—the "Blank misgivings of a creature / Moving about in worlds not realized," as Wordsworth put it—can be transformed into the delicious shiver of beauty. The severed fingers of Sedna become the beautiful warm-blooded marine mammals by which the Eskimos survive; the sun goddess Amaterasu is lured forth from her cave by the newly invented mysteries of dance, comedy, and the mirror of self-awareness; Adam and Eve get knowledge as well as death, and give birth to history and to human redemption; Cain's descendant Jubal invents music; the infant Jesus is attended by Magi with splendid gifts; the genitals of Cronus arise from the sea foam as the beautiful goddess of love; the corn god's golden hair waves in the wind as the silk of the ripening maize; and the pratfalls and transgressive gaucheries of the aboriginal tricksters are the source of all human arts and graces.

The painful feeling of shame is the cause of devastating pathologies of feeling and cognition—emotional traps and feedback spirals and stunted capacities and self-destructive behavior. But perhaps all this damage is not so much the result of shame itself as of our attempts to deny it, disavow it, sweep it under the rug, blame it on others, or ignore it. What the creation myths seem to indicate—and similar examples from the arts, literature, scriptures, traditional wisdom, and ritual practice could be multiplied—is that when shame is properly accepted and acknowledged, it can be the portal to our freshest, deepest, and most positive experience of the world.

Shame and beauty, then, share a common root. The work of the myths cited in this section is both to show us how to experience the beauty we have paid for with our shame and to remind us that if we attempt to avoid or repress the shame, we will find ourselves as cut off from beauty as the world was from sunlight in the myths of Amaterasu and Persephone. Both conscious joy and shame involve the emergent and aroused reflexivity, self-reference, and feedback of nature, both within and beyond the sphere of human culture. Certainly there never was an unalloyed purity in the universe; the cosmos hides its privates with a fig leaf, and, if the cosmos is the body of God, then God, coyly, hides his or hers too. The blush, which Darwin saw as one of the defining characteristics of humanity, is the very condition of physical existence, and there is no way back to a time before the blush. It is the painful path from earlier and less reflexive modes of being to later and more reflexive modes, and the subsequent coexistence of the two in their complex historical product. The blush is time itself.

Many of the major institutions of traditional societies—ritual in general (especially sacrifice, but also funerals, initiations, birthing ceremonies, puberty rituals, and purifications); religious codes of behavior; customs of modesty in clothes and deportment; courtship and marriage; hereditary privilege; etiquettes of education; the traditional forms of the arts—may be seen in this light as other ways of ensuring a productive passage through shame to beauty.

Sacrifice transforms a shameful act—the public killing of a living being or its substitute—through collective acknowledgment of our condition and recognition of the nature of the universe, into an experience of beauty. Other rituals similarly accept, frame, organize, and elaborate the chaotic shame inherent in death, life crisis, birth, sexual awakening, and pollution, in such a way that we recognize the beauty that also attends those moments of embarrassing emergence and self-reference. Religious moral codes give us clear boundaries to transgress and ways of seeking beautiful repentance when we do transgress. Modesty, by explicitly concealing our animal nature, draws attention to it; the blush brings out the special conscious beauty of the face. Courtship and marriage accept and concentrate the shame of sexuality and thus allow its strange mutually mirroring beauty, the lovely pathos of its nakedness, to be revealed.

Institutional privilege thematizes and renders acceptable the shame of inequality, whether that inequality stems from lucky genetic differences of talent or from the luck of the social circumstances of birth and upbringing; our shame at the relative paucity of our achievements is accepted as integral to the beauty of service to what is nobler than we. The necessary and institutionalized inequality of parent and child during the child's minority is the source of both humiliation and the most exquisite tenderness. The traditional relationship of teacher and student—one of the few other examples of explicit and prescribed personal inequality that remain in the modern world—transforms what is potentially the most murderously shameful situation of all, one person telling another what to think, into a beautiful and mutual pursuit of the truth. (Perhaps, ironically, it is a misplaced bad conscience about this inequality that makes the contemporary academy so furious a scourge of hierarchy and domination.)

The traditional forms of the arts are also, in a less immediately obvious way, both reminders of our shame and revealers of beauty. The traditional pan-human artistic genres—metered poetry, storytelling, visual representation, music, drama, and so on—are keyed to our neurophysiological makeup in such a way as to remind us of our materiality, our mortality, and the automatism of our delight, as well as the strange reflexivity of our awareness. We are embarrassed by our pleasure in rhyme, by the sweetness of melody, by stories with neat endings, by gorgeous color combinations, and by the great natural genre of representation in general. It is in and through this very corniness, this shameful twinge of natural response, that the mysterious powers of beauty take flesh and reality. But many have felt that the beauty was not worth the concomitant twinge of shame. The aesthetic severity of the modernist has its precedents: in the Hebrew prophets and the Islamic mullahs with their shame-denying injunctions against representation, in the Athenian feminists who in their destructive fury castrated the statues of the gods, in the Byzantine iconoclasts, in the followers of Savonarola who burned the Botticellis, and in those of the puritan John Knox who forbade the beauties of church decoration and ritual, and who smashed the stained glass and abolished the old church music. But these movements could arguably be seen as attempts to renew and refresh the shame that our rituals had so beautifully *managed* that it had almost been buried and forgotten. Something rather different, I believe, has happened in the last one hundred and fifty years: the systematic cultural attempt to deny shame altogether.

It is a truism of sociology that modernity was the period during which, for a multitude of reasons—greater personal mobility, the contraction of the unit of production from the extended family to the individual worker, the drive toward political liberty, the spread of literacy, urbanization, and so on—many of the traditional institutions of preindustrial society fell into decline. Myth, ritual (especially sacrificial ritual), religion, traditional customs of modesty, courtship, marriage and family, hereditary privilege, and the traditional art forms all lost their hold upon the allegiance and imagination of the people. Modernity can also be usefully defined as that period in which politics came to be polarized into Left and Right. Thomas Carlyle, writing about the French Revolution, was the first writer we know of in the English language to use the term "left" in its political sense, in 1837. The French words *gauche* and *droite* had been in political use in France since before the turn of the century, having originated in the seating customs of the political factions of the revived *Parlement* that sparked off the Revolution. By 1887 the Left-Right distinction was a regular and recognizable description of the two wings of the British parliament.

It has been precisely since politics divided itself into Left and Right that beauty began to be rejected by artists and critics, or euphemized and denatured as aesthetics. The term "aesthetic" itself was coined by Immanuel Kant at about the same time as the French "left" and "right," and came to replace the older word "beautiful"; the sublime was preferred to the beautiful, and the process that led to Dadaist and later postmodernist invectives against beauty was inaugurated. Are these events connected? How, in other words, may we relate these four interesting facts: the function of traditional institutions in accepting shame and thus releasing its mysterious twin, beauty; the decline of those institutions in the nineteenth and twentieth centuries; the replacement of beauty by aesthetics and sublimity; and the rise of the Left and the Right? The most compelling explanation seems to be that in our eagerness to deny shame—rather than to manage it in such a way as to make beauty possible—we took two routes. The right-wing route was to project the dirty failings and sensual indulgence of one's own physical body onto inferior Others—foreigners, the poor, the ethnically different—and arrange society so as to keep them down. The left-wing route was to deny the authority of the judging superior consciousness, translate one's own feelings of failure, humiliation, and inadequacy into pity for the oppressed, and turn all the accumulated rage of denied shame murderously against the bourgeoisie, the rich, and the Jews. In the process the search for beauty was largely abandoned by the modernists and postmodernists, and it is only now being revived by a new generation of writers, artists, musical composers, and architects (whom I have discussed in my book *The Culture of Hope,* The Free Press, 1995).

The reason that we are so angrily suspicious that cheating might have gone on in the market—despite the fact that the evidence of the inflation rate would seem to indicate a fairly low percentage of discrepancy between what goods are worth and what we pay for them—is that we are ashamed and have lost the way to accept that shame and transform it into beauty. Shakespearean economics can be for us a recovery of that way: a recognition of our messy contractual relationships with others, and the messiness of our individual and collective ways of imprinting value upon the material universe. But it is also a promise of a universe that is much more generous and creative than we could have imagined, and an invitation—if we accept the shame—to participate in that creativity and to profit by it both materially and spiritually. True humility is the source of joy.

The Economics of the Future

Let us imagine a twenty-first-century economy based on Shakespearean principles. To envisage such an economy requires that one first postulate a Shakespearean way of getting there; but an examination of the great secular changes in technology, demographics, capital, labor, and culture that are currently going on would seem to indicate that we are already well on the way. Successive waves of economic energy are passing through our civilization, changes of paradigm whereby the nature of wealth alters and the interests that drive human effort migrate and transform. A modern economy is not like the old notion of a balanced ecology, in which every species occupies its own fixed ecological niche and a mysterious set of feedbacks preserves a homeostatic harmony among them; instead, it is much more like the present model of ecological succession, where clusters of species rise, replace their predecessors at the top of the food chain, and are demoted, giving way to others, and the very shape and identity of the ecological niches undergo continuous irreversible metamorphosis. We live in a world of economic transvaluation, in which each wave of succession reaches and passes its point of maximum capital flow, employment, and cultural influence, to be succeeded by a further wave. Obsolescence disrupts people's lives, and at the same time society as a whole becomes—erratically but inevitably—richer and more full of opportunities for those willing to use them. As each new wave comes along, the disparities in wealth between the rich and the poor first increase, and then decrease, leaving the average person with much more disposable income than before.

Two hundred years ago America was an agrarian nation, in which the majority of the people worked on farms and the majority of the capital commitment and cultural energy was going into agricultural production. Prices were relatively high enough, and the production system labor-intensive enough, to support a large rural population. Wealth was widely distributed, reinforcing the American political ethic of equality that de Tocqueville celebrated. Then with the introduction of such devices as the cotton gin and the combine harvester, the cost of production dropped rapidly, prices collapsed, production sharply increased, the number of workers needed fell off sharply, and, after an initial increase in investment for mechanization, the capital requirements for farming relative to the rest of the economy went into steady decline. Rural unemployment sent thousands of jobless farmers out on the roads. Farming simply bulked less large in the nation's economy, society, and culture: it took up a smaller share of its interests. Today perhaps 5% of our national treasure and work goes into farming. One odd little countertrend, however, may be significant: there is an increasing number of gentleman and lady farmers, freed from more pressing economic necessities, who have taken up ranching or planted gardens or bought vineyards for the sheer joy of doing so. Like aristocrats of an earlier agricultural era, who hunted, rode, bred animals, sailed, or fished, preserving in their leisure the ancient work patterns of the hunter-gatherer past, the new leisure classes have rediscovered as a pleasure and spiritual recreation what was once the drudgery of survival.

It is already clear that what happened to farming is already happening to the extractive and manufacturing sectors. In the developed countries manufacturing employment and capital investment rose until it tied up the bulk of the available labor, capital, and cultural energy. At first, huge fortunes were made. Then wealth became widely shared; the essential and collectively powerful assembly line workers could ask a decent fraction of the earnings of their masters. Then automation, robotics, computer assisted design and manufacturing, materials science, miniaturization, "just-in-time" inventory techniques, discount retail, and global competition created successive leaps in efficiency, cutting costs, prices, and labor requirements, increasing volume, and maximizing the utility and durability of the product. Manufacturing, like farming, became more capital-intensive and less labor-intensive; Marx's nineteenth-century proletariat withered away; unemployed industrial workers crowded the decaying inner cities. The rust belt succeeded the dust bowl; and we are now reaching the point that the capital requirements for manufacturing are likewise dropping—until, perhaps, they will be no more than the 5% or so we need for farming. The amounts of money to be made out of manufacturing are also shrinking, and thus the amount of the world's interests tied up in it. Finally, perhaps, a few dozen biotech/nanotech factories, with some bored troubleshooters and elite staffs of designers and marketers, will make all the world's necessary stuff. We may even, in what will appear to be a decadent and deplorable cultural development, create gentleman factories, like our present dude ranches, to provide the old thrills of heroic industrialism; theme parks of the assembly line; civil peace reenactments. The present vogues for furniture making and home improvement may already be examples of this trend.

So far this is a familiar story; and according to its script the third wave, the information age, is upon us, the golden dawn upon the economic horizon. However, it takes a little more imagination to see that the same thing will happen to the information industries, presently ascendant, that happened to the farms and factories. There is no reason that the technologies of data acquisition, storage, management, and retrieval should not perfect and miniaturize and cheapen and streamline themselves almost out of existence like their predecessors. If the historical analogy holds, employment, investment, and cultural commitment in the information industries will rise to about 90% of the given resources; at first huge fortunes will be made; then as the labor demand rises, economic equality will increase; there will follow the predictable collapse of the labor market as the information industries become more and more cost-efficient, smaller and smaller on the world's horizon, less and less labor-intensive, and finally less capital-hungry and less profitable, leaving a few cash cows providing all the world's needs. Eventually their operation will take up 5% of our money and our people. Hordes of information workers will be turned out on the streets, asking the employed if they can spare a dime. Moreover all this will happen much faster than the rise and decline of manufacturing, just as the manufacturing age happened faster than the agricultural age. Everything is getting faster and faster. Information resources will be virtually invisible, at our mental fingertips, perhaps even wired into us by neural/cybernetic interfaces, activated by an unconscious movement of the will as are our own brains—as natural, cheap, and convenient as a hammer. Will we then create clunky antique data devices, requiring programming and the memorization of command codes, for the leisured and the nostalgic?

But there is a more important question; What will succeed the knowledge industries? An economic wave or paradigm loses its hold on a civilization not because of inefficiency, but because of efficiency. Earlier waves of economic activity are not suppressed by succeeding waves. The reason there are so few farmers in the United States and so little money tied up in farming, when once 90% of the nation was agrarian, is not the failure of farming or its defeat by manufacturing; but its astonishing success, its achievement of productive perfection earlier than manufacturing. It now needs only a small fraction of the country's human and economic resources to supply more than enough foodstuffs and raw materials. Likewise, manufacturing and information processing will perfect themselves into relative economic insignificance. Finally, we will be left with the irreducibly labor- and capital-intensive human industries of what we might call "charm": tourism, education, entertainment, psychoanalysis, adventure, crafts, religion, sport, fashion, art, history, movies, ritual, healing, personal development, politics, literature, gossip, the eternal soap opera of relationships. Once the world's wages have leveled up to those of the developed countries, a process already well in train, the service industries will begin to starve for labor and be forced to raise their pay scales. At the same time the job descriptions and the actual content of service employment will begin to approximate those of artists, entertainers, educators, and sports professionals. One can already see this process at work in the restaurant industry in such wealthy cities as Dallas, New York, Phoenix, or Los Angeles; good waiters, sommeliers, and cooks are wooed and tempted by rival establishments, and each evening is conceived as a little work of art. Eventually restaurant staffs and adventure tour guides and falconers and perfumiers and masseurs will be as highly regarded as painters, professional athletes, and musicians are today; they will be reviewed in the journals, exhibited, and highly paid.

But even these trends do not yet capture the extent of the transformation that is coming. We can see the beginnings of the great change in the experimental pension policies that have been established in some countries, for instance Chile and Britain, and in the current retirement planning practices of much of the American middle class. In Chile the government has privatized the social security system, requiring workers to invest tax-free a proportion of their incomes toward retirement. At foreseeable rates of return it will accumulate handsomely, to the point where it will be sufficient to support a person's livelihood. Much of the savings will remain unspent by the end of a person's life, because of the uncertainty of the date of death and the need to keep a reserve on hand. It will thus be passed on to the heirs, and this investment should, in about two generations, turn the entire population of Chile into independently wealthy property owners. Though Britain is proceeding more cautiously with this extraordinary piece of social engineering—fulfilling Marx's dream of worker ownership of the means of production, but by methods that would make him turn in his grave!—the same will happen there too in time. The American middle class has abandoned its trust in the Social Security system, has begun its own private retirement planning, and will no doubt press its politicians to privatize social security in the near future, thus extending the benefits to all workers and providing a huge boost of long-term investment to the economy. Once other nations perceive that they too can be rentiers and owners, they will surely adopt the same policies in self-defense. A further tendency will accelerate the whole process: as financial security increases, a drop in birthrates will inevitably follow, thus decreasing the numbers of the new generations amongst whom the inheritance will be shared.

Thus the dream of Jacob, of the servants in the parable of the talents, that one might transform oneself from a debtor in whose enterprises the master has a bond with a severe rate of interest into a shareholder and co-owner of the firm, may be on the horizon. The whole human race can be masters of the vineyard. If everybody is an owner, and the technology can provide as a cheap utility all the necessities of life, work will become a high privilege, and service of others will be the most sought-after of all activities. It will be the most intense pleasure and the deepest form of play. As we have seen, there will be no need for huge numbers of workers, except in the charm industries where work will be inherently interesting and attractive (for if it is not, nobody with a private income would do it). The world will begin to approximate the condition of the Shakespearean theater while a play is being performed—everybody provided for and paid up, an entrancing entertainment going on, and work performed by artists who are supremely good at it and privileged to be in the position: Ferdinand and Miranda holding hands at the masque.

In such an economy the huge rift that now lies between moral and economic relationships will be healed. Personal rights and property rights will become merely different locations on the same legal spectrum. As owners of the world and of its endlessly productive processes of creation, we shall have an interest in its health, rather than in its exploitation and sequestration from our rivals. We will be learning which inscriptions of human meaning and value will stick on the world and which will not; and in the process of negotiation with the rest of nature in establishing such coinages, we will become once more the insiders of nature, as subtly part of its ecosystem as were our hunter-

gatherer ancestors. Farming and manufacturing take matter and energy from
the universe, and when such matter and energy is taken, it ceases to exist
where it is taken from—what is now food and electricity and automobiles
ceases to be topsoil and petroleum and iron ore. These resources can be used
up, and therefore must be fought over militarily or legally. But the new industries will be taking chiefly information from the universe; and information
does not necessarily cease to exist where it is taken from. It can be copied
without loss. We may contest the ownership of the research work that uncov-
ers it, but there is no "tragedy of the commons"—no exhaustion of the resources owned in common that nature provides.

The universe has over the last thirteen billion years or so discovered by
trial and error how to fit everything in it together without radical contradiction, despite the changing conditions imposed by its expansion and cooling,
and the spontaneous symmetry breakings that have resulted. In the process
the universe has generated the fantastic riches of physical, chemical, and living order. It is thus a supremely "intelligent" expert system in making things
work, so cleverly arranged that many philosophers have argued that it is the
product of an intelligent designer, and most folk religions regard it as popu-
lated by intelligent spirits. Through science this enormous stock of natural
information now lies at our disposal. As a delightful bonus, we can "mine"
this wealth with minimal damage to the ecosystems in which it lies. Any
child growing up is already cannibalizing this "natural intelligence" that lies
around her, as she learns how to use her own body, learns in her muscles and
cerebellum the ratios of inertia and the acceleration of gravity, learns with
her lenses and retinas the consequences of the inverse square laws of candle-
power, and the orderly projective geometry of perspective. She uses the
chemoassay of her nostrils and tongue to sample the basic chemistry of the
world, and the vibratory interface of her eardrums and cochleas to analyze
the harmonic structure of its waves. Gardens and pets teach her the things
she has in common with animals and plants.

But until recently in the history of the world the process of acquiring and
piggybacking upon the natural cleverness of the world stopped there. Thus
grotesquely inaccurate theories about how things could be fitted together
have flourished, crippling the human mind as effectively as organic damage
to its tissues themselves—"buggy" software that interrupts clear thought at
a myriad of junctures, many of them apparently unconnected with the original error. Much mental illness and emotional dysfunction is a result of such
software errors, mistakes in programming, so to speak, that come from bad
basic science.

Even though the gates of good science are partially opened, and its healing and productive information is available, it is not in such a form as to be
assimilable by nonscientists. What is needed is art that can transform this information into usable knowledge and in turn into human wisdom. Such art
cannot merely be good science education and popularization, though we
have a desperate need for these as well. It must, like the poetry of Dante
Alighieri that taught Italians the brilliant natural philosophy of Thomas

Aquinas, or the canvases of Monet and Seurat that taught the French the wave theory of light, or the novels of Thomas Mann that showed his readers the world of modern biology, be so utterly melded and incarnated into human aspirations and experience that our intelligence is debugged and enhanced almost without our knowing it. Human subjects have been shown to undergo a fifteen-point temporary improvement in their intelligence quotient simply by listening to Mozart. Why? Because Mozart understood at some very deep level how the world works harmonically, and his music provides a bridge for us to the inexhaustible intelligence of the universe. When through the experience of music or drama or viewing visual arts we replay the software of a great genius in our heads, we not only take on a moiety of that person's own intelligence, but plug in to the intelligence of God.

The experience of Shakespeare is perhaps the most potent form of this intelligence enhancement and "debugging" program that we can find. And Shakespeare, as we have seen in this book, can also help us to connect to the wisdom of the universe's own vast economy and our own part in it. He has, for instance, already guessed that above the biological miracle of propagation and evolution he describes in the Sonnets there is an even greater miracle of artistic propagation and evolution, "That in black ink my love may still shine bright" (65). Perhaps the greatest artistic challenge for the new generations of artists and poets who are now growing up in the ruins of modernism and postmodernism will be to build upon what the artists of the past have done, listen to the scientists, learn—as did our mythical predecessors Solomon and Orpheus and Taliesin and Vyasa—the language of plants and animals and stones, and create a grand channel of metaphorical and narrative commerce between ourselves and the rest of nature. No enterprise could be more enriching to both the human economy and the divine.

How might an economy based on the superabundance I have suggested here actually work in practice? We need only look to trends already well established in those areas of the economy that have discounted the costs of automated production—that anticipate the postagrarian, postmanufacturing, postinformational regime of the next century. These trends include the decoupling of currency from precious metal reserves; the permitting of national currencies to float against each other; the widespread substitution of credit for cash; the dematerialization of money into electronic information; the breakup of old multiethnic states into ethnic nations and the formation of transnational currency unions; the widespread use of barter among individuals and corporations to avoid taxes and other costs associated with money exchange; the increase in the amount and frequency of unreported tips and gratuities; the recognition of the gray and black markets as major creators of wealth; and the increased liquidity of assets previously held to be outside the economic sphere, such as social and cultural heritage, personal talent, insurable goods like invulnerability to litigation, environmental considerations like clean air and water, patentable genetic strains of living organisms, the "look and feel" of software. The net result will be three large changes: the penetration of the market into all areas of human life; the refinement of the market so that it is no longer a crass and reductive instrument of exchange; and the differentiation of currency into forms more appropriate to the nature of the exchange.

This last change requires some explanation. Marx's complaint that the market commodifies human values and alienates the worker from the fruits of his or her labor was well taken. Money as it has traditionally been used—what Bassanio calls the "pale and common drudge / 'Tween man and man" in *The Merchant of Venice* (III.ii.103)—with its simpleminded, quantitative, and stereotyped evaluations, cannot adequately express the more complex exchanges that take place among human beings. Money is not an unjust measure but an inarticulate one, which cannot make us feel the flow of gratitude; justice must not only be done, it must also be shown (and felt) to be done. When we supplemented the weak human memory for obligations with the efficient device of money, we lost a large part of the personal feeling that gave economic exchange its moral foundation and spiritual significance. We cut off bonds from their biological and affective roots.

But the computer has no such human limitations on its memory. Remembering is what it does best, and at a vanishing cost. When we receive a credit card report or bank statement, all those exchanges that we had forgotten are recovered in detail, the where and when and what. In theory, then, money is no longer necessary for personal transactions. One could imagine a computer network that might never use actual money figures but could continuously observe people's actual exchanges—what they considered to be a fair reciprocation for goods and services received, in terms of goods and services rendered. It could then calculate the relative state of obligation in which each of its subscribers stood and report that state to them in a qualitative, rather than a quantitative manner, along several dimensions such as moral onus, social obligation, due aesthetic accolade, practical benefit, reasonable gratitude, and so on. Large obligations to a few could be weighed explicitly against small obligations to the many. The effect would essentially be to give each person a currency of his or her own, which could float in several dimensions against the currencies of others. The current trend toward credit cards that bear a photograph—and perhaps eventually a fingerprint or retinal pattern—identifying the bearer, together with a chip containing the bearer's account balance, anticipates this development. Naturally, in transactions among corporations and other abstract bodies, the old one-dimensional numerical measure would continue to be most useful. A corporation cannot and need not feel either alienation or gratitude, though of course it must act as if it did. But human beings would no longer be constrained into the value world of an abstract financial institution, and could begin again to know their wealth or poverty for what it truly is—the index of our moral, aesthetic, emotional and cognitive standing among our fellows. The increasing invisibility of such exchanges to any central authority would preserve their privacy and integrity. Our hunter-gatherer-farmer social instincts could be recoupled to our economic life, and our morality reconnected to our livelihood.

When we place these developments in the context of the
dance that we have already postulated—where all persons
vidual owners of the means of production and thus wou'
through existential need to work for a living—what we get
economy that Shakespeare describes in those plays wher
cratic world is functioning properly. It is a world of personal g.......
tude, of an almost unconscious generosity; it is also one in which honor and
shame compel compliance to decent human standards and the acknowledgment of debt. But this world, emphatically, is not a utopia. Terrible things
can happen in it—Leontes can fly into a jealous rage, King Harry can break
his old friend Falstaff's heart; and there is always the danger of cheating, of
the retreat into more atavistic theories of what is valuable, such as those of
Edmund and the evil daughters in *Lear*. But in such a world there is no
moral muffling of the actual exchanges among humans. A Shakespearean
drama is an ideal market, a fully communicative system, in which information can, unhindered, transform itself by exchange into knowledge and
thence into true wisdom. Emotions are appropriate to their objects, and
moral consequences, good and bad, can come home to roost. There is none
of that triviality we see in the faces of so many of our contemporaries; if
there is one crime to be laid at the feet of this postmodern world we live in,
it is the crime of the lack of dignity. So many of us are shame deniers, our
anxious little countenances shut off from the current of karma, the cold but
welcome blast of the moral gale that blows through a truly lived life. But this
condition cannot survive the explicitness of the Shakespearean market,
where a spade is called a spade and fair value, good and bad, is given and
received.

Wealth and Morality: The Choices

The fact that machines will take the place of the Elizabethan servants, peasants, tenant workers, and hirelings in providing the economic base for the
new gift exchange economy will offer a large challenge to our moral understanding of wealth. Do we value things for themselves and for the benefits
they give to our lives? Or do we rather value them because others cannot
possess them if we do, because we are envied for our possessions, because
we have seen others want them and, as the philosopher René Girard suggests, we copy their desire and acquire what they want because we covet the
happiness we imagine it might bring them, gaining power over others by
having in our gift what they cannot otherwise acquire? If material and informational goods are available to all, as rentiers or independently wealthy in-
vestors, we will have to face up to our own fundamental moral worth. There
are two choices. We can be miserable and make others miserable by making
wealth mean the possession of those things—unique original works of art
or craft, perfect real estate locations, access to individuals of genius and
charisma, an exquisitely tasteful upbringing, and suchlike—that can be con-

trolled and kept from others. If we take this choice, to be rich will be to be sadists and dogs in the manger, hoarding those unreproducible goods but letting others get enough of a peep at them to make their mouths water; and to be poor will be to eat one's heart out with envy and resentment at the apparently satisfied spiritual desires of others, despite the fact that one's every bodily need or want can be taken care of. Or we can find a way of creating value and continuously exchanging it in such a way as to increase the happiness of each through a systemic pleasure in gift giving. → what sort of gifts?

It is artists and writers who must bear the major responsibility for making the new age of abundance one of gift exchange rather than one of hoarding, envy, sadism, and snobbery. Their track record in this century has not been good: left-wing cultural leaders have taught the have-nots the arts of murderous discontent and resentment, and right-wing cultural leaders have taught the haves the arts of contempt and seduction. Shakespeare stands as a gigantic counterexample: a genius who gave his whole soul to creating a nationwide social drama that would bring out the finest side of all human beings. Arguably the achievements of the English nation since Shakespeare's time in science, the arts, commerce, and government have been energized by Shakespeare's brilliant impulse, though there are signs since the First World War that its impetus has at last begun to slacken. The next century offers an opportunity for artists and writers to do for the world what Shakespeare did for England. We can, in the light of this study of Shakespeare's economics, formulate a new primary long-range goal for the world's governments: to make everybody rich and thus to make their own existence as political institutions largely unnecessary. But it will be equally important to guide the meaning of those riches so as to make them truly means of human happiness rather than the occasion for an anguish that is the more intense for lacking the excuse of physical want.

This guidance must reconnect economic with moral obligation, market goods with ethical, aesthetic, and cognitive goods. The words we live by contain within them the secret of how we ought to live. To be a husband is to seal oneself to a house bond. To "have" is to "have to." The word "ought," our modal auxiliary for moral onus, is the old past tense of "owe." "Freight," "fraught," and "earn" are all cognates of "ought." The word "owe" was once a variant of the word "own," which can mean "possess" but can also be used as a reflexive intensifier for such words as "my," "your," "his," "her," "their." What we have is what we have to do; what we ought to do is what we owe to do; what we own is what we owe; and this owning, or "owning up," is the central freight of our selfhood. It is our bonds, our entering into bonds, that makes us human; we only *are* the promises we keep. Their weight gives our freedom its meaning; the grace period for their repayment is the time of our lives; and the repayment, with interest, is the way not only to redeem our bond but to redeem ourselves.

further reading

Argyros, Alexander. *A Blessed Rage for Order* (Ann Arbor: University of Michigan Press, 1991).

Baldwin, A. Dwight, Jr., Judith de Luce, and Carl Pletsch, eds. *Beyond Preservation: Restoring and Inventing Landscapes* (Minneapolis: University of Minnesota Press, 1994).

Benedikt, Michael, ed. *Value: Center 10* (Austin, Texas: The Center for American Architecture and Design, 1997).

Botkin, Daniel B. *Discordant Harmonies* (New York: Oxford University Press, 1990).

Burckhardt, Sigurd. *Shakespearean Meanings* (Princeton: Princeton University Press, 1994).

Burkert, Walter. *Homo Necans: The Anthropology of Ancient Greek Sacrifice Ritual and Myth,* trans. Peter Bing (Berkeley: University of California Press, 1983).

Channell, David F. *The Vital Machine* (New York: Oxford University Press, 1991).

Clausen, Christopher. *The Place of Poetry: Two Centuries of an Art in Crisis* (Lexington: University Press of Kentucky, 1981).

Cooke, Brett, and Frederick Turner, eds. *Biopoetics* (Lexington: ICUS, 1999).

Corrigan, Robert W. *The World of the Theatre* (Glenview, Ill.: Scott, Foresman, 1979).

D'Aquili, Eugene G., Charles D. Laughlin, Jr, and John McManus, eds. *The Spectrum of Ritual: A Biogenetic Structural Analysis* (New York: Columbia University Press, 1979).

Darwin, Charles. *The Origin of Species* (1851; New York: Collier, 1962).

Davies, Paul. *God and the New Physics* (New York: Touchstone, 1983).

———. *The Cosmic Blueprint* (New York: Simon & Schuster, 1988).

DePryck, Koen. *Knowledge, Evolution, and Paradox* (Albany: State University of New York Press, 1993).

Fox, Robin, ed. *Biosocial Anthropology* (London: Malaby Press, 1975).

——. *Encounter with Anthropology* (New Brunswick, N.J.: Transaction Publishers, 1991).

——. *The Challenge of Anthropology* (New Brunswick, N.J.: Transaction Publishers, 1994).

Fraser, J. T. "Out of Plato's Cave: The Natural History of Time," *Kenyon Review,* New Series, 2:1 (Winter 1980), pp.143–62.

——. *Time as Conflict* (Basel: Birkhäuser, 1978).

Gioia, Dana. *Can Poetry Matter?* (St. Paul, MN: Graywolf Press, 1992).

Girard, René. *The Girard Reader.* Ed. James G. Williams (New York: Crossroad, 1996).

Gleick, James. *Chaos: Making a New Science* (New York: Viking, 1987).

Griffin, David, ed., *The Reenchantment of Science* (Albany: State University of New York Press, 1988).

——. *God and Religion in the Postmodern World* (Albany: State University of New York Press, 1989).

Hans, James S. *The Play of the World* (Amherst: University of Massachusetts Press, 1981).

——. *The Origins of the Gods* (Albany: State University of New York Press, 1991).

——. *The Golden Mean* (Albany: State University of New York Press, 1994).

Hofstadter, Douglas R. *Gödel, Escher, Bach* (New York: Basic Books, 1979).

Hyde, Lewis. *The Gift: Imagination and the Erotic Life of Property* (New York: Vintage, 1983).

Lorenz, Konrad. *On Aggression* (New York: Harcourt, Brace, 1966).

Mandelbrot, Benoit B. *The Fractal Geometry of Nature* (New York: Freeman, 1977).

The Marx-Engels Reader, 2nd edition. Ed. Robert C. Tucker (New York: Norton, 1978).

Parry, Jonathan, and Maurice Bloch. *Money and the Morality of Exchange* (Cambridge: Cambridge University Press, 1989).

Prigogine, Ilya, and Isabelle Stengers. *Order Out of Chaos: Man's New Dialogue with Nature* (New York: Bantam, 1984).

Redman, Tim. *Ezra Pound and Italian Fascism* (Cambridge: Cambridge University Press, 1991).

Rentschler, Ingo, Barbara Herzberger, and David Epstein, eds. *Beauty and the Brain: Biological Aspects of Aesthetics* (Basel: Birkhäuser, 1988).

Rotman, Brian. *Signifying Nothing: The Semiotics of Zero* (Stanford: Stanford University Press, 1987).

Scheff, Thomas J. *Microsociology: Discourse, Emotion and Social Structure* (Chicago: University of Chicago Press, 1990).

Sexson, Lynda. *Ordinarily Sacred* (New York: Crossroad, 1982).

Shell, Marc. "The Wether and the Ewe," *Kenyon Review,* New Series, 1:4 (Fall 1979), pp. 65–92.

——. *The Economy of Literature* (Baltimore: Johns Hopkins University Press, 1993).

Turner, Frederick. *Shakespeare and the Nature of Time* (Oxford: Clarendon Press, 1971).

——. *Natural Classicism* (1985; Charlottesville: University Press of Virginia, 1992).

————. *Beauty: The Value of Values* (Charlottesville: University Press of Virginia, 1991).

————. *Rebirth of Value: Meditations on Beauty, Ecology, Religion, and Education* (Albany: State University of New York Press, 1991).

————. *Tempest, Flute, and Oz: Essays on the Future* (New York: Persea Books, 1991).

————. *The Culture of Hope: A New Birth of the Classical Spirit* (New York: Free Press, 1995).

Turner, Victor W. *The Ritual Process* (Chicago: Aldine, 1969).

————. *Dramas, Fields, and Metaphors* (Ithaca: Cornell University Press, 1974).

————. *From Ritual to Theater* (New York: Performing Arts Journal Publications, 1982).

Wechsler Judith, ed. *On Aesthetics in Science* (Cambridge: Massachusetts Institute of Technology Press,1978).

Wilson, Edward O. *On Human Nature* (Cambridge: Harvard University Press, 1978).

————. *Consilience: The Unity of Knowledge* (New York: Knopf, 1998).

Wheeler, John Archibald. "World as System Self-Synthesized by Quantum Networking," *IBM Journal of Research and Development,* 32:1 (Jan. 1988), pp. 4–15.

Whitehead, Alfred North. *Science and the Modern World* (Cambridge: Cambridge University Press, 1967).

index